Also by H. R. McMaster

Battlegrounds: The Fight to Defend the Free World

Dereliction of Duty: Lyndon Johnson, Robert McNamara, the Joint Chiefs of Staff, and the Lies that Led to Vietnam

AT WAR W
OURSELV

H. R. McMASTER

AT WAR WITH OURSELVES

MY TOUR OF DUTY IN THE
TRUMP WHITE HOUSE

HARPER

An Imprint of HarperCollinsPublishers

HarperCollins books may be purchased for educational, business, or sales promotional use. For information, please email the Special Markets Department at SPsales@harpercollins.com.

FIRST EDITION

Library of Congress Cataloging-in-Publication Data has been applied for.

ISBN 978-0-06-289950-7

24 25 26 27 28 LBC 5 4 3 2 1

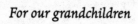

For our grandchildren

CONTENTS

NOTE TO READERS

*To tell the tale plainly is now much more difficult than to tell
it treacherously.*
—G. K. CHESTERTON

Those who despise Donald Trump will want to read in these
pages confirmation that he was a narcissist unfit for the highest office in the land. Those who revere him will want to read
how Trump the anti-hero fought to save the United States
from establishment politicians and bureaucrats who had for
too long been derelict in their duty to the American people.

But I wrote this book to get past the hyper-partisanship
and explain what really happened. I wrote with no political
agenda; the politics of our day are pulling this country apart.
And I wrote with no desire for requital. I wrote to recount
what I experienced.

As a historian, I have been a consumer of books like this
one, and I have always approached them with vigilance and
skepticism. I expect that you will do the same.

AT WAR WITH OURSELVES

CHAPTER 1

"YOU'RE FIRED"

Trump Lashes Out at National Security Adviser H.R. Mc-Master for Describing Evidence of Russian Meddling as 'Incontrovertible' . . . **MCMASTER COULD LEAVE WH AFTER MONTHS OF TENSION WITH TRUMP** . . . Report: H.R. McMaster to Be Fired—at Kelly and Mattis's Behest . . . Putin Praises Trump, Assails Sanctions, Vows to Defend 'Great Power' Russia . . . *SERGEI SKRIPAL, EX-DOUBLE AGENT, POISONED IN UK* . . . Nerve gas attack unsettles residents in English cathedral city . . . *NICHOLSON SAYS SITUATION IN AFGHANISTAN HAS FUNDAMENTALLY CHANGED . . . NSA AJIT DOVAL HEADS FOR WASHINGTON TO GET INDIA-US 2+2 BACK ON TRACK* . . . US Pastor Faces Espionage Charges In Turkey . . . Trump Meets With Saudi Crown Prince And Talks About Money . . . White House has been expelling its top officials like a deflating balloon . . . **TRUMP REPLACES MCMASTER WITH BOLTON AS NATIONAL SECURITY ADVISER . . . MCMASTER, LEAVING WHITE HOUSE POST, WILL RETIRE FROM ARMY THIS SUMMER . . .** "I am thankful to President Donald J. Trump for the opportunity to serve him and our nation as national security advisor."

[THE PHONE CALL, 4:30 P.M., THURSDAY, 22 MARCH 2018, FORT LESLEY J. MCNAIR, WASHINGTON, D.C.] The Situation Room announced, "Stand by for the president."

"Good afternoon, Mr. President," I said after I heard him pick up.

"Hello, General," he said. "I am calling to let you know that I have decided to go with John." He meant that he was replacing me with Ambassador John Bolton.

Trump thanked me for my service. "You did a great job, General. I agreed with you ninety percent of the time; the other ten percent of the time, not so much."

I told him I had appreciated the opportunity to serve as his national security advisor. "Hopefully, you saw that I never tried to get you to agree with me. I tried to give you the best analysis and multiple options."

After President Trump and I hung up the phone, Trump tweeted:[1]

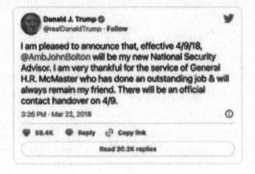

My communications director, Michael Anton, released the statement I had prepared earlier in the day:

After thirty-four years of service to our nation, I am requesting retirement from the U.S. Army effective this summer[,] after which I will leave public service. Throughout my career it has been my greatest privilege to serve alongside extraordinary servicemembers and dedicated civilians. I am thankful to President Donald J. Trump for the opportunity to serve him and our nation as national security advisor.

*   *   *

I KNEW when I took the job thirteen months earlier that this day would come. I had resolved to do the best I could as long as I was effective and not to fight to keep the job or try to parlay it into a promotion or another position in the administration. I felt disappointed that I would no longer be in a position to help Trump implement long-overdue shifts in foreign policy. But my relationship with him had become fraught, and we both knew my tenure with the administration was up.

A constellation of forces had undercut my relationship with the president and led Trump and me to conclude that it was time for me to go.

Nine days earlier, Trump had fired Secretary of State Rex Tillerson, and in turn, those who wanted me gone intensified their efforts to get the president to ditch me, too. They had employed the time-honored Washington tactic of leaking to the press. Multiple outlets cited unnamed sources saying Trump would fire me imminently.[2]

Getting me out was part of a larger plan hatched by men who thought their job was to protect Donald Trump from himself. They hoped for a long interim period following my departure during which my old friend Ricky Waddell, the deputy national security advisor, would serve as acting national security advisor. White House Chief of Staff John Kelly and Secretary of Defense James Mattis would then have time to convince Trump either to keep Ricky on or to hire someone of whom they approved.

But I knew whom Trump would select—someone who had not stopped campaigning for the job since he was passed over for it the last time. That person was John Bolton.

★　　★　　★

THE DAY before I was fired, I met for dinner with my Indian counterpart, Ajit Doval, at Quarters 13, Fort McNair, a quiet place at the intersection of the Anacostia and Potomac Rivers, just south of the U.S. Capitol. Doval is a character straight out of central casting. Betraying his background as the former director of his country's Intelligence Bureau, he would lean into conversations, cock his head to the side as he spoke, and use hushed tones, even when discussing the most routine subjects.

During our walk after dinner, he whispered, "How much longer will we work together?" It did not take someone with Doval's intelligence background to figure out I was departing the Trump administration. Without answering directly, I told him it had been a privilege and expressed confidence that there would be continuity.

We knew each other well enough for Doval to be direct. "What happens in Afghanistan after you leave?"

I reminded him that President Trump had approved the South Asia strategy last August and that it was the first reasoned and sustainable strategy in seventeen years of war. Doval knew this, but sometimes you cannot be fully candid with even your closest foreign counterparts. In fact, I shared Doval's concern, and I knew that my response was less than convincing. Trump was unconventional and impulsive. Sometimes his impulses were good. Other times, to use one of his turns of phrase, "not so much."

★   ★   ★

[9:30 A.M., THURSDAY, 22 MARCH 2018, TEN HOURS BEFORE THE PHONE CALL, WEST WING OF THE WHITE HOUSE.] I went into my office early. I said good morning to my chief of staff, Ylli Bajraktari, who was always upbeat.

Ylli, like so many others on the National Security Council (NSC) staff, did his best every day to transcend the byzantine politics and vitriolic partisanship that could easily have distracted all of us from our duty. As he did every morning, Ylli gave me an update on the substantive issues of the day—in this case, the poisoning, on March 4, of former Russian military intelligence officer Sergei Skripal and his daughter in Salisbury, England, using a banned military-grade nerve agent that was easily traced to Moscow. Russian spy agencies—the Foreign Intelligence Service (SVR) and the military Main Intelligence Directorate (GRU)—were the perpetrators. The use of a nerve agent had placed hundreds, maybe thousands, of lives at risk. It was with this particularly heinous method that Russian president Vladimir Putin had apparently decided to assassinate Skripal, a former

KGB double agent who had been imprisoned for thirteen years in Russia but was then released by Moscow in an exchange in July 2010, the biggest spy swap since the Cold War.

I placed a call to my UK counterpart, Mark Sedwill, whom I had known since we served together in Afghanistan seven years earlier. We agreed that such an egregious attack required a strong response. Unless Putin believed there were costs to such actions, Kremlin aggression would continue unchecked.

It came to me to present this evolving intelligence picture to the president and to develop options for a coordinated U.S. and multinational response.

Since beginning my time as national security advisor, I had found that discussions of Putin and Russia were difficult to have with the president: Trump connected all topics involving Russia to special counsel Robert Mueller's investigation of Russia's attack on the 2016 U.S. presidential election and the allegations (which were found to be false) that the Trump campaign, including the president himself, had "colluded" with Russia's disinformation campaign to sway the election toward Trump.

Since Trump's election, Democrats and others opposed to Trump kept looking for evidence of collusion or corruption with Russians or for compromising information—such as that in the discredited Steele dossier, a document filled with false allegations about Trump that was funded by the Hillary Clinton campaign and presented to the FBI as fact.

All this had created opportunities for the Kremlin.

Like his predecessors George W. Bush and Barack Obama, Trump was overconfident in his ability to improve relations with the dictator in the Kremlin. Trump, the self-described "expert dealmaker," believed he could build a personal rapport with Putin. Trump's tendency to be reflexively contrarian only added to his determination. The fact that most foreign policy experts in Washington advocated for a tough approach to the Kremlin seemed only to drive the president to the opposite approach.

Putin, a ruthless former KGB operator, played to Trump's ego and insecurities with flattery. Putin had described Trump as "a very outstanding person, talented, without any doubt,"[3] and Trump had revealed his vulnerability to this approach, his affinity for strongmen, and his belief that he alone could forge a good relationship with Putin: "It is always a great honor to be so nicely complimented by a man so highly respected within his own country."[4]

Moreover, Trump's tendency toward moral equivalence made him relatively unconcerned about some of Putin's brazen acts of aggression. When Fox News host Bill O'Reilly asked Trump in February 2017 why he respected Putin even though "he's a killer," the newly inaugurated president responded, "There are a lot of killers. We've got a lot of killers. What do you think? Our country's so innocent?"

So, on Putin and Russia, I had been swimming upstream with the president from the beginning—but recently, the current had intensified. Less than two weeks before the Skripal poisoning, I had attended the Munich Security Conference. A Russian member of the Duma, the lower house of the Federal Assembly, asked me if the United States would work with Russian cyber experts to improve cybersecurity. I smiled and said, "I doubt that any Russian cyber experts would be available, because they all seem to be occupied with attacks against the United States and our allies." I went on to observe that recent indictments brought forward by Mueller against thirteen Russian agents and three entities for election interference had revealed clear evidence of Russian efforts to discredit the U.S. election.

Those eager to undermine me told Trump that I had described the preliminary Mueller Report as "incontrovertible," and they got exactly the reaction they wanted. Trump tweeted:[5]

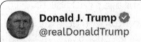

Donald J. Trump ✔
@realDonaldTrump

General McMaster forgot to say that the results of the 2016 election were not impacted or changed by the Russians and that the only Collusion was between Russia and Crooked H, the DNC and the Dems. Remember the Dirty Dossier, Uranium, Speeches, Emails and the Podesta Company!

8:22 PM · Feb 17, 2018

To amplify the message, Russian state-controlled Sputnik News reported that "National Security Advisor H. R. McMaster directly contradicted President Trump, saying that there was Russian meddling in the 2016 election."[6]

Predictably, John Kelly called me to tell me the president was furious. I offered to call the president and clarify that we were talking about separate questions. First, did Russia meddle in the election? Second, did the Kremlin favor one candidate over another? And third, did the Russian interference have an effect on the election result? The answer to the first question was yes. As to question two, I believed that the Kremlin did not care who won the 2016 American election, as long as a large number of citizens doubted the legitimacy of the result. And there was no way to determine the answer to the third question.

Kelly discouraged me from calling Trump. "Just wait until you see him."

It was no surprise that Trump was still angry when I returned from the Security Conference. And his aversion to me would only grow. I think this was because I was the principal voice telling him that Putin was using him and other politicians in both parties in an effort to shake Americans' confidence in our democratic principles, institutions, and processes. Putin was not and would never be Trump's friend. I felt it was my duty to point this out.

Sedwill told me that British prime minister Theresa May was concerned that Trump would not support a strong response to the Skripal poisoning. I shared her concern. For over two weeks, then-CIA Director Mike Pompeo, Director of National Intelligence Dan Coats, and I had presented the president with mounting evidence that the Kremlin was behind the poisoning. Tillerson had said as much publicly. But Trump struggled to understand why Vladimir Putin would authorize such an aggressive attack, and when he talked with May, he raised doubts that Putin's government was directly involved.

Sedwill and I had been working with our counterparts across Europe and beyond to secure pledges that their governments would impose significant costs on Russia. We reached agreement with several countries but had sensed reluctance in Berlin, Paris, and Rome. The U.S. Treasury Department completed work on a new round of sanctions designed to impose costs on Russian entities for a range of offenses, including those associated with the Kremlin's earlier disinformation campaigns designed to delegitimize the 2016 U.S. election and pit Americans against one another over issues of race, immigration, and gun control. When I brought those sanctions to Trump, he approved them, but he grumbled, "How are we ever going to have a better relationship with Russia if we keep sanctioning them?"

I thought, *Okay, this is one more association between me and information he doesn't want to hear and decisions he'd rather avoid.* I knew it would not be any easier when I brought him additional actions in response to the Skripal poisoning.

After the check-in with Sedwill, I walked briskly past the Oval Office, through the Rose Garden, and into the Executive Residence, which lies between the East and West Wings of the White House. I jogged up the three flights of stairs to the second floor of the Residence and entered the Treaty Room. Kelly and Pompeo were already there.

The president was sitting at the desk eating breakfast. I told them all that I had just gotten off the phone with Sedwill. I summarized the progress we were making on a coordinated response among allies to the Skripal poisoning and reminded Trump that I would bring him options for a decision the next day, before he departed for Mar-a-Lago.

I changed the subject to the call Trump was about to take from Turkish president Recep Tayyip Erdoğan. I had four minutes to prep him, which was not unusual. He hated to prepare, especially when he was grumpy. I predicted that Erdoğan would again complain, as he had during their last meeting, about arming and supporting the Syrian Democratic Forces (SDF), which he viewed as a separatist force.

Erdoğan was also angry about Muhammed Fethullah Gülen, an erstwhile ally turned opponent of his, who now lived in the United States, in the Poconos. The Turkish government labeled Gülen a terrorist. Erdoğan believed Gülen was responsible for the failed 2016 military coup against him. The Turks imprisoned the American pastor Andrew Brunson after the coup, holding him under specious charges of spying for the CIA and helping to plot the overthrow of

Erdoğan's government. I told Trump that Erdoğan would not release Brunson unless we threatened severe consequences.

"Mr. President, if you ask Erdoğan for something, you'll get nothing. We'll have to impose costs on him."

Trump, who was in his usual contrarian mode, told me I was wrong, that he intended to ask Erdoğan to release the pastor, and that he was confident Erdoğan would do so.

"Mr. President, Erdoğan is a bully. He will keep pushing us until we push back hard."

The call with Erdoğan went exactly as predicted. Erdoğan refused to release Pastor Brunson and harped on Gülen, a clear admission that Erdoğan was holding the pastor hostage. Aware that Trump and I were on the outs, Erdoğan suggested that I had delayed their conversation. Trump scowled at me from behind the desk. I shrugged, indicating that this was typical Erdoğan behavior.

By the end of the conversation, Trump was frustrated—in part due to Erdoğan's intransigence, but also, I believe, because I had been right about how the call would go.

After he hung up the phone, Trump brought up the subject to which he defaulted whenever he wanted to chastise me—Afghanistan. He echoed those who were advocating for the complete withdrawal from Afghanistan. In recent months, the isolationist right had pilloried anyone who presented alternatives, including "loser generals" whom they accused of perpetuating a futile forever war.

Trump brought up one of their favorite targets, Mick Nicholson, the commanding general of the NATO-led Resolute Support Mission and Operation Freedom's Sentinel in Kabul. As he had said several times, Trump remarked "that general over there doesn't know what he is doing."

I had defended Nicholson before, and this time I was more strident. "The people you are listening to don't know what they are talking about. Have you ever spoken to Nicholson? I can get him on the phone right now."

Trump ranted: "I don't need to talk to him. You know I did the Afghanistan thing for you, General," he said, referring to the decision he made in August 2017 to approve a long-term strategy for Afghanistan and South Asia.

I replied, "Mr. President, you made the decision based on what was best for the American people. You should never do anything for me."

His face became more flushed.

I told the president, Kelly, and Pompeo, "My Saudi counterpart, Dr. Musaed, is in my office, so I should go."

Kelly followed me into the hallway and stopped me before I headed down the stairs. I turned to face him and, completely fed up, said, "Give me a fucking date."

Kelly nodded.

I would have one when Trump called me at home seven hours later.

★　　★　　★

BEYOND THE fundamental incompatibility of our personalities, the "three As," allies, authoritarians, and Afghanistan, became millstones that ground down my relationship with Trump. Trump had made a tough and, in my view, correct decision on Afghanistan, but when members of his political base objected to that decision, he blamed me. Strongmen like Putin and Erdoğan had come to see me as an impediment to their agendas and portrayed me as sabotaging Trump's relationship with them. I saw U.S. allies as bestowing tremendous advantages, while Trump tended to view them as freeloaders on U.S. security.

When I returned to my office, I told Ylli that it was likely my last day. I intended to work hard until the end and carry on with the lunch I was hosting at my home with national security advisors Dr. Musaed bin Mohammed Al Aiban of Saudi Arabia, Sheikh Tahnoon bin Zayed Al Nahyan of the United Arab Emirates, and Haneef Atmar of Afghanistan. After the one-on-one meeting with Musaed, I drafted the public statement and an email to send to the National Security Council (NSC) staff for release after the president announced my departure.

Ricky Waddell came into my office. He was upset. He had been put in an awkward position by Kelly, who had enlisted him to convince me to compete for promotion and take another job in the military.

Kelly had assured Ricky that his efforts to expedite my departure were based on his desire to protect me from reputational damage associated with continued service in the Trump White House. I told Ricky that this was not his fault. I saw no point in remaining as national security advisor any longer than I was effective for the president and the nation.

With Donald Trump, most everybody gets used up, and my time had come.

As I headed home, Ylli called to tell me that John Bolton was in the West Wing lobby waiting to see the president.

★   ★   ★

THOSE WHO wanted me out of the job included members of the alt-right who saw me as an impediment to their nativist agenda; neo-isolationists; members of the Republican Freedom Caucus; and self-described "economic nationalists" who accused anyone who questioned their policy prescriptions as being a "globalist." These disparate groups used a variety of tactics to undermine trust between the president and me, including unfounded accusations of disloyalty and insubordination and ludicrous allegations that I was anti-Israel, soft on jihadist terrorists, and weak when it came to confronting Iran. What these groups had in common was a desire to use Donald Trump as a vehicle for advancing their agendas and a belief that I was frustrating that desire. These groups would portray me as disloyal to Trump, but I was doing my best to give the elected president options so he could determine his own agenda. Paradoxically, my replacement, for whom many members of these groups advocated, would push his own policies until he was fired and then would publish a damning tell-all while Trump was still in office and running for reelection.

By the end of my run, it was clear that Bolton was angling for the job and that his Fox News appearances were an extended audition. Fox News personalities friendly with Trump, such as Sean Hannity and Laura Ingraham, gave Bolton an assist by reinforcing the narrative that I was a globalist obstructing Trump's agenda. This built on earlier campaigns, including the #FireMcMaster social media barrage of August and September 2017. The effort to get me out brought together a strange cabal of useful idiots in the alt-right ecosystem who believed their own disinformation about me and devised ludicrous schemes—such as having an attractive woman approach me at a restaurant, buy me a drink, and secretly record me as I disparaged my commander in chief. I was gone before they could hatch their plan.[7]

The press got a lot wrong during this period. Some, especially in the alt-right pseudo-media of digital sites that mimic legitimate news outlets, deliberately aided these groups. Meanwhile, the left-wing media pursued an unrelenting false narrative of Russian collusion and rarely reported on positive policy developments. Many reporters were manipulated. Many were willing to be manipulated if the story made for good copy. I decided not to waste time parrying the onslaught of attacks and to focus instead on what I could control—doing the best job I could for the president for as long as I was effective.

I knew when I took the job that my shelf life would be limited. Reports that I had "never really clicked" with Trump were accurate. I was fine with that. I did not need Trump as a friend, and I did not crave affirmation from him. But I did need him to trust me. Those who wanted me out worked hard to erode that trust.

★   ★   ★

AFTER I hung up the phone with Trump, I called my wife, Katie, to let her know.

"The president called. It's over. I transition with John Bolton on April ninth." She would soon hear the news breaking on the radio as she drove home from her job at the Catholic Diocese of Richmond, Virginia. Katie cried, but not due to regret; she was relieved. I was inured to the vitriol of social media and other attacks, but I had underestimated how much stress it placed on her.

I then called my chief of staff, Ylli, to tell him it was officially over. My core staff had gathered in my office waiting for the news. They had worked tirelessly to support me and serve the president. Their futures were uncertain, but I urged all of them to stay on to ensure a smooth transition.

That evening, I put on my U.S. Army dress mess uniform for a black-tie event hosted by Saudi Crown Prince Mohammed bin Salman to commemorate the twenty-seventh anniversary of the 1991 Gulf War. The event was held in the Andrew W. Mellon Auditorium, a grand building on Constitution Avenue. Doric columns rise over sixty feet to a ceiling known for its acoustic resonance. The hall was full. As I walked in, I recognized several government officials and reporters. Someone saw me, stood, and began clapping. Then everyone in the hall joined her. I was surprised at and appreciative of the display of support.

Several speeches followed dinner, including one by former Florida governor Jeb Bush, who was representing his father, George H. W. Bush, who had been president during Desert Shield and Desert Storm. Jeb mentioned the Battle of 73 Easting, a lopsided victory over a Republican Guard division in which I took part as commander of Eagle Troop, Second Armored Cavalry Regiment. I was reminded of the tremendous rewards of service in our military, especially being part of teams bound together by mutual respect, trust, and common purpose, teams that can take on the quality of a family. Despite setbacks and failures, I had never stopped trying to foster that same commitment to the mission and to colleagues as I led the National Security Council staff and ran the national security decision-making process.

★   ★   ★

AS SOON as I departed the job, family, friends, acquaintances, and strangers asked a similar series of questions, ranging from the innocuous "What was it like?" to "How did you get along with Trump?" to the leading "Is Trump really a (fill in the blank)?"

This book goes beyond answers to those questions. As a historian, I consider it my responsibility to explain what the Trump administration achieved and failed to achieve in the areas of foreign policy and national security during a pivotal moment in American history. I want readers to understand better how government should work and the roles and responsibilities of senior officials. As with a previous book of mine, on President Lyndon Johnson and the Vietnam

War, this book explores how personalities and relationships influenced decision-making and policy. It will also help readers understand better the demands of the office of the president, the qualities and traits important to satisfying those demands, and how Donald Trump's personality and character frustrated his ability to realize his potential and fulfill his duties to the American people.

Everything in the Trump White House was much harder than it needed to be. I tried to understand the perspectives and motivations of the president and of all who struggled to get Donald Trump the best advice, help him set the course for his foreign policy, and coordinate the implementation of his decisions.

This book exposes how the extreme polarization of America's polity afflicts more than our national psyche. Polarization is a weapon that malicious domestic factions and hostile external foes wield to undermine governance at the highest level. Donald Trump emerged from profound divisions in American society and politics. But once he was in office, the forces that he had exploited to win the presidency interacted with those who despised him and subjected him to constant stress and attack. In the war with ourselves, Donald Trump had become the antagonist in his own story.

A follow-up question many people ask about my tour of duty in Washington is "Was it worth it?" My answer is yes. I'm a soldier. I love the United States of America, have risked my life for her, and have asked other men and women to fight, take risks, and make sacrifices in her name. Donald Trump was the sixth commander in chief under whom I served since taking the oath to "support and defend the Constitution of the United States" at the age of seventeen, on the parade field known as "the Plain," 150 feet above the Hudson River at West Point. I tried to serve Donald Trump as I had his five predecessors—to the best of my ability.

How well did I fulfill my duty to Donald Trump and the Constitution of the United States? After you have read the story of my thirteen-month-long tour of duty in the Trump White House, I would ask you to be the judge of that.

CHAPTER 2

"YOU'RE HIRED"

TRUMP SECURITY ADVISOR FLYNN RESIGNS . . . The Cost of the Air War Against ISIS Has Reached $11 Billion . . . North Korea tests new ballistic missile . . . *LAST MAN STANDING: MCMASTER FOR NSA?* . . . **TRUMP CHOOSES H.R. MCMASTER AS NATIONAL SECURITY ADVISER** . . . Trump says, "Our country is lucky to have people like this" . . . The selection Monday of the Army lieutenant general is earning Trump **RARE PRAISE FROM BOTH SIDES OF THE POLITICAL AISLE . . .** McMaster will join the ranks of numerous generals serving at high-level positions in the Trump administration, including Defense Secretary James Mattis and Secretary of Homeland Security John Kelly . . . **WHO IS TRUMP'S NEW NATIONAL SECURITY ADVISOR LT. GEN. H.R. MCMASTER? . . .** Trump, announcing his decision, called McMaster "a man of tremendous talent and tremendous experience" . . . *MCMASTER'S TAKEAWAYS: DON'T LIE, DON'T BLAME THE MEDIA, DON'T RELY ON AN INNER CIRCLE* . . . Lt. Gen. H.R. McMaster hasn't shied away from expressing strong public opinions on military and strategic issues . . . **MCMASTER KNOWS HOW NATIONAL SECURITY POLICY CAN GO WRONG. WILL THAT HELP HIM?**

FEBRUARY 17, 2017, the Friday before the start of Presidents' Day weekend, was unseasonably warm in my hometown of Philadelphia. I had taken the train from Washington after two days of frustrating meetings with Department of the Army staff in the Pentagon. My job was to design the future Army, but the Pentagon is a place where ideas are crushed under the weight of bureaucracy.

I checked into my hotel and headed over to the Foreign Policy Research Institute, a think tank, to brief fellows and guests on the results of a study I had commissioned roughly eighteen months before. The subject was what we were then calling Russian new-generation warfare (RNGW), what many now refer to as hybrid warfare.

Before leaving Washington, I had watched morning news anchors speculate about who would replace retired lieutenant general Mike Flynn as national security advisor. Flynn had been subjected to an FBI interview that the Department of Justice later concluded was conducted without any "legitimate investigative basis," and he had resigned after only twenty-four days on the job.[1] He and I had served together in Iraq and Afghanistan, where he was a professional, collaborative, and effective intelligence officer. Years later, I would find it hard to recognize the man who was amplifying absurd conspiracy theories, endorsing the false "stop the steal" claims about the 2020 election, and encouraging the January 6, 2021, assault on the Capitol Building.

My cellphone rang as I walked down Walnut Street. The call was coming from a partially blocked Washington, D.C., number. I answered.

"Hello, General McMaster, this is the White House deputy chief of staff, Katie Walsh. President Trump would like you to travel to Mar-a-Lago this weekend to interview for the position of assistant to the president for national security affairs. May I tell the president you're coming?"

I replied yes, thanked her, and called my wife, Katie, who was used to phone calls that suddenly changed our lives. That was one of them. Over the last thirty-three years, Katie had been my full partner in serving our nation.

"Of course you have to do it," she said.

★ ★ ★

SOON AFTER, I called the magic Pentagon number for "DoD Cables," a team of military communicators who can instantly reach almost any senior Department of Defense official anywhere in the world. I asked to speak with Secretary Mattis. He was midway across the Atlantic Ocean, en route to the Munich Security Conference. I told him about the call from the White House and the scheduled interview at Mar-a-Lago.

"Secretary Mattis, I'll only do this if you want me to."

"Yes, I want you to do it, H.R.," he responded, "it would be great to work with you."

Although I had never served with Mattis, I knew and respected him. We held similar views on the failures and shortcomings of U.S. strategy toward Iran and in the fight against jihadist terrorist organizations.

I made several more phone calls, to family and friends, and asked them to keep the news confidential. I spoke to my sister, Letitia, and to my father. I would see both of them in a few hours. My father would join me in downtown Philadelphia that evening for the First Troop Philadelphia City Cavalry formal "dining in," a military ceremony involving dinner, drinking, and rituals, including a punch bowl ceremony and singing to foster camaraderie and esprit de corps.

In between calls to make travel arrangements, I spoke with White House chief of staff Reince Priebus and with Steve Bannon. I had never dealt with either man but was aware of the controversies surrounding Bannon, who had described himself as "virulently anti-establishment" and determined to "destroy the state"—statements that had made his appointment as the president's "chief strategist" alarming.

Bannon's daughter, a West Point graduate and U.S. Army officer, had told him that junior officers in the Army respected me and that I was a "soldier's general." Bannon now asked me, "Is that true, or is that bullshit?"

I suggested that he reserve judgment on that question for himself. I told both men that it was an honor to be considered for the job and that I looked forward to meeting them at Mar-a-Lago.

I was beginning to piece together how my name had gotten to the president. After General Flynn resigned as national security advisor,

Sen. Tom Cotton had put my name in the hat. Cotton had told me that I was "partially to blame" for his decision to go to Officer Candidate School after graduating from Harvard Law School and then to serve as an Army infantry officer. I later discovered that Cotton had called several people to recommend me, including Priebus, Bannon, Pompeo, and Jared Kushner, who had been one of Cotton's students at Harvard.[2]

The officers of the First Troop were gracious hosts. My father, who would turn eighty-four in two months, had done serial active-duty tours as an Army Reserve officer toward the end of his career and had retired three decades earlier as a lieutenant colonel. He had missed military camaraderie, and he had a wonderful time at the dining in. When the news broke that I—along with Ambassador John Bolton; the superintendent of West Point, Lieut. Gen. Bob Caslen; and Lieut. Gen. (Ret.) Keith Kellogg—was a candidate for the national security job, my phone buzzed constantly with incoming messages, but I ignored them and enjoyed the amusing, mildly profane proceedings of the dining in with my dad. At the end of the year, when he encountered severe health challenges, I was grateful we had shared that evening together with our fellow soldiers.

Back at Fort Eustis, I met my aide-de-camp, Maj. Kevin Kilbride, and my executive officer, Col. Neal Corson, to make contingency plans for a rapid departure. Then I went home to see Katie. I also tried to catch up on the many phone calls I had missed over the past eighteen hours. Many were from people who knew Donald Trump, hoped I would be selected, and wanted to tell me what to expect during the job interview. A few urged me not to interview because they found Trump so detestable. I knew, based on the negative reactions Trump elicited from many Americans, that I would lose some friends if I took the job. One friend would even suggest that my service in the Trump administration was the equivalent of serving Vichy France.[3] Gen. Mark Milley, the Army chief of staff, predicted that Trump would hire me and pledged to do all he could to help me with the transition if that were the case. I spoke with my old friend and rugby teammate William Coyle, who observed, "Some people hate Trump so much that they want him to fail. But he's the president of the United States. We can't afford for him to fail."

I slept well that night and went to the gym early Sunday morning before my flight to Palm Beach. I packed my Army blues—Priebus had told me to interview in uniform—and pulled down the late Peter Rodman's excellent book *Presidential Command*, to reread it on the flight, which I did. As the plane took off, my eyes were drawn to a line I had highlighted years earlier, in the book's conclusion, which explained why the job was important:

> An effective national security adviser remains indispensable—to arm the president for the policy engagement that is required; to ensure that the bureaucratic process provides what the president needs; to help protect presidential interests. The security adviser is the guardian of the president's independence of judgment, and is also in a position to provide a strategic overview of the whole of national security policy.[4]

While no one is ever fully ready for the broad scope of responsibilities associated with the national security advisor job, I was grateful for the range of experiences across thirty-three years of service on which I could draw, if selected. I had assessed policy and strategy from the ground up while watching the iron curtain part and the Soviet empire disintegrate; fought in the U.S.-led coalition's lopsided victory over the Iraqi Army in the 1991 Gulf War; prepared units for combat in a post–Cold War period, when many thought that peace enforcement would be the main mission for the U.S. Army; commanded a regiment that defeated ruthless terrorists and insurgents in Iraq; rewrote wartime strategies to cope with realities in theaters abroad, rather than fantasy in Washington; led multinational teams to combat corruption and strengthen the Afghan state; trained America's warriors to prevail in battle; and designed the future Army to ensure America's ability to fight and win future wars as part of the U.S. joint force. But the most valuable experience may have been the opportunity to study and teach history and to research and write about how and why Vietnam became an American war. I had learned from that research and from my wartime experience that policies developed in Washington are often written by those who do not understand what it takes to implement them.

As I walked out of the airport in West Palm Beach, I got a call from Mike Pompeo.

I had never met or spoken to the former congressman and fellow West Point graduate. He was supportive. "I recommended that Trump select you," he told me, and he warned me that President Trump would move quickly among topics: "You are going to get rapid-fire questions. Think about what is your thirty-second answer for everything." Pompeo also told me to relax, and that Trump, in contrast to his combative public persona, would be engaging and gracious.

A driver met me and took me directly to Mar-a-Lago, where I changed into my Army uniform in a room used by the president's military aides. Then I walked into the main guest entrance under the portico, down the steps, and through the gilded living room. I took in the hooded fireplace and gazed up at the twenty-one-foot-high gold leaf ceiling—a copy of the Thousand-Wing Ceiling in the Gallerie dell'Accademia in Venice, Italy.

Priebus, Bannon, and Kushner met me in the Tea Room, which offers panoramic views of the lawn and the beach beyond it. We sat at a round table to talk while Kushner took phone calls and moved in and out of the conversation. I was to meet with the president in about an hour; it had become clear that this was the pre-interview. Priebus and Bannon asked questions about geopolitics, but Bannon, who had a penchant for using war metaphors for significant policy issues as well as for personal confrontations, wanted to know about our cavalry troop's experience in the 1991 Gulf War.

I noted that it was a long time ago, as we were one week away from the twenty-sixth anniversary of the Battle of 73 Easting. I then explained that the main reason for the lopsided outcome of the battle was the bonds of confidence, trust, and affection among our 136 troopers. I tried to leave it at that, but Bannon pressed for details. Using salt and pepper shakers and sweetener packets to represent armored vehicles and the enemy's defenses, I described the courageous actions of our soldiers, crews, and platoons and emphasized how every trooper took initiative. I described how our soldiers had attacked a much larger force without hesitation and noted how history had informed our cavalry troop's preparations. Having studied armored combat in North Africa during World War II, we had based our battle drills—rehearsed responses to predictable sets of circumstances in combat—largely on German field marshal Erwin Rommel's papers and on U.S. major general Ernest Harmon's "Notes on Combat Actions in Tunisia and North Africa."[5]

I also told them that many captured enemies wept when our soldiers gave them water, rations, and spare pairs of boots. The enemy had been told that Americans would execute them. I stressed the discipline and humaneness of our soldiers as well as their courage.

Bannon and Priebus thanked me for sharing the account and told me that the president would likely ask me about the battle, too.

It was time. I walked into the bar, greeted the president, shook his hand, and thanked him for considering me for the position. I took the chair across the rectangular table from him as Priebus, Bannon, and Kushner sat around us. Hanging on a wall behind Trump was a portrait of him, wearing tennis whites and looking about thirty years younger. The backdrop was an apocalyptic orange sky.

Trump was warm and welcoming. He had "heard many good things from many people" about me. As Pompeo predicted, Trump asked several questions in quick succession. When he asked for my assessment of the war in Afghanistan, I described the sixteen-year-long war as a one-year war fought sixteen times over with short-term, inconsistent, and fundamentally flawed strategies. I highlighted that the Obama administration had been negotiating from a position of weakness. By no longer designating the Taliban as an enemy while bargaining with them, it had removed military pressure on the terrorist group.

Trump asked about the Middle East and the ongoing U.S. war against ISIS in Syria and Iraq. I observed that jihadist terrorist organizations and Iran were perpetuating a destructive cycle of sectarian violence. I shared the president's distrust of the theocratic dictatorship in Iran and lamented the sanctions relief under the Joint Comprehensive Plan of Action (JCPOA), the Iran nuclear deal negotiated by the Obama administration.

Trump agreed that, across multiple administrations, we had not imposed adequate costs on Iran to deter further aggression. He was also sympathetic to my general assessment that the United States had not competed effectively in recent years, and our power and influence had diminished.

"Mr. President, if selected, I will work with you to challenge assumptions that underpin U.S. policies and develop options for you that bolster our competitive advantages." I think my intention resonated with a man who, as candidate for president, had promised to make Americans "tired of winning."

Bannon asked me to summarize my book *Dereliction of Duty* and its lessons. Trump told me he had just read it and "liked it very much." (I later met the staffer who had prepared a synopsis of it for him.) "Mr. President, Lyndon Johnson's advisors told him what he wanted to hear instead of what he needed to know to make wise decisions. As a result, the United States went to war in Vietnam without a sound strategy. LBJ failed to consider the costs and consequences of his decisions. Many Johnson administration advisors knew better, but they went along because they were afraid of losing influence with the president." I asked rhetorically, "But what good were advisors if they told LBJ only what he wanted to hear?" I said the key lesson for me was to "ensure that the president gets the best analysis and multiple options so he can make informed decisions."

Trump seemed happy with the answer.

Much of the conversation was light.

"General, do you golf?"

"Mr. President, I do not. If you are looking for a good golfer, you would have better luck with an Air Force officer."

Trump had made me feel at ease, and I was enjoying the conversation. Toward the end of the interview, Bannon prompted me to tell the Battle of 73 Easting story. I quickly summarized the battle, then told Trump that an Iraqi brigade commander whom we had captured pointed to a photo of Field Marshal Erwin Rommel that was taped to the turret shield door of our squadron's command post Bradley and asked a cavalry scout, "Why do you have a picture of your World War Two adversary?" The young soldier had responded "Why don't you shut the fuck up? If you had read a little about Rommel, you wouldn't be sitting in the back of my track." The point was that our soldiers are smart and attuned to the lessons of history.

Trump laughed. He asked me when I could start. He seemed to be hiring me on the spot.

Priebus interjected nervously, "Mr. President, we have more interviews."

I told Trump that I lived in Tidewater, Virginia, but could move to Washington and start immediately. He said that he would like me to stay in the Army as national security advisor and asked what I thought of this. "Mr. President, that would not be unprecedented. Then-Lieutenant General Colin Powell remained in uniform as national security advisor, and Lieutenant General Brent Scowcroft did the job of deputy national security advisor while still on active duty."

It then seemed to occur to the president that staying in uniform might disadvantage me financially. He asked, "How much does a three-star general make?"

"I don't really know," I responded. "Every month my check goes to Katie, and whenever I use an ATM, it works."

"Wow, you really are in this just for the service, aren't you?"

I stood up, shook the president's hand, thanked him again for the opportunity, and walked out.

A question the president did not ask was how I saw my role as national security advisor, how I intended to assist him with his foreign policy and national security agendas. In retrospect, that unasked question proved significant. So did the presence of his "chief strategist," Bannon, in the room for the interview. Trump's poor understanding of the national security advisor's role relative to that of his cabinet and other members of his staff, along with his penchant for pitting people against one another instead of building collaborative teams, would cause friction in his administration and in our relationship.

*   *   *

PRIEBUS AND Bannon emerged a few minutes later and told me to hang around. The president wanted to see me again after the other interviews. It was midafternoon. I returned to the military aides' room where I had changed. I was very hungry but did not want to go back to the main building to order lunch: they wanted to keep the interviewees separate from one another. I found a one-pound bag of pistachios and ate much of it while I made calls and caught up on emails. I left an IOU for Air Force major Wes Spurlock, one of the military aides, for the pistachios, but as I drafted this chapter, I realized I had never made good on it. I have since repaid my debt thanks to Nuts.com.

Around dinnertime, someone came to inform me that the president had run out of time and was on his way to dinner. The next interview would be the following morning. I checked into the Hilton Garden Inn, a short drive away, changed, and went to the hotel restaurant. As I wolfed down a burger, I called fellow job candidate Bob Caslen and asked him to join me for a beer, only to discover we had been put up in separate hotels. Bob told me he was departing on a flight the next morning. I assumed I was one of the finalists, but did not know who else was still under consideration.

I found out the next morning when I bumped into John Bolton in the men's room at Mar-a-Lago.

"Good morning, Ambassador."

"Good morning, General."

He was on his way out, and I was on my way in, for my second interview.

Back in the living room, I joined Priebus and Bannon on a couch between two chairs across from the fireplace. The president walked in. I stood to greet him. He sat down in a chair and told me that another interview would not be necessary. He had decided to appoint me as national security advisor. "I look forward to working with you, General." He then told Priebus to bring in Keith Kellogg, the fourth candidate and acting national security advisor.

Kellogg took the chair across the coffee table from the president. I did not know Keith: his assignments were in light infantry units, and he was a generation older than me. He looked dejected. The president introduced us and asked if I would keep Keith on as chief of staff. "Sure, Mr. President." I turned to Keith, "It'll be a privilege to serve with you."

The president introduced me to his deputy press secretary, Sarah Huckabee Sanders. They began discussing when and where to make the announcement. Sanders suggested the following day, at the

White House. The president asked if Katie could join me for it, and I told him I was sure she could. The plan was for me to fly to Washington on Air Force One later that afternoon. The White House would get me home to Fort Eustis to pack and would then fly Katie and me back to Washington the next day.

We adjourned. As we walked outside into the bright Florida sunlight, I noticed that Kellogg was upset. He said something about quitting and complained that no one had been with Trump longer or was more loyal than he was to the president. I tried to console Keith, telling him I was sure we could make a good team. Unfortunately, his sadness would morph into resentment and malice.

Back in the military aides' room once again, I changed, throwing my uniform into a garment bag. Soon afterward, someone knocked on the door to tell me that the president had changed his mind: he would announce my appointment in front of the Mar-a-Lago press pool in about an hour.

I quickly tried to call Katie, but she was at an appointment. My uniform had become wrinkled, but I found the president's valet, an Army sergeant, who steamed it for me. Wrinkle-free, I returned to the living room to find the president directing how the couch would be arranged for the announcement.

Trump invited Kellogg to join us on the couch. Keith sat awkwardly to his left. Soon, the press pool crowded in. The president waited for them to settle and then said, "So, I just wanted to announce . . . that General H. R. McMaster will become the national security advisor. He's a man of tremendous talent and tremendous experience. I watched and read a lot over the last two days. He is highly respected by everybody in the military, and we are very glad to have him."

I replied, "Mr. President, thank you very much. I'd just like to say what a privilege it is to be able to continue serving our nation. I'm grateful to you for that opportunity. And I look forward to joining the National Security team and doing everything I can to advance and protect the interests of the American people. Thank you very much, sir." Then I shook the president's hand.[6]

After the announcement, I retrieved my phone, which was already buzzing with innumerable texts and voicemails from friends and family. I noticed an incoming call from my boss at U.S. Army

Training and Doctrine Command, Gen. David Perkins, whom I had known for nearly two decades and for whom I had great respect. I asked the president if he would mind talking to him, given that I was leaving Dave's command on such short notice. Trump graciously obliged. Without warning, I handed the phone to the president, who spoke with a surprised Dave Perkins as we walked to the motorcade that would take us to Air Force One.

Once aboard the aircraft, I met other members of the White House staff. Joe Hagin, the chief of White House operations, asked the president to sign a directive to provide me with a Secret Service protective detail and informed me that the detail would meet me in Washington on Tuesday afternoon.

I finally reached Katie. I also called my father, sister, and my aunt Johanne Curcio, my late mother's sister.

After Air Force One landed at Andrews Air Force Base, I made my way over to two U.S. Marine Corps Osprey tilt-rotor aircraft and greeted the crew who flew me home to Tidewater, Virginia. That night, Katie and I discussed what was certain to be an interesting and challenging tour of duty. We decided not to move our home to Washington until our daughter Colleen and her fiancé, Lee, were married in California on April 1.

The next day, the Ospreys returned to fly me back up to Washington.

As the ramp of the Marine Corps MV-22 Osprey dropped, I yelled thanks to the U.S. Marine Corps crew above the roar of the spinning tilt rotors, grabbed my two bags, and walked onto the tarmac to meet members of my new Secret Service detail. Over the next thirteen months, they would become like members of our family. The team took me directly to the White House to begin my first day as national security advisor, almost exactly twenty-four hours after President Trump had hired me.

Some of the friends who called me before and after the interview had recommended that I decline the job. The president was a deeply flawed person, they said. Everyone who works for him gets chewed up or emerges from the experience with a sullied reputation. But I saw it as my duty to serve. Regardless of Trump's personal foibles, I believed I could do genuine good for him and the country. Besides, my commander in chief had asked me to do the job, and I would continue to serve as I had under his five predecessors.

I felt no sense of trepidation or anxiety. One learns in combat that those are not helpful emotions. I knew the job would be challenging, but I felt up to it. The only pressure I would experience was the pressure I put on myself to perform well the job I had studied as a historian. What I did not anticipate fully was that, unlike the units in which I had served in combat overseas, in Washington, the Trump administration was already at war with itself.

CHAPTER 3

"LOVE ALL,
TRUST A FEW"

President Trump Sends Top Aides to Mexico Amid Deep Strains with U.S. . . . **THE ROAD TO POWER IN UKRAINE RUNS THROUGH DONALD TRUMP** . . . Trump Calls for Aggressive Change in Speech to Congress . . . *H R MCMASTER: THE PHILOSOPHER GENERAL WHO COULD TAME TRUMP* . . . McMaster Faces Limits in Overhauling Flynn's NSC . . . McMaster delves into the responsibility for the Vietnam War debacle. He concludes that everyone in political and military leadership shares the blame . . . China to Increase Military Spending by 7% in 2017 . . . Donald Trump Is No Ronald Reagan . . . Pence Visits DMZ as Tensions Rise Between U.S. and N. Korea . . . U.S. split over plan to take Raqqa from Islamic State . . . Erdogan Claims Victory in Referendum to Give President Sweeping Powers . . . *Many Americans Disapprove of Trump but Are Open to His Agenda, Poll Finds* . . . In address to Congress, Trump leaves behind campaign rhetoric and embraces Washington ritual . . . **Muslim majority countries show anger at Trump Travel Ban** . . . TRUMP'S NEW TRAVEL BAN BLOCKS MIGRANTS FROM SIX NATIONS, SPARING IRAQ

I WALKED into the West Wing side entrance, up the stairs, and down the hallway to the office suite for the assistant to the president for national security affairs and the deputy assistant. There, I met Coast Guard captain John Reed, who had been serving as executive assistant to Michael Flynn. Deputy National Security Advisor Kathleen Troia "K.T." McFarland walked out of her office at the back of the suite to greet me. It was K.T. who had held the team together under the strains of the transition between presidents and of Mike Flynn's unexpected departure

John Rader and Navy lieutenant commander Sarah Flaherty emerged from an office not much larger than a walk-in closet. John was serving as my policy advisor, and Sarah as K.T.'s. Sarah had met K.T. through K.T.'s daughter, a fellow naval officer. K.T. and I had a few moments alone in the furnished but otherwise undecorated NSA office. She acknowledged the turbulence associated with the transition and the unexpected departure of Flynn, but said that important work was already under way. She explained that we had a talented team and that she had run deputies committee meetings to develop options for the president on North Korea—the problem that President Obama had told President Trump was most urgent.

I thanked K.T. for all she had done and told her that her understanding of the president and the Trump team would help me transition into the job. Aware that I had never been assigned in Washington, K.T., who had first served on the NSC staff under Henry Kissinger, warned me that the working environment of the White House would be "nothing like your experience in the military."

In Washington, she noted, "friends stab you in the chest."

Others had given me similar warnings. Former Speaker of the House Newt Gingrich told me that "when you find yourself in a snake pit, don't be surprised when you have to handle snakes."

As I entered the Situation Room, in the basement of the West Wing, I sensed trepidation among the NSC senior staff. Megan Badasch, the deputy executive secretary, recalled later that she was thinking, *This is where we all get fired.* K.T. had told me that many members of the staff shared Badasch's anxiety.

I explained that I needed their help because "this was my first assignment in Washington." I acknowledged Keith Kellogg's service in Vietnam and noted how challenging it must have been to lead soldiers under a fundamentally flawed policy and strategy. I shared with them my view that the Obama administration policies and strategies to cope with threats from China, Russia, North Korea, Iran, and jihadist terrorist organizations had been, like U.S. strategy for the Vietnam War, based on fundamentally flawed assumptions. We would scrutinize assumptions, take time to understand the nature of the challenges and opportunities the United States was confronting, identify what was at stake, craft realistic objectives, and develop multiple policy options to accomplish those objectives at an acceptable cost and risk.

I asked the team for their thoughts on how I should prioritize my personal efforts to contribute to the mission. I thought I had allayed their concerns about their being fired, but I sensed reluctance among them to share criticisms and suggestions in such a large group.

Badasch asked me to visit the Eisenhower Executive Office Building (EEOB) to meet members of the Executive Secretariat, the body that coordinates the work of the NSC staff internally and communications between the NSC staff, the White House staff, and the departments and agencies. The team there had been working tirelessly since the transition and could use a morale boost.

As we walked across the EEOB parking lot and up the stairs to her office, I saw looks of surprise as I greeted members of the NSC and White House staff in the hallways. I learned later that most national security advisors rarely ventured out of the West Wing and into the EEOB. Over the next year, I would routinely visit directors in their offices. It gave me the opportunity to see members of the NSC staff more frequently, hear their perspectives, and benefit from their insights. Meeting people on their own turf often makes them feel more comfortable. It is also one of the many aspects of leadership that is common in the Army but unusual in the White House.

*   *   *

LATER THAT first day, I met with my policy advisor, John Rader, and with John Eisenberg, the NSC legal advisor and deputy counsel to the president for national security. Eisenberg stressed that to fulfill his responsibility to the president, he must be present for consequential conversations. He explained that although his responsibility was to the president alone, he would help me avoid pitfalls and ensure that any NSC initiatives were legal and above reproach. For example, Eisenberg had lamented Mike Flynn's decision to grant an interview with FBI investigators without a White House attorney present because it was detrimental to Flynn and could have compromised executive privilege—that is, the power of the president and other officials in the executive branch to withhold certain forms of confidential communication from the courts and the legislative branch. Rader caught me up on how the current NSC organization and process had developed during the transition. The elevation of homeland security advisor Tom Bossert to the equivalent of the national security advisor had blurred the lines of responsibility and also created bureaucratic problems: Bossert and I could both convene meetings with the secretary of defense, secretary of state, and other cabinet officials, which could cause redundancies and confusion.

But the most controversial aspect of the Trump National Security Council, as laid out in a January 28, 2017, National Security Presidential Memorandum (NSPM), was the designation of "regular attendees" of the principals committee (PC) of the National Security Council and the Homeland Security Council.[1] Rader told me that, as the draft of the NSPM went through the clearance process, Priebus had used a red Sharpie to add Trump's chief campaign strategist, Steve Bannon, to the roster of regular members of the principals committee (PC). The document had not listed the director of national intelligence and chairman of the Joint Chiefs of Staff, Gen. Joseph Dunford, as regular members of the PC. Senior policy advisor Stephen Miller had added these edits before Mike Flynn was aware of the change. This was a problem because those who had been removed were important for getting the president the best advice; also, Bannon's membership on it would imply that Trump was allowing partisan politics to intrude on issues of national security.

I made a note to talk with the president about this.

*   *   *

I LEFT the White House that day at around 8 p.m. and jumped into the back right seat of one of the two Suburbans that would be my principal means of conveyance for the next year. It was a short drive across the Potomac River to Fort Myer. My bags were already in the two-room apartment at Wainwright Hall, military lodging named for Gen. Jonathan Wainwright, who, after the evacuation of Gen. Douglas MacArthur from the Philippines in 1941, was forced to surrender to the Japanese Army and endured three years of brutal captivity. Wainwright and I had both commanded the Third Cavalry Regiment. He was the regiment's twenty-seventh colonel, serving from 1935 to 1938, seventy years before I assumed command of that storied unit as its seventy-first colonel. It was a reminder that the Army is a living historical community. The travails of soldiers like Wainwright put into context the relatively trivial concerns that many in Washington regard as crises.

The refrigerator in the apartment was stocked. I found a welcome note from Shannon George, the wife of Maj. Gen. John George, with whom I had served at Fort Eustis. The Army and Army friends would remain a source of support in my new job.

The next day, Wednesday, February 22, my first full day on the job, started early for me. I departed Wainwright Hall just after 7 a.m. I intended to use my first hour in the office each day for reading and thinking. Dr. Seth Center, the NSC director for national security strategy and history, had gathered together the Obama administration's most significant policy documents for me. They were disappointing. I should not have been surprised, as for many years prior, I had been on the receiving end of inane policy papers such as those about Iraq and Afghanistan. Reading the papers in my office affirmed my belief that, in the post–Cold War period, U.S. strategic competence had atrophied.

At 8:30, I met my intel briefer, with whom I would spend a lot of time over the course of the year. I read through the President's Daily Brief (PDB), the "book of secrets" the intelligence community produces each morning for the president and a select group of cabinet-level officials, as my briefer hit the highlights. The PDB's analytical essays have no byline, but briefers know who the author of each one is and will provide feedback to that person based on discussions. I complimented one well-written and well-argued assessment of how jihadist terrorist organizations were evolving. My briefer smiled and said, "It does not surprise me that you like the paper. You know the author very well." PDB papers are scheduled well in advance. In what was a remarkable coincidence, the assessment had been written by my daughter Katharine, who was serving at the National Counterterrorism Center.

What were the chances that Katharine's essay would be in my first PDB or that I would read it and compliment the anonymous author? I was even prouder of her service. *It was an auspicious sign*, I thought.

Mike Pompeo stopped by just prior to what would be my first PDB session with him and the president. He reminded me to give Trump quick, essential information and, if appropriate, to tell a story that illuminated the key dimensions of the given subject. He warned that I would hear what one might consider outlandish ideas during conversations with the president, because Trump was determined to do what he had been elected to do—shake things up. Moreover, he told me, Trump was not of the world of politics and policy, and he tended to think out loud.

Before we walked down the hall to the Oval Office, Pompeo highlighted two aspects of Trump's worldview that were problematic: he undervalued alliances, and he tended toward moral equivalency when discussing threats from authoritarian hostile powers. I would come to appreciate this quick psychological snapshot of the president and how adept Pompeo was at his job and interacting with Trump.

In the small waiting area outside the Oval Office, Pompeo introduced me to the president's briefer. Priebus, Bannon, McFarland, and Kellogg were there, too. Apparently, no one wanted to miss the PDB show. When the president was ready, we all walked into the Oval Office together. The briefer, Pompeo, Priebus, and I sat in chairs across from the president in front of the Resolute desk given to President Rutherford Hayes in 1880 by Queen Victoria. The desk was made of oak wood from the HMS *Resolute*, which had gotten stuck in ice and was abandoned in the 1850s.

The president pointed to a stack of newspapers on the right side of his desk. "General, I have never seen anyone get such good press. Mike, even you didn't get such good press." Trump looked at me. "Did you know that Mike graduated number one in his class at West Point?"

I responded, "No, I did not. That is impressive. You should know that I, too, graduated near the top of my class, but in a different category—demerits."

While cracking the West Point joke, I was also counting heads. I could not imagine that having so many people in the Oval Office for an intel briefing would be effective—and it was not. With a large audience, the president seemed to revert to his role as host of *The Apprentice*, the reality-TV show in which Trump was the center of attention as candidates vied for the privilege of serving as his apprentice.

I came to regard the PDB and other meetings in the early days of the Trump White House as exercises in competitive sycophancy. Some advisors tried to outdo one another with obsequious compliments to the president and attestations to his wisdom. Commiseration about the president's persecution by the media (such as the false claims of collusion with Russia) provided an easy path to an advisor's ingratiation with him. Phrases often heard included "Your instincts are always right" and "You are the only one who can . . ." and "No one has ever been treated so badly by the press." In the PDB show, the presence of an "audience" encouraged the president to stray from the topic at hand or to say something outlandish—like "Why don't we just bomb the drugs?" (in Mexico) or "Why don't we take out the whole North Korean Army during one of their parades?" But I soon learned that Trump asked such questions and made other outlandish statements only to entertain or shock those assembled. The briefer handled the near-constant disruptions brilliantly, with a calm, professional demeanor, waiting patiently for the conversation to return to him so he could summarize succinctly the most important elements of the PDB.

As that first PDB meeting broke up, I made a note to follow up with Pompeo and Priebus on how to make the session more useful for the president. Later, I would pare down the roster for the meeting, only to have Keith Kellogg go directly to the president to be reinstated. About a month later, I told the president I did not need Keith in the meeting and he would no longer attend. My concerns were about security as well as the meeting's dynamic. I also reduced the number of people who would receive the PDB. In a White House that was leaking like a sieve, it was important that the briefing go only to those who had a need to know.

The first full day and every day that followed would be unique, and the fast pace and the intervention of unanticipated events ensured that no day was boring. During the two hours that followed that first PDB meeting, I met with reporters, called a newspaper editor to ask him to remove elements of a story that could undermine national security, had lunch with the president and a follow-on meeting in the Oval Office to discuss the forthcoming budget submission to Congress, and called Iraqi ambassador Fareed Yasseen (whom I knew from my service in Iraq) to hear his concern that a revised executive order known as the travel ban would include Iraq.

I also met with Dina Powell, whom Ivanka Trump had offered to transfer from her staff to mine. Ivanka and Jared knew I would need help navigating the dynamics of the West Wing. Their idea was that Dina would serve as my political "consigliere." But after I learned about Dina's experience on Capitol Hill, in finance, in the White House under George W. Bush, and in the Middle East, I crafted a more substantial position for her. She would serve as deputy national security advisor for strategy, a position critical to shifting the NSC's focus away from short-term tactics and toward the development of long-term integrated strategies. I could use her help. Dina accepted the offer.

Megan Badasch, the deputy executive secretary—who, I was starting to realize, was the de facto executive secretary, despite Kellogg's holding the title—began to discuss the flow of paper associated with the policymaking and decision-making process. She then began to summarize the safeguards she had put into place after leaks of two memorandums of telephone conversations summarizing President Trump's calls, during his first week in office, with Mexican president Enrique Peña Nieto and Australian prime minister Malcolm Turnbull. Kellogg waved his hand in front of her face to cut her off.

"Keith, you cannot do that," I said. "Let Megan say what she has to say." I was already sensing a counterproductive dynamic between Kellogg and other members of the team.

But, overall, it was a good first day. After dinner in the Residence with the president, Priebus, Kushner, Bannon, Mattis, Pompeo, and General Dunford, I walked across Lafayette Square to the Hay-Adams hotel. The Off the Record is one of Washington's great bars, a well-known gathering place in the hotel's basement. It was my good

fortune that Dr. Marin Strmecki and Dr. Nadia Schadlow, both executives at the Smith Richardson Foundation, were in town. Because
Nadia and Marin have an in with the hotel's staff, we sat at the most
discreet table, tucked behind the bar. Over dry martinis, we sketched
out what the NSC staff does for the president—"Coordinate and integrate across the departments and agencies to provide options" was
the headliner. Marin suggested a focus on developing what he called
"game plans" to compete more effectively against rivals, adversaries, and enemies. He, Nadia, and I had often lamented the absence
of strategies to overcome challenges and take advantage of opportunities. U.S. foreign policy was often reactive, as the NSC focused
on discrete tactical decisions without what Winston Churchill described as "an all-embracing view." Thanks to Marin and Nadia, I left
Off the Record with notes for the next day's all-hands meeting with
the NSC staff.

★　　★　　★

THE NEXT morning, I met with Vice President Mike Pence. He
thanked me for serving in the military and shared with me that his
son, Michael, was a Marine Corps officer who would soon deploy
to Afghanistan. Michael had recently graduated from Purdue University and was training to become a pilot.[2] The former governor
and congressman told me that his previous career as a talk radio
host had taught him listening skills and noted that "too many politicians have stopped listening."

Pence shared his intention to resurrect the National Space Council to drive innovation in what had become a contested domain. I
offered to mobilize the NSC staff in support of that effort. He told
me never to hesitate to ask him for advice or assistance. I would take
him up on that offer several times.

I would see Pence's character tested in the coming months. Although he was tactful and reserved in demeanor, he never hesitated
to tell Trump when the president's "instincts" were leading him to
self-defeating rhetoric or behavior on topics like NATO or the alliance with South Korea. Pence did not falter on those occasions nor
would he during the January 6, 2021, assault on the U.S. Capitol.

After the day's PDB meeting in the Oval Office and a short conversation with the president about an upcoming phone call with Prime Minister Justin Trudeau of Canada, it was time for the all-hands NSC meeting. I walked out of the West Wing and across the parking lot to the South Court Auditorium, in the Eisenhower Executive Office Building. The tiered seats were full of NSC staff.

I got a laugh when I told those assembled, "If anyone is surprised that I'm standing here, you're not alone." I also asked them, "Are you happy? I'm happy, because I have the opportunity to serve with you, a great team with an important mission."

I thanked everyone for their service to our nation and to the president at what I believed was a critical time. I made it clear that we were *all* there to help President Trump determine his foreign policy and national security agenda. "I have noticed that some have referred to those who served in the Obama administration as 'holdovers.' We are a team. We must work together to serve our nation and the president well. I do not want anyone to use that term."

I pulled out the sheets of paper I had ripped from my notebook after talking with Strmecki and Schadlow the night before. "I want to begin a conversation with you about our mission, our vision for our organization, our priorities, and the process we'll run to help the president advance and protect American interests. We exist to enable the president to plan and execute an integrated strategy to protect and advance U.S. interests and values. It is also our job to coordinate the implementation of strategy to ensure that initiatives are mutually reinforcing or at least ensure that they are not working at cross-purposes." I gave examples of how, in recent years, the United States had applied one element of national power in a way that cut against others and undermined our objectives.

"We have to earn the trust of the president and officials across our government. We have to eliminate leaks to the press because they distract us from our mission and undermine trust." I noted that a discussion that I had the day before, about changes to NSC structure, had leaked immediately. "The president must trust us, or we cannot do our job for him and the nation. And foreign leaders must trust us to keep the president's conversations with them confidential. If leaks force us to limit deliberations to an ever-shrinking circle, our policies will suffer from the absence of important perspectives. And we need to earn trust across the departments and agencies. We need to lead by charm."

We would focus on outcomes. The president was predisposed to challenging the assumptions on which previous policies were based. "That is a good thing," I told them. "Trump does not intend to be a 'caretaker president.' Over the next four years, we have an opportunity to help him shift the global balance of power in favor of the United States."

"We often talk about black swans, unanticipated events that have unforeseen consequences. But in recent decades we have averted our eyes from what my friend Dr. Frank Hoffman labeled 'pink flamingos,' obvious dangers we ignore because they are inconsistent with our preferences."[3] One pink flamingo was that autocracy was making a comeback. I then summarized the threats from revanchist Russia, Iran's theocratic dictatorship, and the only hereditary communist regime in the world, North Korea. But I gave special emphasis to the new great power competition that had emerged with another authoritarian regime, China, for which a giant *red* flamingo may be a more appropriate metaphor.

I ended by asking the team's thoughts with regard to the following questions:

What are the top priorities?

What strategic shifts have we seen in the past fifteen years?

What strategic shifts do we want to create?

What do we want the world to look like in four years?

What are we missing? What are we not talking about that we should be working on?

I took a few questions, until John Reed reminded me that I had a meeting in the Oval Office in five minutes. I thanked the team again and urged them to take care of themselves and look after one another and their families. Our staff then handed out five-by-eight index cards, and I asked everyone to use the cards to give me feedback, whether anonymously or while identifying themselves. In my past career, when I took command of a squadron and, later, a regiment, I had found this to be an effective way to get a fast, candid assessment of an organization.

Some who had arrived in the White House with their own agendas confused my comment that I was apolitical with a reluctance on my part to advance Donald Trump's foreign policy and national security agenda. For example, Keith Kellogg, who seemed to find it impossible to overcome his resentment over not having been selected for my job, wrote later that "in Washington, D.C., no one gets to be apolitical. Every national security decision is guided by administration policy and strategy, which means politics."[4]

I underestimated the difficulty of insulating the NSC from the vitriolic partisanship afflicting Washington and the nation. Some on the NSC staff were so resentful of Donald Trump that they leaked what they perceived as damaging information to the press or to former Obama administration appointees, who then posted the leaks on social media. Others, including Kellogg and some members of the NSC staff who were close to Mike Flynn or Steve Bannon, used those leaks to reinforce this us-versus-them mentality. The constant false allegations of collusion with Russia motivated some staffers to assume the role of defenders of the president. But no matter how noble their motives, that was not their job. They, like those who leaked to undermine the president, fomented distrust and distracted the team from our responsibilities. Directorates responsible for the most dramatic policy changes, such as the Middle East directorate, were the most distrustful and distracted. I also underestimated the degree of distrust between the NSC staff and some members of the White House staff.

*   *   *

I MET many of my new colleagues during my first chief of staff meeting, which Reince Priebus hosted in his office. Most attendees sat at Priebus's large conference table; others took seats on both sides of the fireplace opposite his desk. I sat next to National Economic Council director Gary Cohn, whom I had met at Mar-a-Lago. He and I would work well together to integrate economic and national security policy. I joked with Gary, the former president and chief operating officer of Goldman Sachs, that I had worn a uniform to work since I was seventeen and would have to get some new suits. Cohn, who was always impeccably dressed, nodded to my attire and said, "That suit doesn't look bad." I held open the jacket to show him the label, "Mobin Tailor; Kabul, Afghanistan," and told him, "The bad news is that it would set you back ninety bucks." We both laughed. I'm sure Gary's socks alone were more expensive than my suit.

As the meeting began, Priebus asked Stephen Miller to provide an update on the president's first speech to Congress, scheduled for the following Tuesday, February 28, part of which was meant to honor veterans. The plan was to showcase a veteran who was also a convicted felon.

I was astonished, thinking, *Who is doing the vetting?* Then I realized that this was one of the reasons I was there.

I then explained that, even if the ex-felon were reformed, using him as an example could be insulting to veterans and those serving today. "While we should not stigmatize those who suffer from mental health challenges after traumatic combat experience, a felon is not a good representative for the vast majority of veterans, who emerge from combat strong, resilient, and who go on to make tremendous contributions to society." President Trump, I suggested, would not want to reinforce Hollywood's and popular culture's portrayal of veterans as fragile, traumatized human beings. "Soldiers do not view themselves as victims," I explained, "and veterans do not want to be pitied."

Priebus directed Miller to select a different veteran.

In addition to meeting the White House and NSC staff, I prioritized meeting with or phoning former national security advisors, which I would accomplish over the next few weeks. Since the National Security Council's inception in 1948, the role of its staff has evolved from acting as a small executive secretariat to coordinating and integrating the president's foreign policy and National Security Strategy.

Each former national security advisor shared their perspectives and experiences.

On our first call, Secretary Condoleezza Rice expressed concern that our international partners had perceived U.S. withdrawal from the world under President Obama and were bracing for greater disengagement based on the nativist language Trump had employed during the presidential campaign. She noted that Russia was not strong but would fill vacuums left by perceived or actual U.S. disengagement and warned that in the United States' so-called pivot away from the Middle East, we risked missing real opportunities in the region.

Retired Marine Corps general Jim Jones foreshadowed the difficulties I would encounter with Kellogg and Bannon. He recalled struggling to bond with colleagues who had been through the crucible of the election campaign and had assumed the role of true partisans for the president and his agenda.

Obama's other national security advisors, Tom Donilon and Susan Rice—after making what I am sure they knew to be an infeasible recommendation to prioritize climate change as the most important national security issue—focused on organization and process in my calls to them. They both stressed the relationship between the Homeland Security Council and the National Security Council and recommended strongly that the HSC convene only at my direction, to avoid confusion across the government.

Zbigniew Brzezinski emphasized the threat from North Korea and the importance of galvanizing the world to block Pyongyang's path to the most destructive weapons on earth. Brzezinski also described his relationship with President Carter. Once he determined how Carter liked to receive information, Brzezinski would use newspaper articles to spark his interest in a particular topic. He also suggested that I brief the First Lady weekly, because a good relationship with her could solidify my relationship with the president. "Remember," he told me, "your relationship with the president will determine your effectiveness and your survival." I wanted to heed his advice, but I knew that my natural aversion to "networking" would make any attempt to foster a relationship with the First Lady awkward and probably ill-fated.

Colin Powell was kind enough to host me at his home for lunch during my second week in Washington. Powell had served as deputy national security advisor and national security advisor while serving as a lieutenant general under President Ronald Reagan, after which he was promoted to four-star rank and eventually appointed as chairman of the Joint Chiefs of Staff. During lunch, he said that, these days, "having an active-duty officer in there could help tremendously, because you can set the tone that foreign policy should not be infected by the same kind of vitriolic partisan discourse that we see the country engaged in." Powell was familiar with taking over a post in a time of turbulence, having assumed responsibility in the wake of the Iran-Contra scandal. Unsurprisingly, he warned me about overzealous senior directors who might be tempted to run operations out of the White House. I told him that I had already shut down a communications line between the NSC staff and a head of state.

Dr. Henry Kissinger visited me in the office during my first week. He described the national security advisor as the only person in the foreign policy and national security establishment who has the president as his or her only client. He noted the natural tension between the national security advisor and the secretary of state and joked that the relationship between the two was never better than when he held both positions.

During our sit-down, I expressed agreement with Kissinger's observation, published in a long interview with *Atlantic* editor Jeff Goldberg, that the Obama Doctrine was "an essentially reactive and passive foreign policy" that sought "vindication of its values by withdrawing from regions where we can only make things worse."[5]

★   ★   ★

TO BEGIN to build relationships, I scheduled one-on-one meetings with each of the NSC principals and with senior members of the White House staff. Jared Kushner described his broad portfolio, which ranged from Israeli-Palestinian-Arab relations to trade deals to the relationship with Mexico to planned presidential travel. I assured him that the NSC would be the best way to coordinate his initiatives with the departments and agencies.

Secretary of the Treasury Steven Mnuchin gave me good insights into the president's decision-making and worldview. The U.S. ambassador to the United Nations, former South Carolina governor Nikki Haley, stopped by with her chief of staff, Jon Lerner. Joe Hagin, White House deputy chief of staff for operations, took me to a great Italian dinner at La Perla. A season ticket holder for the Washington Nationals, Hagin would also offer Katie and me tickets to several games during baseball season.

Whenever I could, I went on the road to meet my new colleagues in their departments. When I visited then-Department of Homeland Security secretary John Kelly and his chief of staff, Kirstjen Nielsen, at DHS headquarters, we discussed the failed initial travel ban that suspended travel from seven Muslim-majority countries for ninety days and how members of the White House staff had forced that executive order on the president without proper coordination. "Stephen Miller completely bypassed [DHS], and it was a disaster," Kelly told me.

Kelly also discussed a debacle during his and Secretary of State Tillerson's visit to Mexico City to meet with President Enrique Peña Nieto, a trip meant to patch up relations after Trump described Mexican immigrants as criminals and insisted that Mexico would pay for construction of a southern border wall. As Tillerson and Kelly met with Mexican foreign minister Luis Videgaray, they were alerted that Trump had made a speech in which he said, "We're getting really bad dudes out of this country and at a rate that nobody's ever seen before, and they're the bad ones, and it's a military operation." And any goodwill that Kelly and Tillerson had built with Peña Nieto promptly crumbled.

After my first few days on the job, I knew I needed to pare down the attendees at Oval Office meetings, rein in the White House staff on national security issues, and help Trump align his words and actions with what he wanted to achieve. He had clearly gotten in his own way on immigration and Mexico policy.

★   ★   ★

MEXICAN OFFICIALS were not the only foreign counterparts nervous about the Trump administration. The sudden change of national security advisors had heightened concern. Many senior foreign officials visited in my first two weeks.

Japanese national security advisor Yachi Shotaro and Indian foreign secretary Subrahmanyam Jaishankar both shared their grave concerns over China's increasingly aggressive behavior. Would President Trump reverse U.S. policy and begin to compete with China?

Egyptian foreign minister Sameh Shoukry was eager to discuss the dangers of the Muslim Brotherhood. He asked if the president was willing to take on the Muslim Brotherhood and its sponsors in Turkey and Qatar.

Ukrainian foreign minister Pavlo Klimkin worried about Trump's Putin-friendly rhetoric and wanted assurances of continued U.S. support. He wondered out loud if the president knew that Putin was a liar who was manipulating history to justify his aggression against Ukraine.

Iraqi National Intelligence Service director Mustafa al-Khadimy (whom I had known since 2003) gave his assessment of the ongoing U.S. campaign to defeat ISIS. He wanted to know if the United States would stay until the job was done.

Others called, including Afghan president Ashraf Ghani, whom I had known for over a decade. He was anxious about Trump's many statements about Afghanistan over the years.[6] He asked, does the president really believe that the war effort in Afghanistan is a waste?

I initiated calls to counterparts, including Canada's national security advisor, Daniel Jean, who was concerned about the president's views on trade and the chances of the United States' pulling out of the North American Free Trade Agreement (NAFTA). "Is the President serious about withdrawing from NAFTA?"

I did not yet know the answers to any of their questions, and neither did Donald Trump. But they were some of the questions I would have to help him answer for himself and the nation.

Having served for years in multinational commands abroad, I was comfortable coordinating with allies and partners, and I understood the value of doing so. I believed that our alliances were only growing in importance, that we would need them more than ever to counter predatory pressures from revisionist powers Russia and China. On my second full day at the White House, I held a videoconference with national security advisor counterparts from the other "Quint countries"—an internal coordinating group comprising France, Germany, Italy, the United Kingdom, and the United States. Christoph Heusgen of Germany was running a little late, but Mariangela Zappia of Italy was right on time. After suggesting that Germany and Italy must have been trying to confuse me by reversing stereotypes, I asked my four colleagues to share their advice on the job of national security advisor and their greatest national security concerns and priorities, given that I was the newest member of our "club." I then suggested that we take our top-five shared national security challenges and each lead an effort in the coming months to frame that challenge and determine how we might apply our competitive advantages in concert to advance our mutual interests. I was sold on the value of alliances. Clarifying how we would work together on our top priorities could help convince Trump that Winston Churchill was right when he observed, "There is only one thing worse than fighting with allies, and that is fighting without them."[7]

* * *

I KNEW that my most important relationship besides Trump would be with the secretaries of state and defense. Former NSAs Tom Donilon and Stephen Hadley hosted weekly lunches and discussions with their counterparts, and I would propose something similar with Mattis and Tillerson. I respected both men. Our views on America's interests and the threats to those interests were generally aligned. But from the very beginning, our relationship was uneasy.

Immediately after the Quint meeting, I departed for the Pentagon to meet with Secretary Mattis and General Dunford. Mattis met me at the stairs outside the Pentagon and saluted in what I thought was an extraordinary expression of humility and comradeship. We walked up the steps, into what those in the military refer to as "the building," and then up more stairs, to his office on the third floor. Mattis sat behind his desk, and I sat on a chair to his front left. It was just the two of us. He told me that he had postponed my meeting with General Dunford because he wanted to have some time alone with me.

"H.R., I think you should retire from the Army."

"Mr. Secretary, I don't have to tell you how onerous the retirement process can be, and I'm already in the job. And the president told me he'd like me to stay on active duty."

Mattis looked down. He seemed to be suppressing anger or frustration.

Anticipating what I thought might be an unspoken concern that I would try to parlay the job into a promotion, I told him, "I have decided already that I'll retire out of this job. I'll decline any offers to compete for promotion or another assignment."

Mattis told me what I knew already: "You'll have to be confirmed by the Senate." He reached behind his desk for a binder of materials that his personal staff had clearly assembled for him. He then raised the case of two officers who, after graduation from the United States Military Academy at West Point, had arrived for the Infantry Officer Basic Course at Fort Benning, where I was then commander. They had been accused of committing sexual abuse and sexual assault while at the Academy. I had issued a "General Officer Memorandum of Reprimand" based on those serious charges, an administrative action that, once filed in an officer's record, can be career-ending. I deferred filing the letters and deciding how to dispose of their cases (such as with court-martial proceedings) until the investigation was complete. In the meantime, I permitted the two officers to continue training in Ranger School after they graduated from the Basic Course, a routine progression for infantry officers. Soon after they began Ranger School, a related investigation of another alleged perpetrator uncovered exculpatory evidence that exonerated all three subjects. The allegations were found to be incontrovertibly false, so I duly withdrew and destroyed the letters of reprimand.

Subsequently, members of Sen. Kirsten Gillibrand's staff, who had found it difficult to accept the facts of the case, discovered that, instead of me, the Army G-3 (another three-star general in the Pentagon who serves as deputy chief of staff for operations), by regulation, should have been the authority to allow the officers to go on to Ranger School. Because sexual assault in the military is, quite rightly, such an important issue, the Army vice chief of staff issued me a sternly worded "letter of concern," stating that I should have known who had the waiver authority to allow the two officers to continue training while the investigation progressed.

Now, years later, Mattis opened the binder and, without referring to the circumstances, read from the original allegations, telling me that senators were likely to do the same and accuse me of being complacent about sexual harassment and assault. I told Mattis that all those allegations had been discredited, that I had done the right thing, and that I had been absolutely intolerant of sexual harassment and sexual assault. I had merely afforded the accused due process, and they were later exonerated by the evidence. I had made a mistake, with the advice of counsel, only in allowing the accused to continue training at Ranger School without consulting the Army G-3.

"None of that will matter," he said. "The hearing will destroy your reputation."

I responded that if certain senators tried to misrepresent the facts, I would be happy for them to "bring it on." I told him that I would explain all this to the president and vice president and get back to him.

I did so, and Trump and Pence preferred that I remain on active duty. If Mattis was concerned that I might dilute his influence in the area of military advice, he would see soon enough that it was my intention to amplify, rather than muffle, the voices of the cabinet

I called Mattis to tell him my decision to remain in uniform. He responded perfunctorily, "Okay, H.R."

When I arrived at the Pentagon for my second visit later that week, my reception from Secretary Mattis was not as cordial.

Tom Bossert and I were meeting with Mattis to discuss the plan to defeat ISIS that the president had directed Mattis to deliver to him within the first thirty days of his presidency. I was just getting familiar with the draft plan, but it seemed incomplete: there was no clear concept for consolidating the military defeat of ISIS into a sustainable settlement. I would study the plan further before commenting.

On the way back to the White House, Bossert suggested that he, as homeland security advisor, should convene the principals committee to seek approval of the plan. In the first of what would be several differences of opinion on the delineation of our responsibilities, I told him that, due to the strategy's strong foreign policy and military components, I would convene the NSC meetings on it.

After reading the draft of the "Comprehensive Strategy and Plans for the Defeat of ISIS," I found my initial impression confirmed. Our strategy lacked a clear political and security end state and a description of how the United States intended to work with others to achieve it. I thought that Secretary Mattis would agree. In a principals committee meeting in the White House, he had observed that our military operations in Syria had "outrun our headlights." I thought he meant we needed a political vision for the region into which those military operations (as well as diplomatic, economic, law enforcement, and informational efforts) would fit. But instead of the "comprehensive strategy" the president had called for, the document was a military operational plan to support proxy forces in the offensive against ISIS's physical caliphate in Syria and Iraq. I saw the draft strategy as essentially a continuation of the Obama strategy, but I thought it best to continue the discussion at a later date, with only Tillerson and Mattis, rather than raise those concerns in front of all the principals.

Besides, another issue demanded immediate attention, one that would require the principals to stay at the White House a bit longer.

⋆   ⋆   ⋆

I ASKED Mattis, Tillerson, Attorney General Jeff Sessions, Bossert, and a few others to walk upstairs and join me in my office. The purpose was a final review of the president's executive order entitled "Protecting the Nation from Foreign Terrorist Entry into the United States," aka the travel ban, version 2.0.

The first travel ban executive order had not gone through a normal NSC-run review process. It had contained legal flaws, such as violation of due process rights for those with valid visas or green cards and discrimination against people based on religion. Because of those and other flaws, the executive order had created tumult at airports, and a federal court and a court of appeals had blocked its implementation the day after Trump signed it.

The new draft had seen several changes, including exempting people who possessed valid visas or green cards, but it still included a ninety-day ban on entry to the United States from the following countries: Iran, Libya, Somalia, Sudan, Syria, Iraq, and Yemen.

I was most concerned about the inclusion of Iraq. Tillerson and Mattis were, too, because Iraqi soldiers were bearing the brunt of the fight against ISIS in northern and western Iraq. I had worked on the revised EO draft with Eisenberg and Rader. We made pen-and-ink modifications to language and removed Iraq from the list. But I wanted to make sure everyone agreed before we brought the document to the president. I had already gone to Stephen Miller, who used to work on Senator Sessions's staff, to confirm his assent.

Sessions sat to my left at the head of the small conference table in front of my still-bare bookcase. I gestured toward Mattis and Tillerson. "General, all of us agree that Iraq should be off the list. The Iraqi people are the victims of ISIS, and Iraqi soldiers are making tremendous sacrifices in the fight to defeat the terrorist organization. Besides insulting our partners, the ban would be a propaganda victory for ISIS and the Iranians, who would use it to foment divisions between our small advisory forces in Iraq and Iraqi soldiers, casting the United States as an untrustworthy, spiteful partner. Loss of trust would increase the risk to our forces."

Sessions looked at me and said, "I am not impressed."

"General, but you should be impressed," I replied.

I got up, walked over to my desk, and pulled a photo off the wall. Aside from a photo of Katie and our daughters, it was the only personal item I had brought with me on my first day in the White House less than a week earlier. I put it in front of him and said, "This man is why you *should* be impressed."

I explained that the photo was of Mayor Najim Abed Abdullah al-Jibouri, Iraqi brigadier general Khalaf Qais, and me, the three of us surrounded by joyful children in a city that had a year earlier been rendered desolate by al-Qaeda. I described how Najim had led courageously as chief of police and mayor. His mediation between local and tribal leaders to break the cycle of sectarian violence and isolate terrorists and militias from the population had been essential to defeating al-Qaeda and to allowing life and the happiness (as captured on the faces of the children) to return to the city.

Because he was so effective, Najim had risen to the top of al-Qaeda's assassination list. The Iranians also saw him as a danger, in their designs to keep Iraq perpetually weak and mired in civil war; they actively undermined Najim within the Iraqi government.

I told Sessions how my own family had sponsored the al-Jibouri family of six under special "benefit parole" visas. They were now homeowners in Northern Virginia. The rest of the al-Jibouris had applied for citizenship, but Najim had maintained his permanent resident status so he could return to Iraq when needed to continue to fight for his native land. Indeed, when ISIS later took control of Mosul and territory in Iraq and Syria, the new Iraqi prime minister, Haider al-Abadi, had called Najim to ask that he leave the comfort and safety of Northern Virginia to do again what he had done in Tal Afar: lead Iraqi forces to defeat ISIS, regain control of territory, and restore trust between the Iraqi government and the Sunni communities. Najim was currently fighting in Iraq, but he had to return to the United States periodically to keep his residency valid. The travel ban would not only humiliate him, but also impede his ability to care for his family and fight our common enemy.

My story either struck a chord or tired Sessions out. He replied, "Okay, take Iraq off."

I thanked him and asked everyone to follow me to the chief of staff's office to make the change stick. As we walked down the hall, I put my arm around the attorney general's shoulder. "I really appreciate this. I look forward to working with you."

Priebus pulled in Bannon and Miller as we sat around the conference table in his office. I told Priebus that "the attorney general and secretaries of defense, state, and homeland security all approve of our edits to the new EO, including that Iraq would not be on the list. So, let's take Iraq off and stop going back and forth on this." I asked for his and Bannon's assurances that no one would work behind our backs to convince the president to put Iraq back on the list. All agreed, and I thanked them.

In an extraordinary coincidence, soon after the meeting on the new EO, I learned that, three days later, one of General Najim's daughters would take the oath of allegiance to the United States and become a citizen, the first in her family to do so. I cleared my calendar for the ceremony. Najim was in Iraq, but it was wonderful to see his wife, Zahra, and the children and to be with them to celebrate the important occasion. After he swore in the new citizens, the judge called on me to make a few remarks. I thanked our newest citizens and told them "You are our nation's greatest source of strength." I noted that they appreciated far better than most citizens who were born in the United States the "great gifts of our republic, gifts that too many of us take for granted."

One of the biggest missed opportunities for the Trump administration would be a failure to deliver a positive message on legal immigration and take advantage of what I do believe is one of our nation's greatest competitive advantages, our democracy's power to attract families like Najim and Zahra's. We spent a lot of time talking about whom we didn't want in the country and not enough time talking about whom we needed.

At the end of my first two weeks on the job, I called Katie to tell her that, despite some feuds and a lot of troubling signs of tension, my initial days there had been promising. The experience with the president's speech and the travel EO demonstrated how frank, transparent discussions with colleagues could deliver positive results. I told her, "It's not going to be easy, but I'm convinced the NSC team and I can do good work for the president and the nation." It was an accurate assessment. But I had not yet realized the scope and persistence of the difficulties we would encounter.

I tend to assume that everyone is motivated by good intentions until their behavior proves otherwise. In retrospect, I should have heeded the advice of the Countess of Rousillon in Shakespeare's *All's Well That Ends Well*: "Love all, trust a few."

CHAPTER 4

DJT AND LBJ

McMaster needs Senate confirmation because he's a 3-star general . . . McMaster is expected to appear, face a vote in the committee soon after and at some point afterward, a Senate floor vote . . . **SENATE APPROVES NATIONAL SECURITY ADVISOR McMASTER** . . . Afghanistan: IS gunmen dressed as medics kill 30 at Kabul military hospital . . . *NORTH KOREA FIRES FOUR MISSILES INTO SEA NEAR JAPAN* . . . *Malaysia Formally Identifies Murder Victim as Kim Jong Nam* . . . The Trump administration is considering sweeping sanctions aimed at cutting North Korea off from the global financial system . . . **THREE WORDS—RADICAL ISLAMIC TERRORISM— EXPOSE A TRUMP ADMINISTRATION DIVIDE** . . . Islamism has become interchangeable with "RADICAL ISLAMIC TERRORISM," which President Trump has vowed to "ERADICATE FROM THE FACE OF THE EARTH" . . . **THE TRUMP ADMINISTRATION IS SENDING MORE TROOPS TO SYRIA** . . . *Hundreds arrested at anti-corruption protests in Russia* . . . Iran and Russia Team Up with Taliban to Undermine U.S.-led Mission in Afghanistan . . .

ON FRIDAY, March 3, 2017, Air Force One touched down at Palm Beach International Airport. I walked down the back steps and jumped into a Suburban, joining the motorcade behind the president and First Lady for the short drive to Mar-a-Lago. The streets were cleared of traffic, but people were lined up several deep, carrying MAGA signs and messages of support for the couple. The Palm Beach Police had cordoned off a smaller but equally impassioned group of anti-Trump protesters.

The polarization of our society along partisan political lines seemed to reach an extreme under Donald Trump. As a military officer, I had remained deliberately disengaged, but as a historian, I knew that political divisions were part of America's story dating back to the Revolution. We had been through worse, but I thought it was past time to focus more on points of agreement concerning how to overcome challenges to our security and prosperity and build a better future. Differences of opinion are part of democratic governance. But the polarization that results in demonizing and disparaging the opposition erodes our common identity as Americans and impedes our ability to compete internationally. I hoped that, despite the divisiveness surrounding Donald Trump, I could help him develop a coherent foreign policy agenda that was true to his priorities and would help bring Americans together.

Staffing the president during weekends at Mar-a-Lago gave me time to think, assess, and plan. We scheduled calls to heads of state for the flights to Florida, the return flights, and even for Saturday afternoons after his rounds of golf.

The president was more enthusiastic about golfing and relaxing away from Washington than spending time with me, and he was often not in a great mood when I arrived in the sitting room outside his apartment with work for him to do. I once joked, "Mr. President, asking you to do the things that you enjoy the least is apparently part of my job description."

Still, he was personable and genial on the calls with foreign leaders. He often ended these conversations with "If you are in Washington, please come by," which caused confusion as to whether this constituted an invitation to the given head of state for an official visit to the White House.

The communications team installed a secure phone in the guest room at Mar-a-Lago where I was lodged, which was along the road from the main resort to the beach. There, I interspersed reading with phone calls to several of the eleven U.S. combatant commanders positioned around the world who had responsibility for geographic or functional commands.

I had told Secretary Mattis of my intention to make these calls. He discouraged me—he felt my doing so would bypass the chain of command that runs through the secretary of defense to the president—but my intention was not to circumvent him. Rather, I merely wanted my fellow officers to help me understand the geostrategic landscapes in their regions. Besides, it was a morale boost to talk with old friends for whom I had tremendous respect.

My first call was to Gen. Mick Nicholson, the commander of the NATO-led Resolute Support Mission in Afghanistan. Mick had unmatched experience in Afghanistan, across more than six years. He had just completed a forty-two-page paper that assessed the situation in Afghanistan and Pakistan, recommending changes to the policy and strategy there. Secretary Mattis had forbidden him from sharing his assessment with anyone. I thought that was a bad idea. One of the lessons of the Vietnam War that had impelled the Goldwater-Nichols Department of Defense Reorganization Act of 1986 was that presidents needed to hear unvarnished advice from combatant commanders as well as from the secretary of defense and the chairman of the Joint Chiefs. But Nicholson and I adhered to Mattis's directive. It was an early sign that Mattis was giving top priority to controlling and metering the assessments and recommendations that went to the president.

On our call, Mick stressed the need for a fundamentally different approach to Pakistan, to use what he called a "spectrum of conditionality" to convince the Pakistanis that it was in their interest to curtail support for the Taliban and other terrorist organizations. "We never apply any 'sticks' to Pakistan, only 'carrots and baby carrots,'" he told me.

As for U.S. support of Afghan forces, I could hear the frustration in my old friend's voice as he described how the U.S. Army was deploying "hollow units" to comply with the arbitrary limits the

Obama administration had placed on the number of troops. The State Department was not helping, either. The special representative for Afghanistan and Pakistan (SRAP), Laurel Miller, was pursuing negotiations while U.S. forces were disengaging and executing the Obama policy for a scheduled withdrawal. The SRAP and others in the U.S. government seemed unaware that the Taliban had no incentive to negotiate. We needed to change course. The Afghan war effort was like a plane on autopilot in the process of crashing while the pilot, crew, and passengers paid no attention.

Other calls confirmed how existing policies and strategies—ranging from North Korea to China to Russia to Iran and the Middle East—rested on flawed assumptions.

That Sunday, back on Air Force One for the flight to Washington, I reviewed my notes. We had work to do.

*   *   *

ON MONDAY morning, March 6, my thirteenth day on the job, I made the first of several visits to Capitol Hill. National security advisors do not spend much time on Capitol Hill. The appointment normally does not require Senate approval, but the Senate had to approve my reappointment to the rank of lieutenant general in my new position.

Over the following nine days, I met with senators in advance of my confirmation. The White House legislative affairs team assigned Virginia Boney to help me through the process. Virginia, who had been director of appropriations for Sen. Lindsey Graham, was competent and well-versed in the personalities and politics on the Hill.

Sen. Bob Corker of Tennessee hosted me for lunch in the Senate Dining Room and pledged his assistance in pushing initiatives important to the president. Corker and the Democratic ranking member of the committee, Sen. Ben Cardin, would be helpful as we tried to forge bipartisan support for policies.

I then met with members of the Senate Armed Services Committee, the committee that had to approve my reappointment before a full Senate vote. Sen. Tom Cotton smiled as he explained how he had taken the lead in advocating for me with Trump because endorsements from Senators John McCain and Graham would have torpedoed me. I had met and briefed other members of the SASC many times in Washington, Kabul, and Baghdad, including Senators Graham and McCain, and Democratic senator Jack Reed. Sen. Dan Sullivan, then a major in the Marine Corps, had served on a task force I directed in 2008–9 to develop a sustainable strategy for the greater Middle East. How could my reappointment be hard? These senators knew me, and we respected one another.

But Boney urged me not to take my reappointment for granted. Given the slim majority, if even one Republican voted against me, "Democrats will sense blood in the water and vote against you just to complicate things for Donald Trump." I received a phone call from Senator McCain, who confided that Mattis was urging him and others to force my retirement from the Army. Mattis had told McCain that he was going to "give me a talking to like a four-star gives a three-star" and direct me to retire. Boney heard later that Mattis had made similar calls to Sen. Joni Ernst and other senators.

My office call with Ernst validated Boney's concerns. Ernst, a fellow Army officer, had served in the Iowa Army National Guard from 1993 to 2015, retiring as a lieutenant colonel. She had commanded a battalion in Kuwait and southern Iraq during the early months of the Iraq War. She worried that my serving as national security advisor while on active duty might drag me and, by connection, the military into partisan politics. Her concerns were legitimate. But I explained that I was confident that I could transcend partisanship.

A few days after those first meetings, Vice President Pence asked me how my engagements on the Hill had gone. I told him they had gone well, but I also related, without mentioning Mattis, Senator Ernst's unease and said that one Republican vote against me could precipitate an avalanche of Democratic "nays." I discovered later that Pence had called Ernst to persuade her to vote "yea."

The hearing before the Senate Armed Services Committee was amicable. Thanks to Senators McCain, Sullivan, Cotton, Reed, Ernst, and Graham, and the hard work of Virginia Boney and the support of the vice president, the Senate voted nine days after the first meeting on the Hill. The tally was 86 to 10 in favor of my reappointment.

As newcomers to Washington who had lived in Army communities that were studiously apolitical, Katie and I found Washington's pervasive partisanship perplexing. The two Democratic senators who thanked me most effusively in private for taking the job, Senate Minority Leader Chuck Schumer of New York and Sen. Elizabeth Warren of Massachusetts, voted against my reappointment.

Months later, at the annual Alfalfa Club Dinner, Katie ran into Democratic senator Cory Booker and, before he knew who she was, asked him what he thought of the new national security advisor. Booker said he was very happy I was in the position. Katie asked, "Then why did you vote against him?" He replied that he had to "protect his political capital." Katie jokingly punched him in the arm and said, "My husband is not political capital." Booker laughed and hugged her. He and the majority of those ten Democrats who had voted against me would become candidates for their party's presidential nomination in the 2019 primaries.

The partisanship in Congress is maddening, but Congress would be critical to resourcing any of President Trump's foreign policy, defense, and national security initiatives. My philosophy for engaging members of Congress was consistent with the adage "If you want them with you at the landing, they had better be with you on take-off." In addition to securing needed resources, bipartisan support would, I hoped, generate a higher degree of consistency in foreign policy, especially on challenges like the long war against jihadist terrorists and the long-term competition with the Chinese Communist Party (CCP).

*   *   *

ON MARCH 6, the same day I traveled to Capitol Hill for my first pre-confirmation meetings, Kim Jong-un had launched four ballistic missiles that landed off the coast of Japan. The United States would need to coordinate the response with South Korea and Japan.

Trump had given me clear guidance on North Korea. During my first Oval Office meeting with him on February 22, he had told me to make sure Kim Jong-un and his regime know that "if they threaten us and our allies, they will face a response that is overwhelming." The president would remain consistent on this point. Six months later, he stated that if North Korea made any further threats against the United States, they would be met with "fire and fury like the world has never seen." Although his statement was strident and unconventional—like his tweet that the button on his desk was "bigger and more powerful" than the button on Kim Jong-un's—his comments were consistent. Moreover, it was not as if past "conventional" statements had worked.

During an Oval Office discussion with Matt Pottinger, senior director for Asia, and Secretaries Tillerson and Mattis, we discussed the potential motivations behind Pyongyang's pursuit of the most destructive weapons on earth. Pottinger and I believed—as did the director for Korea, Allison Hooker—that the idea that the regime wanted nuclear weapons only for deterrence was wrong.

We disagreed with pundits and government officials who argued that the least risky and least costly course of action would be to accept North Korea as a nuclear power and then deter its use of nuclear weapons. If North Korea was concerned mainly with deterring South Korea and the United States, it did not need nukes. Its vast conventional weapons and munitions included more than 21,000 artillery and rocket systems able to bombard the city of Seoul, which lies only thirty-one miles from the demilitarized zone (DMZ). That is sufficient firepower to deter South Korean aggression. Kim, we thought, really wanted to reunify the peninsula under Pyongyang's control.

The picture we painted for Trump was not pretty. Across several meetings on North Korea, he agreed that we had to base our approach on the possibility that Kim's dictatorship wanted the most destructive weapons for more than deterrence or defense and that North Korea would become more aggressive and prone to initiate a war once the regime had its weapons.

There were other reasons that a nuclear-armed North Korea would be a grave danger. As with Iran and the Middle East, accepting and deterring a nuclear-armed North Korea would create strong incentives for the further proliferation of nuclear weapons in the region. If North Korea were in a position to strike the United States with a nuclear weapon, South Korea and Japan might doubt the reliability of America's "nuclear umbrella" and pursue their own nuclear weapons. And soon enough, other countries across Asia and beyond might conclude they needed them, too.

In addition, the Kim regime would likely try to sell its capabilities abroad: Pyongyang sold a nuclear reactor to Syria that Israeli jets destroyed in 2007. Kim would likely share his missile and nuclear technology with Iran. It was not unreasonable to envision North Korea selling nuclear devices to the highest bidder, even if that bidder was a terrorist organization.

With Tillerson and Mattis present in the Oval Office, Pottinger leaned over the Resolute Desk to show Trump a time line with photos to illustrate the historical pattern of previous efforts to denuclearize North Korea. Trump enjoyed these discussions—especially if they entailed challenging the conventional wisdom of the "stupid people" who had preceded him. The graphic depicted the cycle of the Democratic People's Republic of Korea (DPRK) provocation: U.S. concessions to get Pyongyang to the negotiating table; long, frustrating negotiations during which the United States and others made concession after concession resulting in a weak deal that included more payoffs and was locked in the nuclear status quo; and, finally, North Korea's violation of that agreement to restart the cycle.

The contours of what would become the strategy of "maximum pressure" were coming into view. We would try to convince Kim Jong-un that his regime would be safer *without* the most destructive weapons on earth. Trump directed us to "fully isolate North Korea" and to make Chinese leader Xi Jinping "pay a price for backing Kim Jong-un."

Over dinner that evening in the Blue Room in the Residence, Tillerson, Gary Cohn, and I summarized for the president the three "don'ts" we had agreed to in a principals committee meeting earlier in the day. First, don't rush to the negotiating table or accede to weak initial agreements just to talk with North Korea. In the past, we had agreed to a "freeze-for-freeze" in which the United States and South Korea suspended military exercises in return for flimsy North Korean promises to stop testing nuclear weapons and missiles. Second, don't view diplomacy and the development of military options as separate, sequential efforts. Successful diplomacy depends on demonstrated will and the capability to employ force against North

Korea if necessary. Third, don't lift sanctions prematurely to reward the DPRK government just for talking. We needed to keep sanctions in place until there was irreversible momentum toward denuclearization. The president agreed with those guidelines, and they would help shape our approach over the next year.

Trump asked if Xi Jinping would help on North Korea. Tillerson and I doubted it. Cohn argued that China was "weaker than we think" and might pressure Pyongyang if CCP leaders faced economic or financial consequences. Trump said he would confront Xi on North Korea and for not honoring Beijing's commitments on trade. The topic of trade led, as it often did, to a diatribe on NAFTA and the Korea–United States (KORUS) Free Trade Agreement.

Trump saw China's exploitation of the "free trade system," with its statist, mercantilist model, as a threat to American prosperity. I was not unsympathetic to his belief that Washington's political and foreign policy elites had failed to compete effectively and advance U.S. interests. He saw the loss of manufacturing jobs and the trade imbalance in goods as the result of "stupid people" allowing others to prosper at Americans' expense. That is the primary lens through which he viewed not only China, but also U.S. allies (for example, the European Union, South Korea, and Japan) that used protectionist trade policies and subsidized industries to gain unfair economic advantage.

* * *

I was learning that Trump was open to new ideas and perspectives, but he was also prone to changing his mind based on whoever had his ear last. For example, after reviewing the draft of his first address to Congress, I had suggested that the phrase "radical Islamic terrorism" was inaccurate and counterproductive. "Mr. President, we should call these people what they are. Jihadist terrorists are criminals who use a perverted interpretation of Islam as cover for their criminal and political agendas." I suggested that he make a subtle change from "Islamic," which describes the entire religion, to "Islamist," which focuses on their *political agenda* and does not reinforce the terrorists' narrative of a clash of religions. Trump agreed.

But Steve Bannon went to the president and Stephen Miller to ensure that "Islamic" remained in the address to Congress. And the press, oftentimes more enthralled with machinations in the White House than the substance of policy, was happy to keep score. After the speech, the *Washington Post* reported the president's use of the phrase "radical Islamic terrorism" and described it as a rebuke of my position and an indication of a growing divide in the administration.[1] The next day, Bannon's assistant, Sebastian Gorka, said the phrase was "the clearest three words" in the speech.

I had been in the job two weeks and was starting to understand how members of the staff persuaded Trump. The phrase "radical Islamic terror" appealed to Trump's self-described persona in his book *The Art of the Deal*, which is "a little different or a little outrageous."[2] I was also learning about his character, personality, and worldview.

I do not consider myself a pop psychologist, but I believe that personalities and relationships have a strong influence on the course of history. And understanding how Trump's personality and experiences shaped his worldview was necessary for me to help him consider alternatives, overcome rigid patterns of thinking, and make good decisions.

I saw in Trump traits similar to those in Lyndon Johnson. As with LBJ, Trump's insecurities and desire for attention left him perpetually distracted and vulnerable to a mainstream media that was vehemently opposed to him. Also, like LBJ, he had a loose relationship with the truth and a tendency toward hyperbole.

On one of my first days in the White House, as we were walking to the Residence, he stopped next to the Secret Service desk just inside the West Wing, by the door that opens to the Colonnade, the walkway past the Rose Garden. He pointed to a photo taken of the Mall during his inauguration ceremony and said, "Look at that, General, unlike what you saw in the fake media, there were many more people at my inauguration than Obama's."

Trump also shared LBJ's belief that the media were making "a concerted move to discredit him."[3] Besides portraying himself as a victim and believing the narratives he created, Trump shared with LBJ the tendency to belittle others to make himself seem bigger and to hide his own insecurities, fears, and flaws. While LBJ employed the famous "Johnson treatment," which included using his large frame to invade people's personal space, Trump preferred verbal means, often employing mimicry to belittle his target of intimidation— whether it was a disabled reporter in 2015; Sen. Elizabeth Warren, whom he nicknamed "Pocahontas" after she made dubious claims of Native American heritage; or Attorney General Sessions, with whom he was angry because Sessions had recused himself from the Russia collusion investigation. In 2018, when Trump began to mock unnamed generals with "sir, yessir," to insinuate that the senior military were unthinking automatons incapable of grasping his unconventional approach to foreign and defense policy, I knew that my time with him had almost run its course.

As with LBJ, Trump's insecurities made him distrustful and short-tempered, and inspired behavior in others that undermined teamwork. Trump, a real estate developer, often pitted parties against one another to get the deal he wanted. On his reality-TV show *The Apprentice*, he would pick people apart, divide them, and watch them undermine one another. If he sensed weakness or reticence in someone, he would bully them—particularly the contestants who were eager to ingratiate themselves with him and undermine the other contestants. I had already begun to see this behavior with Bannon and me. Trump had told me, for example, that he did not think Bannon should be a formal member of the NSC principals committee, but he told Bannon that the decision to remove him had been mine alone.

Trump and LBJ both wanted to play the role of unrivaled protagonist in an opera they created. I had written about how many of LBJ's advisors were intimidated by him and afraid to give the president advice contrary to his preferred course in Vietnam. I knew that to fulfill my duty, I would have to tell Trump what he didn't want to hear.

★   ★   ★

JOHN POINDEXTER, who served as President Ronald Reagan's fourth national security advisor until he was forced to resign due to his involvement in the Iran-Contra scandal, told me that the first year of the Reagan administration was "very chaotic," observing that the White House under Reagan was "at war with itself and with the secretary of state."

Poindexter recalled how Chief of Staff James Baker allied with longtime trusted Reagan aide Mike Deaver against Ed Meese III, whom Baker described as "counselor to the president for policy." But the tension was greatest between the White House and Reagan's first secretary of state, Gen. Alexander Haig, who had declared himself the "vicar of foreign policy."[4]

Poindexter contrasted that first year with the teamwork among Reagan's second secretary of state, George Shultz, Secretary of Defense Caspar Weinberger, Director of Central Intelligence William Casey, and him. Poindexter even set up a monthly lunch for the four of them in the Family Dining Room in the Residence.

I was confident that, like Poindexter, I would have a good relationship with the secretaries of state and defense. When I told Kissinger and Brzezinski of my intention to work cooperatively and implement a process that amplified the voices of key cabinet officials, they cautioned me never to allow the State Department and the Defense Department to control the policy process. Both of them had clashed with secretaries of state and prevailed in competitions for influence with the president. Kissinger was adamant that if the national security advisor was weak, the secretaries of state and defense would try to determine the president's policy themselves.

I had led multinational task forces overseas and had experience overcoming cultural and personality-based obstacles to collaboration. How hard could it be to forge a cooperative relationship with Tillerson and Mattis? I had also studied LBJ's personality and understood the dangers of responding to an overbearing president with passivity or behavior designed to curry favor. How hard could it be to convince Trump that I was serving him well by getting him the best advice and multiple options even if what he got challenged his predilections?

Much harder than I thought.

CHAPTER 5

INTRIGUE, ELBOWS, AND SEPARATE AGENDAS

WHITE HOUSE INTERNAL RIVALRY POSES A CHAL-LENGE TO MCMASTER . . . Steve Bannon's reach extends to Trump national security team . . . Donald Trump's Russia relationship leaves Washington puzzled . . . TRUMP AND THE GENERALS . . . The few grown-ups in Trump's Cabinet are getting sidelined . . . **CHAOS IN THE WHITE HOUSE: 'THERE'S NEVER BEEN ANYTHING LIKE THIS'** . . . IN ONE ROCKY WEEK, TRUMP'S SELF-INFLICTED CHAOS ON VIVID DISPLAY . . . The Strategic Nous of H.R. McMaster . . . *Saudi Arabia: Trump meeting a 'historic turning point'* . . . Two months into Donald Trump's presidency, it is clear that Trump cannot control himself or his own administration . . . In Greeting to Iranian People, Trump Leaves Out Their Government . . . A Trump and Modi Bromance? . . . The status of Obama holdovers remains a source of tension within the National Security Council . . . **MCMASTER: NATIONAL SECURITY TEAM 'NOT MISSING A BEAT' BECAUSE OF TRUMP CONTROVERSIES** . . . **South Korean President's Ouster to Trigger Shift on U.S. Policy**

I FIRST met Secretary Tillerson on Friday, February 24, 2017. When I tried to schedule a meeting, Tillerson's office said he was too busy to come to the White House. I was happy to make the short drive to the Harry S Truman Building, commonly known as the State Department, or Foggy Bottom.

Tillerson was with his chief of staff, Margaret Peterlin, who had served as his "sherpa" to help him through Senate confirmation, joined his team, and would turn out to be nearly ever present with the secretary during his time in office. Tillerson and I shook hands. He is a prepossessing figure. He exudes gravitas, and I, like many others, had high expectations for what the former chairman and chief executive officer of ExxonMobil would accomplish as our nation's top diplomat.

I asked him about his priorities and assured him that "my intention is to be an honest broker. Although I work for the president, I also work for you and the rest of the cabinet." I shared my early assessment that the National Security Council had become too tactical under the Obama administration and that the White House had centralized too many decisions. "Mr. Secretary, I am already helping the president devolve authorities back to the departments."

Tillerson seemed appreciative of those efforts and told me he was looking forward to our working together.

Three days later, I returned to the seventh floor for a second meeting with him. After waiting in a conference room across the hall, I was ushered into the John Quincy Adams State Drawing Room, where the secretary of state receives distinguished guests. The furnishings are early American masterpieces selected for their connection to the founding of the republic. I was surprised to see Secretary Mattis there, occupying one of the two upholstered wingback chairs across from Tillerson. I sat down in one of the smaller chairs across from Peterlin, who was again accompanying Tillerson.

The meeting started well. We discussed the need to address what Mattis had described as the "strategy-free zone" in Washington, and I summarized plans to develop integrated strategies for the most significant challenges facing the United States. Mattis described North Korea as the "crocodile closest to the canoe," but he and Tillerson both agreed that China was the most important long-term competitor. Tillerson, who knew Putin from his time as CEO of ExxonMobil, shared Trump's belief that it was possible to forge an entente with the Russian dictator, reduce tensions, and cooperate in some areas.

A difference of opinion emerged when I raised Afghanistan. Tillerson and Mattis did not want to begin work on a new strategy, in part, because they were concerned that the president might order a precipitate withdrawal. As early as 2013, Trump had tweeted:

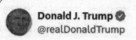

Donald J. Trump ✔
@realDonaldTrump   ...

We have wasted an enormous amount of blood and treasure in Afghanistan. Their government has zero appreciation. Let's get out!

12:06 PM · Nov 21, 2013

We turned to the topic of the Department of Defense's strategy to defeat ISIS. I noted that the proposed new strategy did not go beyond support for the Syrian Democratic Forces and Iraqi Security Forces military operations against ISIS in Syria and Iraq. We needed a strategy not only to defeat jihadist terrorists, but also to influence the resolution of the Syrian Civil War, protect Israel and our Gulf friends from Iran, and limit Russian and Iranian influence in the region.

Mattis was becoming visibly agitated. He raised his voice and scolded me for having the temerity to critique the draft strategy. His tone surprised me, and I could see that Tillerson was surprised as well. I let Mattis get it all out. After a period of silence, I told him, "I have great respect for you, and I did not mean to offend you. But I do not see my job as passively accepting everything that comes to the White House from the departments."

I recalled Kissinger's and Brzezinski's warnings about how tensions between the national security advisor and the secretary of state or defense could undermine the president's ability to clarify and pursue his foreign policy and national security agendas. I tried to forge a good working relationship with Tillerson and Mattis as I had with other members of the cabinet. I would practice what I preached in the all-hands meeting: try to "lead by charm" and win them over with a well-run NSC process.

★   ★   ★

ON MARCH 13, on the way back from a weekend with Katie during which I said goodbye to our friends at Fort Eustis, I received a call on the car's secure phone. Col. Joel Rayburn, a senior director in the Middle East directorate of the NSC staff, told me that before I became national security advisor, Bannon and Priebus had worked with White House and NSC staffers to identify "holdovers" on my staff whom they deemed unreliable or potential sources of leaks. Priebus and Bannon planned to summarily fire those on the list and have them walked off the White House grounds the next day.

I called NSC legal advisor John Eisenberg and asked him if he had heard anything about the scheme. He had not. I then called White House counsel Don McGahn, explained the situation, and told him that this was unacceptable. If it was not illegal, I said, then it was at the very least an egregious violation of trust. Dismissals based on innuendo would harm the reputations of career civil servants and reflect negatively on the president.

I then called Priebus. I try not to use profanity in the workplace, but this was a situation in which profanity seemed appropriate in the form of a rhetorical question: "What the fuck do you two think you're doing?"

Later, in an Oval Office meeting with Bannon and Priebus present, I told Trump that I would like him to hold me responsible for the NSC staff. I knew the leaks were a problem, I said, and assured him that I would make it a priority to stop them. I pointed at Bannon and said, "But I want him out of it."

Trump responded, "Okay, General."

Bannon, as usual, backed off when confronted directly, only to plot his next surreptitious attack. He and Priebus would go on to attribute every leak—I suspect even many of their own—to the NSC staff.

I was surprised and disappointed that Keith Kellogg had known about Bannon and Priebus's effort to dismiss staff members and had not told me of it. But I wanted to get beyond the event and focus on the job we had to do for the president. The following evening, I invited Kellogg, Eisenberg, and NSC staff members whom Bannon had asked to inform on their colleagues to my temporary quarters at Fort Myer for a beer: I wanted to make clear that concerns about any individual should come to me, K.T. McFarland, or Kellogg. I would dismiss anyone who leaked or was otherwise disloyal to the president, but a mass dismissal would give more ammunition to Trump's opponents and put him on the defensive. I noted that many on Bannon and Priebus's list were already near the end of their rotational tours of duty and would soon return to their home departments anyway. As Kellogg and the staff members departed, I told them I wanted us to focus on our work for the president and the nation.

I would soon discover that the "beer summit" did not work.

★   ★   ★

THE PREPONDERANCE of reporting on the first two months of the Trump White House came with headlines like "In One Rocky Week, Trump's Self-Inflicted Chaos on Vivid Display" and "Chaos in the White House."

Reporters knew only half the story. The NSC team had just begun to assemble when Mike Flynn departed. Members of the White House staff were trying to divide and weaken the NSC. NSC staffers, including those who had cast themselves in the role of defending Donald Trump and those who sought to discredit him, were leaking to reporters to advance their agendas.

It was sometimes hard to tell what the motives of leakers were. Sure, the White House was a chaotic, noisy political battlefield, but I was determined to cut through the noise, friction, infighting, and obstruction. We had to establish priorities. During my second weekend at Mar-a-Lago, on March 18–19, I gave Megan Badasch a list.

Prior to Trump's summit with Chairman Xi at Mar-a-Lago in early April, we would prepare a China policy framing document and supporting paper, gain presidential approval of a nascent Northeast Asia strategy designed to prevent North Korea from threatening the United States and our allies, initiate work on integrated strategies for the most pressing national security challenges, and finalize the NSC calendar to capture big events, such as travel and key meetings, and the preparation for those events.

I recruited key members of the team, such as Ricky Waddell, as deputy national security advisor; Ylli Bajraktari, my chief of staff; and Ylli's brother, Ylber, who would serve as senior director for defense policy and strategy. Mike Flynn had already hired Dr. Fiona Hill, one of the foremost experts on Russia under Putin, to serve as senior director for Europe and Russia.

As I recruited new teammates, I learned from those who were already there—like Ken Juster, deputy assistant to the president for international economic affairs, who had extensive experience that included senior positions in the Commerce and State Departments. Over dinner at the Bombay Club, he suggested how to integrate economic goals with national security and foreign policy priorities, while warning me that ideologues who had joined the administration had already launched ad hominem attacks against him and others who had worked on the trade agreements Trump wanted to terminate or revise. I told Juster that I would do my best to insulate our team from slander and backstabbing so we could get the work done for the president.

One might wonder why someone would serve in a White House described daily in the press as chaotic. Some may not understand this, but the simple answer for many was their sense of duty to our nation.

About a month into the job, I went to dinner with Waddell and Col. (Ret.) Rich Hooker in the main dining room of the historic Army and Navy Club on Farragut Square in Washington. It was restorative to be with fellow West Point graduates and friends with whom my life had intersected in combat. Rich, whom I had asked to join Hill's team as senior director for Europe and NATO, recalled later a conversation he had with Rick Waddell while I was away from the table. "Over our brandy," Hooker later wrote, "I admitted to Rick that despite my deep admiration for him and for McMaster, I had serious misgivings about joining the Trump Administration. I have never forgotten [Waddell's] response: 'We are sworn officers of the Republic. When asked to serve, we serve.'"[1] The sense of duty that

Waddell, Hooker, and I had internalized at West Point would prove necessary for us to transcend and endure the attacks that Juster and many other members of the NSC staff would experience.

The team was moving forward on our list of priorities, and morale was improving. One member of the staff described the first all-hands meeting as an "open, candid, intellectual conversation." I held another on March 21. Scanning the faces in the auditorium, I sensed far less angst in the room than I had during my third day on the job.

Behind me on a large screen was the vision for our organization: "A thoughtful, strategic, and effective organization that is valued and trusted as an honest broker across the U.S. government and by key international partners."

To those gathered, I emphasized trust. "Leaks destroy trust," I said, "and they have to stop."

I summarized the changes intended to flatten the organization, including the elimination of two deputy positions and the internal reports that went to those deputies. I emphasized our key tasks as staffing the president and running a process that coordinated and integrated efforts across the government. I then proposed a list of fifteen problem statements that we would refine and use as the basis for policy development over the coming year:

1. How to ensure the DPRK is not a national security threat to the United States and its allies.
2. How to establish a relationship in which the United States and China both enjoy fair and balanced prosperity and neither threatens the other while maintaining U.S. primacy in the Asia-Pacific region and preventing China from establishing new global spheres of influence.
3. How to defeat the Islamic State of Iraq and Syria (ISIS) such that it no longer controls territory or population centers and cannot sustain operations against the United States or its partners.
4. How to resolve the Syrian Civil War while defeating ISIS[-] and al-Qaeda-related groups and denying Iran's influence in a future Syrian political settlement while limiting Russian influence, weakening Hezbollah, and protecting Israel.
5. How to ensure that Iraq is stable and not aligned with Iran.

6. How to neutralize Iran's destabilizing behavior and shape its internal politics such that the Iranian political system ceases its fundamental hostility to the United States and its allies.
7. How to stabilize Afghanistan, reduce Pakistani support for transnational terrorists and the Taliban, and prevent an India-Pakistan military crisis.
8. How to counter Russia's destabilizing influence and deter Russian aggression while cultivating areas of cooperation to improve security and protect the vital interests of the United States and its allies.
9. How to protect the U.S. homeland from terrorism and defeat transnational terrorist organizations and organized crime networks that threaten U.S. security and vital interests.
10. How to solidify the central position of the United States in the global energy system while weakening the power of energy cartels and rogue petrostates.
11. How to reinforce U.S. global economic leadership, promote free and fair trade, and foster an expanded set of like-minded countries.
12. How to dominate cyberspace and deter cyberspace adversaries.
13. How to block the proliferation of weapons of mass destruction by nonstate actors and improve U.S. biodefenses.
14. How to strengthen U.S. infrastructure and increase national preparedness and resilience.
15. How to ensure U.S. dominance in space.

After fielding questions, I expressed confidence that we could "help the president strengthen U.S. leadership in the world and shift the global balance of power in favor of U.S. interests and values."

I briefed the president on all this, and he approved after half-listening and saying, "Okay, General." It was time to get the process running and demonstrate its value to the president and his cabinet.

*   *   *

WHILE MY initial meetings with Tillerson had gone well, I started to notice that we were speaking past each other. On March 27, I brought Dina Powell with me to meet with Tillerson and Brian Hook, the new director of policy planning at the Department of State. Tillerson spoke about how he believed in the "Scowcroft model" of foreign policy and national security planning and decision-making. But it became apparent that he defined that model as the State Department's having primacy over foreign policy.

In an uncanny coincidence, I visited General Scowcroft the next day at his office, just two blocks from the White House. Lieut. Col. Jason Galui of the Executive Secretariat, whom I would soon tap as an interim chief of staff, accompanied me. Memorabilia and photos adorned the general's office, including a photo of an exhausted General Scowcroft asleep on Air Force One.

I did not tell Scowcroft about tensions between me and members of the White House staff and the secretaries of state and defense, though he must have sensed it. "I have been reading about the White House infighting in the papers," he told me. "You should know that what you are experiencing is not unprecedented." He described Reagan's White House while James A. Baker was chief of staff as "a witches brew of intrigue, elbows, and separate agendas."

The general's voice and body had grown weaker, but his mind was sharp. He encouraged me to try to transcend the infighting. "You should try to avoid the kind of relationship with Tillerson that Brzezinski had with [Secretary of State] Cyrus Vance" in the Carter administration, which Scowcroft described as "a veritable nightmare." Scowcroft described relations between Colin Powell and Secretary of Defense Frank Carlucci as counterproductive because Powell was too deferential as a three-star general.

Scowcroft's voice took on a stern tone: "You are not junior to the secretary of defense," he said. "Don't act like it."

He also emphasized my duty to help the president integrate efforts across all government agencies with a role in foreign policy and national security. He told me to focus on two functions: first, making the policy process work and developing options for the president; and second, advising the president with views unalloyed by the departments and their bureaucracies.

I asked him how he had earned his reputation as an honest broker. He responded that "the cabinet has to be confident that their views are getting through to the president. And the president's decisions and priorities have to get to the cabinet. You have to be a conduit both ways."

I wanted to be that honest broker. But after the conversations with Tillerson and Scowcroft—only one day apart—it was clear that Tillerson had a different idea of the "Scowcroft model" than the man for whom the model was named. My understanding of post–World War II U.S. history had convinced me that there was no effective substitute for an NSC-led policy process. I did not yet realize it, but Tillerson had already initiated a tug-of-war over control of Donald Trump's foreign policy.

CHAPTER 6

A WELL-OILED
MACHINE—REALLY

SYRIA DEATHS LINKED TO CHEMICAL AGENT SARIN . . . A suspected chemical attack killed dozens of people in a rebel-held area of Syria . . . **TRUMP TO HOST EGYPT, JORDAN LEADERS IN BID TO IMPROVE TIES** . . . ABDULLAH AND TRUMP ARE UNITED AGAINST ISIS, DIVIDED ON REFUGEES . . . Debate over the effects and future of the NAFTA trade deal have been but one point of contention between Mexico and the US since President Donald Trump took office . . . **TRUMP ADMINISTRATION CONSIDERING REMOVING U.S. FROM NAFTA** . . . President Trump welcomes Chinese President Xi Jinping Thursday at his Mar-a-Lago estate . . . **THE TRUMP-XI SUMMIT: A ROCKY RELATIONSHIP TAKES CENTER STAGE** . . . Since Trump took office, U.S.-China relations have faced a rather dangerous situation . . . Russian forces continue to provide **active military support** to Syrian forces despite extensive evidence that the latter are using chemical weapons and targeting civilians . . . **PUTIN STANDS BY ASSAD** AS FIRM EVIDENCE OF CHEMICAL ATTACK MOUNTS . . . **TRUMP ORDERS MISSILE ATTACK IN RETALIATION** FOR SYRIAN CHEMICAL STRIKES . . . McMaster has succeeded in imposing a more regular process on national security decision-making . . . **MCMASTER'S INFLUENCE** on Trump Security Policy Seen in Syria Airstrikes . . . The White House is standing by President Trump's assertions that former President Obama ordered a **wiretap of his phones** . . .

ON THURSDAY, March 30, 2017, I was traveling west to California for a joyous family occasion, the marriage of our middle daughter, Colleen, to Lt. Lee Robinson of the Seventy-Fifth Ranger Regiment. Katie was already in Santa Barbara.

Thanks to the Secret Service, I avoided the ordeal of Los Angeles International Airport (LAX), a place in which Chaucer's phrase "every man for himself" (from "The Knight's Tale") is apt. Suburbans were positioned below the aircraft. As we drove through the airport gates, an escort of California Highway Patrol officers raced ahead on BMW motorcycles in a high-speed choreography to expedite our entry onto the Hollywood Freeway, U.S. Route 101, and our two-hour drive north.

About halfway, in Camarillo, the CHP officers led us into the parking lot of an In-N-Out Burger, a culinary ritual I regard as compulsory upon returning to California. After indulging in a Double-Double and fries, I went on to meet Katie and our daughters at a hotel in downtown Santa Barbara.

The next day, we joined our extended family at the Alisal, a bucolic guest ranch in the Santa Ynez Valley. Our daughters grew up in the Army. (In two weeks, we would move into our eighteenth house.) Colleen had chosen the Alisal as the venue for the wedding reception because it was a touchstone for her and her sisters, a place they came back to every summer for vacation with grandparents, aunts, uncles, and their sixteen cousins.

The wedding Mass at the nearby Old Mission Santa Inés, in Solvang, was beautiful. Two of our dear friends, Fr. Vince Burns and Fr. Paul Hurley, celebrated the Mass and the Sacrament of Marriage. Father Burns, who retired as a lieutenant colonel, is a fellow Philadelphian. Father Hurley is my West Point classmate and a major general who was serving as the Army's chief of chaplains.

As every father knows, a daughter's wedding is an emotional event. The dominant emotion that day was joy over what a wonderful woman Colleen had become. Besides not crying while walking her down the aisle, making it through the father-daughter dance without stepping on her toes, and delivering a toast at the reception, my main responsibility had been hiring the band. Harold Wherry and his Blue Breeze Band were fantastic. There were times when everyone was on the dance floor, including my eighty-year-old aunt Johanne Curcio, whom everyone knows as Aunt Nan.

Secret Service agents got concerned after Lee's fellow officers had the novel idea to coax a general—namely, me—onto a chair that they then proceeded to heave into the air repeatedly. I returned to earth without incident, however. As the festivities continued at an after-party generously hosted by my brother-in-law Michael Trotter I thought about how I had enjoyed everything about the day—seeing two loving people married, feeling the comradeship among soldiers, getting an opportunity to be with family, listening to some killer old funk and Motown music, and being able to stand outside the Washington Thunderdome to get some perspective.

The next morning, after a head-clearing workout, I went horseback riding with family and friends. A cavalry officer who rode tanks and other machines, I am far from an accomplished horseman, but the wrangler leading the ride set a slow pace. When we returned, Michael, one of the Secret Service detail, who had joined the ride despite never having mounted a horse, remarked that he was happy to have accomplished his objective of "finishing on the same side of the horse that I started on."

One Secret Service agent based in California was a true horseman. He had served on the protection detail for former president Ronald Reagan. As we crested a small rise, he pointed out Reagan's Rancho del Cielo, at the very top of a ridge to the west of Alisal.

Looking out at the place where Reagan had sought solace for about twenty-five years of his life, I was struck by the similarities and differences between him and the president I was serving: Trump and Reagan were both celebrities before entering politics. Both cast themselves as disruptors from outside Washington. Both were elected to the presidency by American voters unhappy with political elites whom they believed were self-interested and had failed them.

Reagan's popularity mounted against the backdrop of the stagflation and oil crises of the 1970s. Reagan voters were disappointed about the economy and foreign policy failures, from the fall of Saigon in 1975 to the Iran hostage crisis, which began in November 1979 and did not end until Reagan's inauguration in January 1981. Trump voters were rocked by the housing and financial crises of 2008–9, the transitions in the U.S. economy based on unchecked globalization, and the associated loss of manufacturing jobs to China and other countries. Trump's political base was frustrated with the length and cost of the wars in Afghanistan and Iraq. The president's campaign slogan, "Make America Great Again," was obviously derivative of Reagan's "Let's Make America Great Again." Both men were effective communicators. Reagan, a former actor, was even known as "the great communicator," as he was particularly effective on the relatively new medium of television. Trump, a former reality-TV star, had mastered social media and delivered impassioned unscripted monologues at political rallies.

But the differences between the two presidents who came into office with similar agendas (including tax cuts, deregulation, judicial appointments, and increased military spending) were as stark as the contrast between Reagan's rustic Western-style White House and Trump's lavish southern White House at Mar-a-Lago.

Trump preferred exquisite surroundings but engaged in a coarse form of communication. He took advantage of social media to reach the American people directly with visceral messages.

Reagan was polished. He had a quick wit and a strong sense of humor, often poking fun at himself. When his age became an issue in the 1984 campaign, he quipped that "Thomas Jefferson once said, 'We should never judge a president by his age, only his works.' And ever since he told me that, I stopped worrying."

Trump had a sense of humor, but his vanity precluded any form of self-deprecation. He could be funny, but his preferred form of amusement was ridicule and name-calling—from "Crooked Hillary [Clinton]" to "Lying Ted [Cruz]" to "Little Marco [Rubio]."

Reagan had been on my mind even before the horseback riding at the Alisal. I had been looking for examples of the kind of strategies we needed to compete with China and Russia and had reread one such strategy, National Security Decision Directive 75, which Reagan approved in January 1983 "to contain and over time reverse Soviet expansionism." But while we prioritized the development of long-term strategies, we also had to be ready to respond quickly to crises such as the one Reagan confronted on September 1, 1983.

On that date, Reagan was at Rancho del Cielo. I was a twenty-one-year-old cadet "firstie" in his last year at West Point, enjoying playing rugby and taking then-Major Peter Chiarelli's Politics and Government of the Soviet Union course. I may have been sitting in that class when Reagan's national security advisor Bill Clark made an urgent call to the president's ranch to deliver a preliminary report that a South Korean airliner, Flight 007, en route from New York City to Seoul, had been shot out of the sky by Soviet fighter planes.

"Bill," Reagan said, "let's pray it's not true." Unfortunately, 269 passengers and crew, including 61 Americans, were lost.

Reagan wrote this in his diary that evening: "We were due to return to Wash. on Labor Day but realized we couldn't wait so we left on Fri . . . When we got in on Friday, I went directly to an NSC meeting re the Soviet affair."

I knew the chances were high that I would have to help President Trump respond rapidly to a crisis. There was no shortage of potential flashpoints. Russia had already shot down a Malaysian airliner over Ukraine, on July 17, 2014, killing all 283 passengers and 15 crew members. After Russia's illegal annexation of Crimea and its invasion of Eastern Ukraine in 2014, it was easy to imagine an intensification of that war or an air or naval encounter with Russian forces in the Black Sea region. China's aggression in the South China Sea increased the possibility of an event analogous to the Hainan Island incident of April 2001, during which an American signals intelligence aircraft and a Chinese interceptor jet collided in midair. North Korea had increased the pace of its missile tests in Northeast Asia. A large-scale collapse of security in Afghanistan seemed possible. The nuclear deal with Iran had given the Islamic Republic more funds to intensify its proxy wars. And the weak international response to crimes against humanity in Syria had emboldened the Assad regime and its Iranian and Russian sponsors.

Unlike Bill Clark, in a time of crisis, I would have access to twenty-first-century secure communications and conferencing. After horseback riding, I conducted videoconferences and phone calls from a hotel in Solvang to prepare for a principals small-group meeting on Tuesday morning to refine the China policy framework and the objectives and agenda for the summit with Chairman Xi that would begin the following Thursday at Mar-a-Lago.

I said goodbye to Katie and caught the last Southwest flight out of LAX. One of the busiest and most consequential weeks of my tenure lay ahead.

★   ★   ★

RETURNING TO Washington from the placid Santa Ynez Valley was jolting. Upon my arrival at the White House, Pompeo called to share reports that the Syrian government had used chemical weapons in an attack that killed scores of people in Syria's northern Idlib Province. Reports suggested sarin gas, a nerve agent. As our Middle East team gathered more information, I left for the principals small-group meeting on the upcoming China summit.

I got to the Situation Room a few minutes early to greet the attendees and thank them for coming at an early hour. We started promptly at eight o'clock. The purpose of the meeting, I explained, was "to refine our framework for a new China strategy, understand how the first Trump-Xi summit fits into that framework, and identify ways to use the summit to advance the new policy."

I then read an excerpt from the Obama administration's China policy that reflected the forlorn hope, across multiple U.S. administrations, that China, having been welcomed into the international order, would play by the rules and, as it prospered, liberalize its economy and, eventually, its form of governance. This framing meeting and the paper we had prepared would ground our approach on a new set of assumptions based on the CCP's ideology and its determination to rewrite the rules in favor of its authoritarian mercantilist system. I noted that we were about to help the president effect the most significant shift in U.S. foreign policy since the end of the Cold War.

Tillerson summarized the nature of the competition with China, what was at stake, and the objectives for a new policy. Trump wanted Chinese leaders to know that the United States and our allies would oppose Chinese efforts to establish exclusionary areas of primacy in the Indo-Pacific. We would insist on fair economic practices and reciprocity in trade and market access. We would also try to convince Xi and his delegation that denuclearization of North Korea was in our mutual interest because a Kim family regime armed with the most destructive weapons on earth was a threat to the entire world. Finally, CCP leaders should leave Mar-a-Lago knowing that we would not tolerate Chinese cyberattacks or cyber espionage.

At the conclusion of the meeting, Director of National Intelligence Dan Coats and Pompeo updated us on those previous reports that the Assad regime had used a nerve agent to murder scores of civilians in Khan Shaykhun, Syria. All indicators, from photographs and personal accounts, were consistent with the horrible symptoms of contact with sarin gas, including decreased heart rate, convulsions, foaming at the mouth, and respiratory paralysis. Soil samples were taken, and our intelligence professionals were working with allies to confirm the nature of the attack and who had conducted it.

I briefed the president on Khan Shaykhun. He reacted as Reagan did after the Korean Air Lines shootdown in 1983. He hoped that the report was not true. Why, Trump wondered aloud, would Assad and his Russian allies do this? I told him that the attack had occurred where a Syrian Army offensive had failed, and it seemed likely it was meant to regain the initiative against the rebels.

He then asked, "Could an attack like this have happened without Russia's knowledge?"

I answered with the consensus intelligence view that Russian military advisors would almost certainly have known. I promised to have more details later in the day.

"Okay, General," he responded, "but I just don't understand why they would do it."

★   ★   ★

I ENTERED the Four Seasons in Georgetown through the back entrance, took the service elevator up several floors, and walked past armed guards to Abdel Fattah al-Sisi's suite. The Egyptian president had met with President Trump the day before, while I was traveling home from Colleen's wedding, and had requested a meeting with me.

Trump wanted to improve our relationship with leaders in the Middle East. Egypt, I thought, would be an easy sell. Then-general al-Sisi took power in 2013, after a coup against the Muslim Brotherhood government of Mohamed Morsi. The Obama administration's embrace of Morsi's Muslim Brotherhood government and criticisms of al-Sisi had helped Russia regain influence in Egypt that the Soviet Union had lost four decades earlier after another military leader, President Anwar Sadat, jettisoned Cairo's fifteen-year alliance with Moscow. The warming of relations with Egypt in the 1970s and the associated geostrategic benefits were analogous to what Trump could achieve with a reversal of Obama's accommodation of Iran and alienation of Egypt and the Gulf States.

Our conversation was amicable. Al-Sisi reminisced about Fort Benning (now Fort Moore), Georgia, where he had attended the Infantry Officer Basic Course in the 1980s. We had attended Airborne School and Ranger School around the same time. He shared with me his concerns about the regenerative capacity of the Muslim Brotherhood and its ties to jihadist terrorist organizations. During the Trump administration's transition, Egyptians, the Emiratis, and the Saudis pushed hard for a presidential designation of the Muslim Brotherhood as a terrorist organization. But the State Department raised concerns that the designation would prevent discourse with less extremist branches of the Brotherhood and drive the group underground, where it could become more dangerous.

Toward the end of our conversation, I adopted a more serious tone to emphasize, as Trump had the day before, the need to remove a significant impediment to improved relations with Cairo. I told al-Sisi that I was "confident that we could accomplish a lot together, but only after you free Americans unlawfully imprisoned in your country." I mentioned several of these by name, including Aya Hijazi, an American who, along with her husband, had founded a nongovernmental organization to advocate for child prisoners in Egypt. Hijazi was imprisoned in May 2014 and had gone without trial. I told al-Sisi that the State Department and Dina Powell would follow up with his team. I left the meeting with the impression that he would move on this issue.

Our prioritization of hostages and those unlawfully detained would pay off. Weeks later, Hijazi was released, and Trump received her in the White House on April 21, 2017.

*   *   *

MY NEXT meeting was also in the Four Seasons, with King Abdullah of Jordan, whom I had first met in 2003, while I was serving at U.S. Central Command, or CENTCOM. As with al-Sisi, our shared military experience fostered good rapport between us. We were both cavalry officers.

I asked the king for his ideas about how to prevent Iran from extending its influence and perpetuating the cycle of violence in the region. He emphasized the importance of stabilizing Iraq and ensuring that Baghdad was not aligned with Iran. King Abdullah was pessimistic about our ability to achieve a resolution to the Syrian Civil War that would result in the removal of Assad, the defeat of ISIS and other jihadist terrorists, and a reduction in Russian and Iranian influence. He hedged on condemnation of Russia, more evidence that Moscow had succeeded in casting itself as an indispensable mediator even as it perpetuated the crisis in Syria.

*   *   *

BACK IN the White House, there were more reports confirming the Syrian regime's mass murder attack at Khan Shaykhun. Our team was moving fast. The deputies had reviewed draft options for the president. Eisenberg, the NSC legal advisor, was analyzing presidential authority under Article II of the Constitution to take military action. A fast response would give the Kremlin less time to obfuscate. I wrote down what I thought were eight key tasks we must accomplish to satisfy our objectives:

1. Destroy facilities and capabilities related to mass murder attacks against civilians.
2. Communicate to Damascus, Moscow, and Tehran our willingness to escalate our military response and hold their assets in Syria at risk.

3. Position military forces to defend facilities and U.S. personnel in reach of the Syrian regime and its allies.
4. Engage Russia and Iran to communicate that we would consider them complicit in any future chemical attacks.
5. Focus communications and diplomacy on garnering support for the response and mobilizing international opinion against Syria, Russia, and Iran.
6. Inform key members of Congress to generate support.
7. Minimize risk of civilian and Russian casualties.
8. Identify and implement additional financial sanctions and other follow-on actions against Assad and his Russian and Iranian sponsors to maintain the initiative.

I had served in Iraq with three members of the NSC's Middle East directorate: Derek Harvey, Mike Bell, and Joel Rayburn. We all spoke the same language, and they knew how to plan under time constraints. I would send draft options to the principals for review in advance of taking them to the president.

★ ★ ★

LATER THAT afternoon, I met with the president to discuss King Abdullah's visit to the White House the following day. I showed him pictures of the horrible aftermath of the attack at Khan Shaykhun and told him that evidence was mounting that Syria's "Unit 450" had prepared for the strikes with the Russians' knowledge.

"On your earlier questions of why Assad did it and why Russia would permit it, I have more detail." I unrolled a map of Idlib Province. "Here is where the Syrian offensive failed. Here are the gains that the opposition militias made. And here is where the sarin bombs landed."

It was clear that Assad wanted to break opposition defenses with a demoralizing chemical attack on civilians.

I continued: "On why Putin permitted it, two reasons: he is unscrupulous, and he thought he could get away with it."

★ ★ ★

THE LAST event of my sixteen-hour day was a meeting with Mexican minister of foreign affairs Luis Videgaray at the Capital Grille. At 9:30 p.m., the deserted dining room and high-backed booths were conducive to discreet conversation. Videgaray asked me, as he had asked Tillerson and Kushner, to tell Trump that Mexico was prepared to cooperate on all issues, including improvements in border security and interdicting the "caravans" of illegal immigrants from Central America who transit through Mexico on their way to the U.S. southern border.

Videgaray leaned forward over a glass of wine to tell me that his president could not tolerate continued claims that Mexico would pay for a border wall. I told him I was confident we could work through the tensions and address President Trump's fundamental concerns about border security and the lack of reciprocity in the trade deal. But I stressed the importance of Mexico's and Canada's demonstrating good faith once trade negotiations began. I assured Videgaray that I would work with Tillerson, Kushner (who had picked up Mexico and NAFTA as part of his portfolio), and U.S. trade representative Bob Lighthizer to turn the recent tensions in the relationship into opportunities. Many months later, the result would be a renegotiated trade deal and an agreement that cut down illegal immigration dramatically.

What I didn't say to Videgaray was that he was right to be concerned. Steve Bannon and Director of Trade and Manufacturing Policy Peter Navarro wanted Trump to terminate NAFTA and knew how to agitate the president about Mexico. Gary Cohn and I, sometimes reinforced by Kushner, Mnuchin, or Secretary of Commerce Wilbur Ross, would tell Trump to first let Lighthizer take a shot at renegotiating the trade agreement; he was extremely competent and aligned with the president's objective of getting a better deal.

Yet Bannon and Navarro planted stories in the alt-right pseudo-media that Cohn and I were "globalists" determined to obstruct the president's trade agenda. The truth was that Gary and I used engagements like my meeting with Videgaray to *advance* the president's agenda.

*   *   *

I GOT some sleep prior to the next morning's PC meeting on Syria at 7:30. I opened the meeting, as always, by stating its purpose: "to hear principals' recommendations on and obtain your approval of the options that we intend to bring to the president this afternoon." Tillerson joined via videoconference. After an intelligence update from Coats and Pompeo, I restated the objectives the president had approved and then summarized the three options for his consideration:

Option 1: Integrated military, diplomatic, and financial actions, including a strike against the Syrian aircraft and airfield from which the strike emanated.

Option 2: No military strike, but an intensified diplomatic effort along with expanded financial and economic sanctions against the Assad regime and the Russian and Iranian entities that enable it.

Option 3: Integrated military, diplomatic, and financial actions, including a broader strike against more Syrian aircraft at multiple airfields and a strike against a Syrian regime target associated with Unit 450.

I summarized the relative advantages and disadvantages of each course of action, noting the risk of escalation associated with options one and three, given the potential for unintended Russian casualties. But I also noted the risk of inaction, which had become apparent over time with increasingly egregious chemical weapons attacks against civilians. From December 2012 to August 2014, the Syrian regime had used chemical weapons against civilians at least fourteen times. President Obama did not retaliate against the regime after an August 2013 attack that killed more than 1,400 innocent civilians, including hundreds of children. The Kremlin volunteered to lead what was, in retrospect, a disingenuous effort to collect all of Assad's chemical weapons. Now half the Syrian population was dead, wounded, or displaced.

The principals approved the courses of action for presentation to the president. We would brief Trump after King Abdullah and Queen Rania of Jordan departed that afternoon.

*   *   *

THE PRESIDENT and First Lady met King Abdullah and Queen Rania at the South Lawn entrance of the Residence. The king and queen proceeded on two separate itineraries. As he did with other allies and close partners, the president met one-on-one with the king in the Oval Office, while the rest of us waited with the king's party in the Roosevelt Room. A luncheon followed in the Cabinet Room.

Over lunch, Trump mentioned the "terrible" Khan Shaykhun attack and asked rhetorically, "Why would they do it?" His penchant for saying whatever was on his mind with no filter was, at times, jarring, but it was also sometimes effective. Heads of state were unaccustomed to unambiguous language, and some found Trump's directness refreshing. The president then noted how confusing the war in Syria was. He said, "Maybe General McMaster can explain it."

I responded with something like "Mr. President, Your Majesty, I would normally defer to King Abdullah, who is closest to this problem, but since you asked, I think that the war is best understood as a civil war between Bashar al-Assad's mainly Alawite regime and the Sunni majority, who had grown tired of living under the Assad family's brutal dictatorship. Bashar jump-started the war with the brutal repression of peaceful protests. The cycle of violence shattered Syrian society like a lightbulb. Various ethnic and tribal groups depended on militias or the government for protection. Iran intervened with a proxy Army on the side of the Assad government, while terrorists portrayed themselves as protectors of beleaguered Sunni communities. The Obama administration thought that the war could be kept in a box, but the massive refugee crisis has strained neighboring countries, including Jordan, Lebanon, and Turkey, as well as countries in Europe. After the unenforced red line in 2014, the Kremlin intervened directly in the war to save the Assad regime from collapse."

I looked at Trump and was surprised I still had his attention.

I continued: "Wars usually end when one side imposes its will or when the violence burns out. But outsiders are pouring an inexhaustible amount of fuel on the fire. Iran is using the war to create a land bridge to the Mediterranean, extend its influence in the region, and threaten Israel with destruction. Turkey fears that the SDF will become a Kurdish Army that seeks an independent state. Gulf states and the Turks are supporting different Sunni militias, and much of that support goes to jihadist terrorists associated with al-Qaeda and ISIS. The humanitarian catastrophe continues to grow, and there is no prospect for an end of the war as long as Assad remains in power."

Trump never would have listened to an explanation like that in a normal briefing. He smiled and looked at King Abdullah. "What do you think?"

Abdullah responded, "It sounded pretty good to me."

The discussion we had that day would double as background for the upcoming NSC meeting on options in response to the Khan Shaykhun attack.

★   ★   ★

I HAD consulted with the vice president about the best venue for the decision briefing on Syria. Priebus and others had suggested a less formal huddle in the Oval Office, but the vice president said, "This is a consequential decision, and it should be taken in the Situation Room."

I agreed.

Trump said, "Okay, let's go," and the three of us walked down the staircase to the basement and down the corridor to the Situation Room.

I opened the meeting with "Good afternoon, Mr. President. The purpose of this meeting is to obtain your decision on options in response to the chemical weapons attack on civilians at Khan Shaykhun." I summarized the objectives and courses of action. Coats and Pompeo gave intelligence updates. Tillerson stressed the importance of restoring deterrence lest the use of those heinous weapons become normalized. Generals Mattis and Dunford provided detail on the two military options.

Before the vice president and the principals had the opportunity to provide their assessment and recommend a course of action, the president asked if he needed to decide at that moment. Mattis and Dunford responded that the assets needed for an ideal strike package would be in place the following evening. I suggested that we reconvene soon after the president's arrival at Mar-a-Lago the following afternoon for the China summit. Trump agreed.

Mattis pulled me aside on the way out: "H.R., why are you pushing another meeting prior to the summit?"

"Mr. Secretary," I said, "it's important to get back to the president before the summit, because the Kremlin is already spreading disinformation. The greater the gap between the chemical attack and a U.S. strike, the more opportunity Russia, Syria, and Iran will have to sow doubts about the origin of the attack."

Mattis grimaced at my explanation and walked away.

*   *   *

ON THE way to Andrews Air Force Base, I made calls to allies to galvanize international support for diplomatic and economic pressure on Assad. Newly appointed UK national security advisor Mark Sedwill pressed me: "Has the president decided?"

I responded, "Not yet. I'll call you when he does."

On Air Force One, the president was in a good mood. He walked back to the four-person office I shared with Kushner, Priebus, and Cohn, located directly behind the galley. I was editing draft press releases and presidential statements for strike and no-strike options and matrices assigning to the vice president and cabinet officials phone calls to be made to foreign counterparts and members of Congress.

The president joked: "General, you are always working."

I replied, "I thought that's why you hired me, Mr. President." My staff and others would encourage me to find opportunities for leisure time with Trump, to bond with him. But even if I were to have overcome my deep aversion to obsequiousness, our interests and personalities were too different for that to work.

I walked into Mar-a-Lago just behind Trump. He immediately went to the dining room where he would host Xi Jinping and his party later that evening. He did not like the candelabras and ordered that they be switched out with a larger, more ornate set. He then walked into the kitchen and began asking questions about the meal. We were running late. I gently reminded him that the vice president and others were waiting on the videoconference and that we could begin whenever he was ready.

"Okay, General. Let's go."

We walked down the steps into a sensitive compartmented information facility (SCIF) and then into a small room in which there had been installed an even smaller tent, for the most sensitive and highly classified discussions. An "overflow room" had been set up elsewhere at Mar-a-Lago, for other NSC members in the traveling party to listen in. Those on the roster for the room with the president included Mattis, Tillerson, Kushner, and Priebus. When I entered the tent, Mattis was already there and had brought a colonel with him. "I hope you don't mind," he said. The broad-shouldered aide made the small quarters even more cramped, as did Secretary Ross, who was supposed to be in the overflow room but who had followed us down the stairs. Another chair was brought in. I sat uncomfortably close to the president, trying to avoid physical contact. It was comical.

After reviewing the objectives of the meeting and the three options with regard to a response in Syria, I asked the cabinet officials to provide their assessments and recommendations, beginning with the vice president. Those joining remotely from Washington—the vice president, Coats, and Pompeo—all recommended option one, which included a military strike against the aircraft and facilities complicit in the chemical attack. The president thanked everyone and said he would make the decision after a brief discussion with those of us in the tent.

Trump distrusted all communications systems. After we disconnected from the call, he stood up, and said, "Let's find a place to talk."

The location he chose was the men's room across the hall.

I whispered to Tillerson that I thought it very important for him to highlight, as the vice president had, the risk of inaction on the chemical attack. We were standing in a small circle between the sinks and urinals.

The president turned to Tillerson and asked, "What do you think?"

Tillerson responded that he supported option one. He noted that we were in this situation, in part, because inaction had eroded deterrence and emboldened Assad, the Russians, and the Iranians.

The president said, "Let's do it."

Mattis had the most work to do in transmitting the order to Gen. Joe Votel and CENTCOM. He told the president that he would miss the dinner with our Chinese counterparts and departed for his makeshift command center at a local hotel.

★　　★　　★

THANKS TO teamwork across all the departments and agencies and the competence and professionalism of our armed forces, our work was almost done. I met briefly with Matt Pottinger, senior director for Asia, then went to my room to prepare for dinner. At 6:30 p.m., we greeted Chairman Xi and his party and then sat among one another, rather than with members of each party on opposite sides of the table, which was now adorned with large crystal and gold candelabras.

Trump welcomed the delegation and mentioned that he had enjoyed his long one-on-one conversation with President Xi before dinner. Xi responded that he, too, had enjoyed the conversation. He and his wife, Lady Peng, a famous singer in China, particularly appreciated the greeting they had received as Jared and Ivanka's daughter, Arabella, regaled them with a traditional Chinese song in Mandarin.

I sat to the left of the First Lady and across from Wang Huning, the director of the Central Policy Research Office, the person most responsible for developing Xi's ideological framework, which would turn out to have more in common with Mao Zedong's despotic rule than with the "reform and opening" era that followed Mao's death. Wang is the ideas man behind the concept of the "China Dream" and of the never-ending purges Xi used to eliminate his political opponents and even many of his allies. He is also a relentless predictor of America's demise. Known as the "gray man," due to his preference for being in the background, and rumored to be an insomniac and workaholic, Wang was, unsurprisingly, not the most affable of dinner companions. Thankfully, Liu He, director of the Office of the Central Leading Group for Financial and Economic Affairs, sat to my left. He was one of the few party officials comfortable speaking without an approved script.

At the president's request, Xi recounted the rendition of Chinese history he had shared with Trump during their one-on-one discussion. The chairman's account was selective and heavy on the century of humiliation, the unhappy era during which China suffered many internal fragmentations, lost wars, made major concessions to foreign powers, and endured brutal occupation. According to Xi, the humiliation began with Great Britain's defeat of China in the First Opium War and ended with the communist victory in the Chinese Civil War in 1949. Missing from this account was the U.S. and British role in defeating Japan and ending its brutal occupation.

But the most glaring omissions were the great traumas and horrors that the Communist Party inflicted on the Chinese people as Mao killed tens of millions of his own population through misrule, deliberately induced famine, and political purges. Trump's lack of historical knowledge made him susceptible to Xi's effort to generate sympathy for him and a party that had killed more of its own people than either Stalin or Hitler. As a historian, I found it fascinating to hear Xi manipulate history. The story he told Trump was also revealing. Xi saw the modern-day leader of the West, the United States, as the greatest impediment to realizing the China Dream.

I excused myself from the dinner for a few moments after the main course of steak. It was "H-hour" for the strike on Syrian military targets. I walked downstairs, confirmed the successful launch of fifty-nine cruise missiles, made final edits on the draft statement for the president, and returned to the dinner before dessert had been served. I asked the First Lady to slip the president a folded piece of paper onto which I had written a short note that the attack had been launched, all looked good, and we would give him an update after dinner. Trump told President Xi about the strike as chocolate cake was served. Xi whispered back that Syria's murder of innocents, including children, justified the use of force.

The president and First Lady walked Chairman Xi and Lady Peng to the door just before 8 p.m. I wondered if Xi's recognition that

Trump was willing to employ force might convince him to do more, short of military action, to denuclearize North Korea.

The president joined the traveling party in the small conference room in the basement of Mar-a-Lago. The vice president and those in the Situation Room joined us by videoconference, as did Secretary Mattis, who briefed the results of the strike. Trump was pleased. He complimented Mattis. I gave the president the short statement that my communications director, Michael Anton, and Stephen Miller and I had drafted.

"Do you think I have to do this?" Trump asked.

"I think that it is important for Americans and for international audiences to hear directly from you," I said.

At 10:22 p.m. ET, Trump went live on television with a statement to explain the strikes: "My fellow Americans, on Tuesday, Syrian dictator Bashar al-Assad launched a horrible chemical weapons attack on innocent civilians. Using a deadly nerve agent, Assad choked out the life of innocent men, women and children." Trump explained that "It is in this vital national security interest of the United States to prevent and deter the spread and use of deadly chemical weapons," and he noted that "Years of previous attempts at changing Assad's behavior have all failed."

Mattis, Tillerson, and I made calls to foreign counterparts. Pence and Coats, both former senators, had already spoken to the "Gang of Eight," the leaders of each of the two parties from both the Senate and the House of Representatives and the chairs and ranking minority members of the Senate and House Committees on Intelligence. All supported the decision. After the strike, those designated to do so placed forty-five phone calls to members of Congress within seven minutes. As the president made his televised statement, Tillerson and I went to the nearby Tideline Ocean Resort and Spa to brief the members of the press staying there to cover the summit. Tillerson noted that Russia had been either complicit or incompetent and stressed that the use of chemical weapons must never become normalized. I had little to add.

The next morning, we hosted members of the Chinese delegation for breakfast. State Councilor Yang Jiechi commented that we must be tired, given the strikes in Syria. I told him that we all had a "good night's sleep." Coordinating the effort had been "easy," I told them. "Our well-trained military carried out the president's decision flawlessly."

We had a lot to discuss over breakfast and in the meetings with Xi that followed, but the Chinese delegation was expert at obfuscation. They spoke from prepared notes that consisted of meaningless platitudes and hollow promises. I told Yang that when I asked our team what dialogues under the Obama administration had delivered and what the nine meetings between Xi and President Obama had accomplished, their answer was "nothing." I suggested that "a good starting point might be to honor agreements already made." I tried to impress on Yang and others that Trump did not care about dialogue. He valued actions more than words and wanted to see results.

Although it is easy to think there is no downside to talking, the truth is that that is naïve. The formal dialogues and summits with the United States were boons for the CCP, mainly because they created false hope that China would change its behavior. False hope prevented or at least deferred U.S. actions to counter various forms of Chinese aggression, from industrial espionage to cyberattacks to the construction and weaponizing of islands in the South China Sea. In the small and large meetings with Xi that followed, the president and all of us emphasized clear objectives, including denuclearizing North Korea, ensuring freedom of navigation in the South China Sea, ending Chinese cyberattacks, halting theft and the forced transfer of intellectual property, and reversing unfair trade practices.

Trump was direct. On North Korea, he told Xi that China "could solve the problem in two seconds" if Xi wanted to. Kim Jong-un's nuclear program and his military were dependent on China for over 90 percent of trade. Pyongyang's dependency on China for critical commodities such as oil and refined petroleum gave Beijing tremendous coercive power. Xi remains customarily stone-faced in formal meetings, but his expression shifted, and I thought Trump may have been getting through.

Gary Cohn was even more direct on the economic front, noting that "years of promises to halt unfair practices have gone unfulfilled" and we would soon have "no option but to respond to the lack of reciprocity" in market access and trade. Chinese officials seemed surprised and concerned with the unmistakable shift from "cooperation and engagement" to competition. They seemed confident, however, that they could lure this new administration back into complacency with the same insincere promises of impending liberalization and cooperation on issues that mattered to the United States. I was resolved to prove them wrong.

After a working lunch, the Chinese delegation departed. We remained in the Tea Room for a quick debrief. I judged the summit to have been a success.

The Syria strikes and the initial phase of the maximum pressure campaign on North Korea may have convinced the Chinese delegation to drop their typical talking points. The Chinese delegation agreed that North Korea was a threat to the world, denuclearization was the only acceptable outcome, and maximum pressure was an appropriate approach.

Moreover, Trump had not stepped into any of the rhetorical traps the Chinese always set for American leaders. Pottinger and I had warned Trump that Xi often used innocuous-sounding phrases like "nonconflict, nonconfrontation, and mutual respect" to perpetuate American complacency and passivity. We told him that the CCP's favorite phrase, "win-win," actually meant that China won twice. We warned him that Xi would love him to use phrases suggesting a "G-2" relationship in which the United States and China divided the world into spheres of influence.

Because Trump is reflexively contrarian, I was careful not to tell him what I thought he should say. I was happy for him to be contrary with Chairman Xi, so I told him what Xi wanted him to say.

It worked. Xi did not get from Trump what he had gotten from President Obama, an endorsement of a "new kind of major power relations"—CCP code for "We're in charge now."

Five months later, Trump would tell an interviewer on Fox News, "We have a lot of love in the administration. The White House is truly, as you would say, a well-oiled machine."[1] Steven Mnuchin bought drinks for everyone at the Mar-a-Lago bar, and as Rex Tillerson and I sipped bourbon, I would not have taken exception to Trump's description. The team had come together and performed effectively for the president on the response in Syria and at the China summit. But the "oil" I was applying through the effort to foster collaboration would, over time, break down under the friction of divergent agendas, malicious actors, and power struggles and from the heat of America's vitriolic partisanship.

★   ★   ★

IT WAS time to follow up and increase pressure on Assad, Russia, and Iran.

After a decision like the one made in response to the Khan Shaykhun chemical attack, there is a tendency in government to move to the next hot topic. But our team sustained the pressure on Assad and his sponsors. A week after the attack and five days after the strikes, we declassified a report confirming that Assad's victims had been exposed to sarin. Ambassador Nikki Haley forced Russia to veto a UN Security Council resolution that would have condemned the April 4 chemical attack, called upon Syria to provide full access to investigators, and vowed to hold the perpetrators accountable. On April 19, 2017, the Organisation for the Prohibition of Chemical Weapons said there was "incontrovertible" evidence that the April 4 attacks had involved the use of sarin or a sarin-like substance. The day after the retaliatory strikes, I spoke with Susan Rice, President Obama's last national security advisor, at her request. She was concerned about what was now incontrovertible: that Moscow and Damascus had duped the Obama administration with false promises to eliminate Assad's stocks of chemical munitions.

She emailed me immediately after the call: "My former boss was appreciative and asked me to convey that he thinks you are serving the country well and is grateful you are where you are. Me, too. Many thanks for your time."

It was a sad state of affairs that partisanship, election denial, and the steady pounding of "Russiagate" reporting interacted with Trump's defensiveness to foreclose on any opportunity for civil discourse between Trump and his predecessor. Rice told me that President Obama would welcome the opportunity to speak with President Trump anytime. I told her that I would pass on the message, but we both knew that a call was not going to happen.

When I first raised the possibility of a conversation with Obama, Trump responded, "Hell, no." When I raised the possibility again, on the way to Mar-a-Lago in early March, Trump had agreed. But someone told him that President Obama had wiretapped his phone during the campaign in 2016. Trump's phone was not tapped, but a 2023 Department of Justice report concluded that the FBI had obtained flawed surveillance applications and warrants for members of the Trump campaign.[2] Trump tweeted on March 4[3]:

Donald J. Trump ✔
@realDonaldTrump

Is it legal for a sitting President to be "wire tapping" a race for president prior to an election? Turned down by court earlier. A NEW LOW!

3:49 AM · Mar 4, 2017

Donald J. Trump ✔
@realDonaldTrump

How low has President Obama gone to tapp my phones during the very sacred election process. This is Nixon/Watergate. Bad (or sick) guy!

4:02 AM · Mar 4, 2017

The reports of wiretapping foreclosed the possibility of a conversation.

American politics had devolved into a vortex of vitriol that destroyed opportunities for speaking with one voice even on the condemnation of Assad and his sponsors for the murder of civilians with chemical weapons.

I was beginning to wonder if my personal effort to transcend partisanship was to be a fool's errand.

CHAPTER 7

DEEP CONTRADICTIONS

TRUMP IS SENDING HIS NATIONAL SECURITY ADVISER H.R. **MCMASTER TO AFGHANISTAN . . .** The top U.S. commander in Afghanistan, Gen. John Nicholson, is asking for additional reinforcements . . . McMaster's trip to the region is part of the on-going consultation process ahead of finalizing the Trump administration's South Asia policy . . . **H.R. MCMASTER visits AFGHANISTAN after MOAB ATTACK . . .** H.R. McMaster has arrived in Kabul just days after the U.S. military dropped its largest non-nuclear bomb on Islamic State (IS) group targets in eastern Afghanistan . . . **MCMASTER ADAMANT THAT TALIBAN WILL BE DEFEATED . . .** McMaster said Pakistan should seek its interests in Afghanistan or any other country through political channels and not through violence . . . AFTER TOUGH TALK ON TERROR, US SECURITY ADVISER HR **MCMASTER ARRIVES IN ISLAMABAD . . .** McMaster on Monday met Pakistan Prime Minister Nawaz Sharif and discussed bilateral ties, Afghan situation and rising tensions between India, Pakistan . . . **CONFUSION, CHAOS AFTER TALIBAN BREACH AFGHAN BASE IN DEADLY ATTACK . . .** Afghan and Indian intelligence agencies gave funds and other assistance to Pakistani Taliban militants to fight Islamabad . . . NEW POLICY WILL APPLY BOTH TO AFGHANISTAN AND PAKISTAN: MCMASTER . . . **MCMASTER CONCLUDES PAKISTAN TALKS WITH CALL TO CONFRONT TERRORISM . . .** President Donald Trump faces a stark choice as his security advisers and military commanders push him to send thousands more troops to Afghanistan . . . **PENCE, MCMASTER TEAM UP TO PUSH MORE TROOPS IN AFGHANISTAN . . .**

I HAD written a book about how poor leadership in Washington was a setup for failure in Vietnam. Now I was at least partially responsible for what I judged to be a failing strategy in Afghanistan.

Over Easter Weekend, April 14–17, 2017, I led a trip to South Asia to jump-start the development of a new strategy. National security advisors should travel on their own only on rare occasions, but developing a sound strategy for a war in which American servicemen and -women were risking their lives and making sacrifices qualified as an exceptional circumstance.

I saw strong parallels between U.S. war strategy in Afghanistan from 2001 to 2017 and in Vietnam from 1965 to 1973. Architects of both wars overlooked the warning of nineteenth-century philosopher of war Carl von Clausewitz that "the first, the supreme, the most far-reaching act of judgment that the statesman and commander have to make is to establish . . . the kind of war on which they are embarking; neither mistaking it for, nor trying to turn it into, something that is alien to its nature."[1]

I told Trump that I shared his frustration about the war in Afghanistan. I understood why he doubted our ability to secure a sustainable political outcome consistent with our vital interests. "Mr. President, America's short war mentality has actually lengthened the war and made it more costly. You are right that we've wasted far too much money in Afghanistan." Across several conversations, I explained how, after an anemic and fragmented effort on reconstruction in the war's early years, the Bush administration in its waning months had initiated massive programs and investments to help establish a functioning state. Money poured in from innumerable national, international, and nongovernmental organizations, but at unsustainable rates and beyond the absorptive capacity of Afghanistan's economy. American taxpayers' money was stolen or wasted. Efforts to build state institutions were erratic and ill-conceived. Advisors prodded Afghans to establish centralized national-level systems incompatible with their traditionally decentralized form of governance. The inflows of money and lack of transparency strengthened criminalized patronage networks that looted aid, profited from the wartime economy, and preyed on the Afghan people. I told Trump that while in command of a multinational task force, I had seen U.S. officials avert their eyes from criminal activity, such as the theft of salaries for "ghost" soldiers and police. In the absence of strong security forces and a rule of law, many Afghans had sought protection from power-ful warlords, criminal networks, and militias, further fragmenting society and frustrating efforts to develop a common postwar Afghan identity and vision for the future. As in Vietnam, a government seen as legitimate by the majority of the people was the most important prerequisite for victory.

I thought that acknowledging previous failures might help Trump realize the possibilities of a new, reasoned approach to the war. But it was a hard sell. Trump often told me that an unnamed "friend who is a real military expert" had said that a Taliban victory was inev-itable because "Afghans are the toughest fighters." Trump's friend echoed the popular "graveyard of empires" narrative that portrayed the "endless war" in Afghanistan as futile. Whenever he mentioned this, I would respond, "Those tough Afghans include those who are bearing the brunt of the fight to protect their country and their way of life from the Taliban." Trump's "friend" had it exactly wrong, but Trump found it difficult to distinguish between those who brought him sound analysis and those, real or imagined, who brought him hackneyed bromides.

"Mr. President," I told him, "the Taliban are not romantic war-riors or an organic rural movement, as your friend describes them. They are a ruthless terrorist organization funded by Gulf donors and the narcotics trade, trained by Pakistan's Inter-Services Intelligence (ISI), and intertwined with other terrorist organizations such as al-Qaeda, with which they share resources and expertise. Afghans fight the Taliban because they've lived under Taliban rule and know that the Taliban will neither share power nor abandon their oppressive ideology."

I tried to help Trump understand that the coalition and the Af-ghans did have authorship over the future. But those who wanted the United States to declare defeat and leave Afghanistan used a term that elicited a visceral reaction from Trump: *nation-building*. That term never failed to trigger a Trump rant about the "stupid people" who wasted trillions of dollars in misguided, moralistic efforts to "promote democracy."

I would again concede the point on wasted money and effort, while helping him understand that Afghanistan had been transformed since 2001. Trump was a visual learner, so I showed him photos of Kabul in the 1970s, during Taliban rule, and in 2017, to illustrate how the city had been vibrant before Taliban rule, how the Taliban had choked the life out of the city, and how life had returned after their removal from power.

On the way back to Washington from the Xi summit, I had told Trump that Tillerson and Mattis had discouraged me from going to South Asia, even though I had invited their representatives to accompany me. Just days before my departure, Mattis and Tillerson asked Trump to cancel the trip. He cut them short: "I want General McMaster to go."

Trump's support did not induce a cooperative spirit. Neither Mattis nor Tillerson attended or dialed into an April 13 principals committee meeting to finalize the objectives for the trip. Mattis did send me a letter calling for a "politically, fiscally, and militarily sustainable strategy" to accomplish three objectives: enable a counterterrorism platform, prevent terrorists from obtaining nuclear weapons from Pakistan, and prevent a war between Pakistan and India with Afghanistan as a proxy battleground. The letter welcomed the initiation of an interagency review but made clear that the Pentagon believed that only a "modest increase in military capabilities and authorities" was necessary.

It was an argument for staying the course. The letter rested on the same implicit assumptions that had underpinned an Obama administration document entitled "Afghanistan 2015" that I had read in Kabul in 2012. That document and Mattis's letter were self-limiting and based on assumptions about the level of effort the American electorate would support. The Pentagon had inverted the approach to strategy development taught at the U.S. military's war colleges: first determine the desired ends, next identify the ways to accomplish those ends, and then commit the necessary means. Mattis's letter began with the means. Moreover, enabling a counterterrorism (CT) platform was not an objective. It was a preferred course of action.

I thanked Mattis for his letter and responded with a suggestion that we test the assumption that "the United States can maintain a viable CT platform and protect vital interests under conditions of state collapse." If that assumption were false, we should consider an objective to "prevent state collapse and assist the Afghan government in gradually strengthening institutions and functions." In Iraq and Afghanistan, I had seen many proposals to transition to a "CT platform" or "over-the-horizon" CT capabilities. But without human intelligence and a reliable partner on the ground, counterterrorism is ineffective.

I had begun to realize that the desire to withdraw from Afghanistan drove a strange affinity for the Taliban. Many in government had conjured an imagined Taliban to replace the actual enemy. I asked the NSC staff to work with the intelligence community on a draft framing paper designed to jump-start the discussion. Like Trump's "friend," the paper I received portrayed the Taliban as a romantic rural Afghan movement whose ideology was based on a stern version of law and order that traditional Afghans found attractive. The paper ignored the Taliban's connections to al-Qaeda and other terrorist organizations, implied that its leadership would be willing to share power, and suggested that, if they returned to power, the organization would be less oppressive to women and those who rejected their perverted interpretation of Islam. I used a bold Sharpie to write across the top of the paper, "Did we outsource this paper to the Taliban?"

I consulted with a wide range of people before the trip, including Afghanistan and South Asia academic experts. My friend and counterinsurgency expert Rufus Phillips urged quick action, because "Morale is collapsing." Phillips, former ambassador to Afghanistan Ron Neumann, and Ashley Tellis of the Carnegie Endowment for International Peace pointed out the folly of trying to negotiate a favorable peace agreement while declaring our intention to withdraw.

My fellow officers urged me to get options to the president as quickly as possible. Dunford was wary about showing any daylight between himself and Mattis, but he pushed for a quick presidential decision—in part, to prompt allies to get behind the strategy during an upcoming NATO conference. The Special Operations Command commander, Gen. Tony Thomas, an officer who never pulled his punches, asked the following two questions: Is the deteriorating situation in Afghanistan reversible? Are Afghan forces able to gain strength? He thought the answer to both was "yes." He noted that the Afghan government had been better under Ashraf Ghani, but pointed out that former president Hamid Karzai was still in the shadows. He observed that "we are crushing ISIS-K," referring to ISIS in Khorasan Province, "but are not authorized to fight the Taliban." He urged me to ask the president for "permission to fight our enemies." The commander of Joint Special Operations Command, Lt. Gen. Scott Miller, noted that Afghanistan and Pakistan remained the "epicenter" of the fight against jihadist terrorists. Like General Thomas, he urged a change in the rules of engagement, noting that we are "starting to see Afghans lose" and that we are "not hurting the Taliban enough." CENTCOM commander, Gen. Joe Votel, agreed with Thomas and Miller while stressing the need, as Gen. Mick Nicholson had, for a new approach to Pakistan that employed more than carrots and baby carrots.

On April 11, the combatant commanders were in Washington for their semiannual conference. The initial plan was for the president to interact with them and the Joint Chiefs of Staff for only an hour at the National Defense University. But the president wanted to meet with the generals and host them for dinner at the White House. Mattis made the change. I would continue to advocate for Trump to have greater access to advice from senior commanders—efforts that only sometimes resulted in such access and always succeeded in generating more tension between Mattis and me. Mattis may have wanted to shield the flag officers from Trump's unconventional and, at times, shocking ideas. But these were perspectives the president needed to hear. I was beginning to understand that Mattis wanted the president to hear one voice from the military: his own.

Trump wanted to just "get the hell out" of Afghanistan. Mattis, who seemed happy to maintain the status quo, was limiting Trump's access to those who might help him see alternatives to retreat or a costly "endless" war. Any chance for a long-term strategy for the war in Afghanistan depended on resolving my two-front conflict with Trump's predilections and Mattis's desire for control.

*   *   *

EARLY ON the morning of Good Friday, I said goodbye to Katie and our youngest daughter, Caragh, amid a sea of half-unpacked cardboard boxes. Katie and our daughters had the moving drill down, and this was not the first time I had skipped out of the experience. Quarters 13 would be our eighteenth residence together as a family. (When I returned from the trip four days later, the house looked like we had lived in it for years.)

I walked up the stairs of the Air Force Boeing 707, greeted the pilots and the flight crew, and said hello to our traveling party as I walked down the aisle to the dual-purpose office/bedroom at the back of the plane. After introductions, I welcomed everyone.

"Thank you for making this trip with me over Easter Weekend. We have an important mission. I believe that our war effort in Afghanistan is failing due to the absence of a strategy. The purpose of our trip is to jump-start the development of options for a new South Asia strategy."[2]

We landed at the Kabul airport and took the short helicopter flight to the landing zone within the secure perimeter of the International Security Assistance Force headquarters and the nearby U.S. embassy. Chargé d'affaires Amb. Hugo Llorens and General Nicholson greeted us. I opted to walk to the embassy with Llorens as our team got settled in. Llorens, who in the early 2000s had witnessed the successful partnership between the United States and Colombia in pursuit of what many described as an impossible mission of defeating narco-terrorists, lamented the "defeatism" permeating the U.S. bureaucracy. The situation was difficult but not impossible. "What we need," Llorens told me, "is a strategic long-term approach that is sustainable. We can do it. Core staff is forty-three percent smaller than it was when you were last in Afghanistan. The cost of programs to support the Afghan government and people has decreased from one hundred twenty-three billion dollars to twenty-three billion a year."

As our team sat down with Llorens and his staff in a windowless secure conference room, memories flooded back. I recalled that, seven years earlier, I had sat across the same table from Amb. Karl Eikenberry and the late ambassador Richard Holbrooke, who was then visiting from Washington as the special representative for Afghanistan and Pakistan. I recalled Holbrooke's intensity. In typical fashion, he had asked rapid-fire questions without giving me time to respond, prompting me to say, "If you give me thirty seconds, I might be able to answer one of those questions."

Now I listened as Llorens's staff lamented the lack of authorities for our military to pursue the enemy, describing the restrictive rules of engagement as a sign that we were "not serious about the war." The deputy chief of mission, Dennis Hearne, observed that an effective counter threat finance effort to constrain Taliban funds had been dismantled. Most important, doubts about a sustained U.S. commitment had "encouraged infighting among Afghan officials and their various factions" as they strove to be in positions of relative advantage after U.S. disengagement. Llorens and his team urged removing time limits on assistance while making aid contingent on further Afghan reforms. I left the meeting more determined than ever to develop an option for the first sound, sustainable strategy for the war.

I then met with the intelligence team. Their candid assessment was that the Afghans were on the defensive and were losing the war.

Later, we drove to Mick Nicholson's headquarters. Mick argued that with "more intelligence and air support, a relaxation of the troop cap, the redesignation of the Taliban as a hostile force, and the ability to put combat advisors in Afghan front line units, success will be evident in four years." A sustained, relatively low-cost effort could convince "the Taliban and their Pakistani sponsors that they cannot accomplish their objectives through force." He continued: "Like South Korea, Afghanistan is taking on more responsibility for their own defense while the U.S. effort is transitioning away from close combat and toward critical support functions at a sustainable level of commitment."

The briefing that followed with Mick's staff confirmed his assessment. I thought it was too bad Donald Trump could not have heard it himself.

I was jet-lagged, but meeting with eight students from the American University of Afghanistan energized me. The students were survivors of a Taliban attack on the university on August 24, 2014, that had killed seven students, a policeman, three security guards, and a university professor and wounded many others. Sitting next to me was a student who was paralyzed from the waist down after being hit by terrorist gunfire. When he received treatment in Germany, he was offered asylum there, but refused. I wished more Americans knew the stories of these young Afghans. The drumbeat from the U.S. media was about terrorist attacks, Afghan and U.S. casualties, corruption, and wasted aid. While all those aspects of the war deserved coverage, so did these young Afghans who were determined to build a better future.

★   ★   ★

THE NEXT day, I drove through the arched sally port and entered the well-manicured grounds of the Arg, the royal and presidential residence for Afghan leaders since the late nineteenth century. Ashraf Ghani had taken over as president from Hamid Karzai in September 2014, the first peaceful transition of leadership in over a century. I had known Ghani since the beginning of the war. On September 11, 2001, he was at his desk when a jet carrying six crew members and fifty-eight passengers, including five terrorists, slammed into the Pentagon, across the river from his office in the headquarters of the World Bank. Ghani knew that there would soon be dramatic change in his country. An academic and expert in state-building who had coauthored a book with Clare Lockhart entitled *Fixing Failed States*, Ghani had found Afghanistan extraordinarily difficult to fix. He was far from perfect, but he was a vast improvement over his predecessor, Hamid Karzai, who, due to exhaustion and Pakistani subterfuge, had become hostile to the coalition keeping him in power.

Ghani and I agreed on the need for a long-term U.S. strategy to restore the confidence of the Afghan people and the other coalition members. I emphasized the importance of reforms to reduce corruption and improve government and security force performance. I suggested that Ghani enter a "compact" with the United States that would make our assistance contingent on his improving transparency and accountability, including ending corrupt practices such as salaries for "ghost" soldiers and police. The compact could help Ghani take on the most entrenched criminal patronage networks. He agreed.

The second half of our discussion focused on the need to counter the defeatist narrative on Afghanistan and highlight the contrast between Afghanistan under the Taliban and Afghanistan today. Finally, I urged him to redouble efforts to lessen divisions and foster unity among the Pashtun tribes and between them and the Tajik, Hazara, and Turkic minorities in the country.

As I met with Afghan national security advisor Haneef Atmar and the heads of security ministries, it became clear that the Ministry of Defense had made progress in reducing corruption, appointing people based on merit, and auditing fuel and critical supplies. But the minister of the interior, Taj Mohammad Jahid, did not seem to understand that reform was critical to the state's survival.

I grew frustrated during Jahid's presentation, which was essentially a list of more things he needed. "You do not seem to understand that American leaders and President Trump in particular have no patience left and will no longer tolerate the theft of American taxpayer-funded assistance." I said. I ended the meeting abruptly.

Back at the embassy, I did interviews with Martha Raddatz for ABC's *This Week* and with the Afghan television station Tolo TV. And that evening, Hugo Llorens hosted a large cocktail reception on the roof of his residence at the embassy, which overlooked the 3,500-year-old city and the hills and mountains surrounding it. I knew most of the attendees from my years in Kabul. That evening, I caught up with many old friends, young entrepreneurs, and government officials who had helped lift their country out of the hell of Taliban rule as refugees returned. Together, we looked out over a city transformed. Lights flickered across the Afghan capital in every direction. The city that had been rendered lifeless under the Taliban now bustled. But I knew that if we did not change course, the Taliban and their sponsors could reverse those gains and extinguish those lights.

As I went to sleep in the guest room in the ambassador's apartment on what was close to my seven-hundredth night in Afghanistan, I wanted to be hopeful, but I could not shake a sense of foreboding. We had a chance, finally, to establish a sound, sustainable strategy to win a long war on a modern-day frontier between barbarism and civilization. But I wondered if the missed opportunities associated with short-term, inconsistent approaches we had taken to the war had done irreparable damage to our will. I was determined to get Trump options to achieve sustainable security in Afghanistan and South Asia, but I was unsure that he had the flexibility of mind to overcome his desire to disengage. And I was increasingly concerned that, in contrast to the commanders in the field, the Pentagon did not see the urgent need for a fundamentally different strategy.

Day three in Kabul started with a short helicopter ride to Bagram Air Base for Easter breakfast with the leaders of the First Armored Division and our Special Operations Task Force. Leaders reinforced what we had heard in Kabul: they were frustrated with the rules of engagement. "How do you fight the Taliban or any enemy without designating them as an enemy?" They also told me how staying below the "force management level," or troop ceiling, had broken up teams and rendered them less effective. I huddled with my director for Afghanistan, Fernando Lujan, and other members of our team before departing for Islamabad with the director for Pakistan, Jay Wise. I asked them to identify "bridging actions" the president could approve immediately to arrest the deterioration while we developed options for a long-term strategy.

★　　★　　★

WE BEGAN our descent soon after we took off. The Islamabad airport was familiar to me. During 2003 and 2004, I had visited as a personal staff officer for Gen. John Abizaid, the commander of CENTCOM, the overall military headquarters with responsibility for the wars in Afghanistan and, by then, Iraq and for military operations across the greater Middle East. That trip was the first of several during which I heard U.S. commanders implore Pakistani generals to recognize that the terrorist organizations they used against their neighbors Afghanistan and India were a menace to them, too. And I would hear many times the response from Pakistani generals: promises that, with more American assistance, they could take on their Frankenstein monsters. Nothing had changed.[3]

Our ambassador to Pakistan, David Hale, greeted us. Hale was no stranger to what some might consider impossible causes: he had been special envoy for Middle East peace. But his work in Islamabad was particularly difficult because the policy he had been asked to implement was flawed, and because his interlocutors were experts in the art of duplicity. Over sandwiches at his residence, we shared our mutual frustrations with the Pakistani government, especially the Army.

Hale argued that whatever options we developed for Trump could not be dependent on Pakistani cooperation. He noted that U.S. prioritization of the relationship with Pakistan even at the expense of stability in Afghanistan had overlooked the interconnected nature of security in both places and encouraged the Pakistani military to continue its self-destructive support of terrorist organizations.

I agreed. So did Lisa Curtis, who had just joined our NSC staff as senior director for South and Central Asia. I hired Curtis after reading a report she had coauthored in which she argued that the United States must "consider Pakistan's strategy of supporting terrorist proxies to achieve regional strategic advantage as a threat to U.S. interests." That was the message I would deliver during my six-hour visit to Islamabad.[4]

My second meeting was with government officials in a large office building in central Islamabad. Our delegation sat on one side of the table, and various ministers and deputy ministers sat across from us. I heard exactly what I had expected to hear: descriptions of all that Pakistan was doing to fight jihadist terrorists and promises to do more if they could secure more U.S. military and economic assistance.

I listened patiently before telling them that President Trump was questioning the deep contradiction in our relationship—that Pakistan had the status of a major non-NATO ally but was supporting enemies who were terrorizing the Afghan people and fighting against the coalition and Afghan security forces. They were probably thinking, *Okay, but Americans never follow through.* I was resolved to surprise them.

Pakistani police cleared the route for our motorcade through the controlled chaos of Islamabad's streets, and I was soon sitting opposite Prime Minister Nawaz Sharif in his office. I told the prime minister and his key officials, "President Trump recognizes that we have essentially been funding our enemies through a middle man. Patience is running out, and soon we might no longer be able to provide economic and military aid." Sharif's body language expressed that he understood Trump's position, but it was clear to Hale, Curtis, and me that someone in the room was there to report to the Army leadership every word Sharif said.

As we walked past the manicured lawn at the prime minister's office, the contrast between the trappings of power in the prime minister's office and the actual powerlessness of that office was striking. Despite U.S., British, and other nations' efforts over many years to reinforce the civilian government of Pakistan, Army headquarters remained the center of power.[5] We therefore had to base our approach to Pakistan on the reality that while most countries have an Army, Pakistan's Army has a country.

Gen. Qamar Javed Bajwa, chief of Army, and Gen. Naveed Mukhtar, director general of ISI, Pakistan's intelligence service, were waiting outside Pakistani Army headquarters. Despite our deep frustrations with one another, the meeting began cordially, with Bajwa chiding me for not staying in Pakistan long enough to share a meal with him. I opened the meeting with condolences for the more than eight thousand Pakistani soldiers who had lost their lives to terrorist groups since 9/11 and the more than twenty thousand Pakistani civilians whom terrorists had killed across those years.

"Generals, as you know, we are assisting the president as he develops his policy toward Pakistan and South Asia. Ambassador Hale and I would like to hear your perspective on current U.S. policy and what changes you recommend."

General Bajwa did not hesitate. His comments seemed crafted to preempt what he expected to hear from me: exhortations to "do more" against the Taliban and the Haqqani network and hopeful expressions that we could, finally, work together to end the violence in Afghanistan.

The conversation with Bajwa and Mukhtar followed a recurring pattern, beginning with a litany of grievances. The first was U.S. abandonment of Pakistan after the end of the Soviet occupation of Afghanistan. From there, the conversation shifted to a portrayal of Pakistan as a victim: a victim of the massive influx of refugees as

Afghans fled the Soviet occupation, the Afghan Civil War, and the brutality of the Taliban; a victim of sanctions imposed by the United States due to its nuclear program; a victim of what the Pakistani generals portrayed as a U.S. war on terrorism; a victim of Indian aggression; and so on.

"Generals," I said, "I promise not to make the same pleas to go after the Haqqanis and other terrorist organizations that you have heard from countless American officers and diplomats. I am assuming that you will not do so, and we will have no option but to impose costs on you. Maybe you can prove me wrong."

I told them that the new administration in Washington would pay far more attention to deeds than words and explained that "President Trump, as a businessman, will see funding our enemies indirectly through aid to Pakistan as a bad return on investment."

On the way out, I passed General Bajwa a handwritten note with a list of names of U.S. and allied hostages held by the Haqqani network. He asked me if I would like him to do something about them.

I replied, "I am confident that you can if you want to."

We said goodbye and pulled away from the pristine grounds of Army headquarters.

On the short drive to the airfield, Hale and I discussed the sad pattern of U.S. policy toward Pakistan since 9/11, a pattern consistent with the definition of insanity attributed to Albert Einstein: doing the same thing over and over again while expecting a different result. It was time to break the pattern of serial gullibility. Trump was clear about halting aid if Pakistan did not stop supporting terrorist organizations, but the greatest influence over Islamabad would come with a long-term commitment to support Afghanistan. Without that commitment, the Pakistani Army and the Taliban could just wait Washington out.

★   ★   ★

I WAS eating my way across Central and South Asia—a heart-stopping Army Easter breakfast in Bagram, sandwiches at Hale's residence in Islamabad, and now a delicious dinner at national security advisor Ajit Doval's official residence, on Janpath Road in Delhi.

The conversation was easy, as Doval, Foreign Minister Subrahmanyam Jaishankar, and I believed we had a tremendous opportunity to work together in pursuit of our mutual objectives. We spoke about the war in Afghanistan and the threat to India from nuclear-armed Pakistan, but Jaishankar and Doval spoke mainly about an increasingly aggressive China. The two men were open to unprecedented cooperation thanks to Xi Jinping's aggression. The deepening partnership between the world's largest and the world's oldest democracies seemed logical, but India is fearful both of entrapment into competitions from which it would prefer to abstain and abandonment based on the short American attention span and ambivalence over South Asia. Those "schizophrenic" anxieties and the legacy of India's leadership of the Non-Aligned Movement during the Cold War had led to hedging behavior, especially with Russia, an important source of arms and oil for India.

On the final day of our trip, Lisa Curtis; the U.S. chargé d'affaires in New Delhi, MaryKay Carlson; and I met with Prime Minister Narendra Modi at the Rashtrapati Bhavan, the prime minister's official residence. Modi gave us a warm welcome. It was clear that deepening and expanding our relationship was a top priority for him. He expressed concern over China's increasingly aggressive efforts to extend its influence at India's expense and over its growing military presence in the region. He suggested that the United States, India, Japan, and like-minded partners emphasize the concept of a free and open Indo-Pacific as an inclusive effort to benefit all, in contrast to China's "One Belt One Road" initiative, which we should describe as a one-way street meant to advantage Beijing.

At the end of the meeting, the prime minister gave me a hug, put his hands on my shoulders, and blessed me. "You have an aura around you, and you will do good for humanity."

As I headed back to Washington, I was happy for any help I could get.

CHAPTER 8

TIGHTROPE

TRUMP, ARGENTINE PRESIDENT MACRI HOLD WHITE HOUSE TALKS. President Trump on Wednesday told the leaders of Mexico and Canada that he will not pull out of the **North American Free Trade Agreement,** just hours after administration officials said he was considering a draft executive order to do just that . . . TRUMP'S 100 DAYS ON WORLD STAGE: **RALLYING SOME AND REPELLING OTHERS** . . . Trump called the five-year-old trade pact with South Korea "unacceptable" and said it would be targeted for renegotiation after his administration completes a revamp of the North American Free Trade Agreement (NAFTA) with Canada and Mexico . . . **TRUMP VOWS TO FIX OR SCRAP SOUTH KOREA TRADE DEAL, WANTS MISSILE SYSTEM PAYMENT** . . . A series of North Korean missile tests this year—which are banned by the UN—has sparked international alarm and raised tensions with the US . . . CONTRADICTING TRUMP, **MCMASTER SAYS U.S. WILL PAY FOR SOUTH KOREAN THAAD DEPLOYMENT** . . . SOUTH KOREA SAYS MCMASTER AFFIRMS THAAD FUNDING DEAL UNCHANGED . . . **TRUMP FIRES FBI DIRECTOR JAMES COMEY** . . . President Trump hosted Russian Foreign Minister Sergey Lavrov at the White House, one day after firing the man whose agency is investigating Russia's meddling in the 2016 election that brought Trump to power . . . INSIDE THE OVAL OFFICE WITH TRUMP AND THE RUSSIANS: BROAD SMILES AND LOOSE LIPS . . . **MCMASTER: TRUMP'S SHARING OF SENSITIVE INTELLIGENCE WITH RUSSIA WAS 'WHOLLY APPROPRIATE'** . . . A huge suicide bomb ripped through a secure area of Kabul at the height of the Wednesday morning rush hour . . .

ON FRIDAY, April 21, 2017, as the president departed for his golf retreat in Bedminster, New Jersey, I headed to the Sedona Forum at the invitation of Sen. John McCain. The senator and his wife, Cindy, hosted me at their Hidden Valley Ranch. At a reception on the lawn of their home, under the sycamore trees lining the bank of a fast-running stream, McCain roasted colleagues from both political parties and made fun of himself. I found his sense of humor the perfect antidote to the pomposity and malice afflicting so many in Washington.

After the dinner party broke up, the senator and I walked into his kitchen.

"So, H.R., tell me how it's going."

I reflected on my first two months in the job. Despite the headlines describing the White House as "chaotic," the adhocracy that had produced unvetted executive orders in the early weeks of the Trump administration was gone.

McCain was happy to hear this, but skeptical. "Will he listen to you?" Despite his acrimonious relationship with Trump and the unconscionable insults Trump had leveled at McCain, the former naval officer was careful not to share or elicit direct criticisms of the president.

"Senator, the process is working," I said and used the strategy of maximum pressure for North Korea as a positive example. Then I summarized the high points of the Mar-a-Lago summit with the Chinese and described how we had managed the concurrent activity of the meetings and the Syria strikes.

McCain wanted to know about Afghanistan. I knew from my previous conversations with him in Kabul and Washington that he shared my assessment that U.S. policy and strategy in Afghanistan were the opposite of what was needed.

"You know, H.R., Afghanistan will be the biggest test of your decision-making process, because it cuts against Trump's desire to get out, and the neo-isolationist Republicans have his ear." I told him that the problem was larger than Trump and the neo-isolationists, though. Few people shared our sense of urgency on Afghanistan, and most were happy just to muddle through under the Obama administration's withdrawal policy.

As McCain poured us nightcaps, I told him I had encountered problems with those members of the White House staff who were pushing their own agendas and with members of the cabinet who saw me and the NSC as an adversary rather than a partner. "But, Senator, I am working on it, and I am confident that they will see the benefit of collaborating."

"I wish you luck," he said, "but some people are just jerks."

★   ★   ★

ON THE morning of April 27, I went to the Oval Office to brief Trump in advance of his meeting with his old friend Mauricio Macri, president of Argentina. Trump had been reading newspaper accounts of two devastating Taliban attacks, one on a military base in Mazar that had killed more than 160 people and another in Kabul that had killed more than 180 and wounded more than 400. He looked up from the paper and asked me, "How could attacks like this happen?" He suggested that the war in Afghanistan was futile: "Why don't we just leave, General?"

"Mr. President, Taliban attacks are meant to break the will of the Afghan and American people." I explained that Afghan morale was low due to large losses. Seven thousand Afghan security forces had been killed in action in the last year. "But, Mr. President, Afghans are even more concerned that you will stick with the Obama policy and withdraw on a time line. What we owe you is an assessment and options other than losing slowly, which is what we are doing now."

The next day, I began the principals committee meeting with what I had told Trump. The situation in Afghanistan was urgent. If we did not change course, a collapse of security was possible. But my sense of urgency was not shared. The memo I had sent to the cabinet in March established the goal of getting options to the president by April 28. We would not do so until mid-August. When I asked Afghan director Lujan why it was so hard to get the Departments of State and Defense to shake flawed assumptions, he told me that every time there is a policy review, the "documents go to the same bureaucrats, and they write in the same old stuff."

In early May, as the situation in Afghanistan became more

tenuous, I joined Trump in the back dining room adjacent to the Oval Office, where he was having lunch. As Fox News played on the television, I said, "Mr. President, if we continue with the Obama strategy, options other than withdrawal may no longer be tenable." I asked him to consider a "bridging option" to lift the restrictions on the Department of Defense and relax constraints such as the force management level (FML), or troop ceiling, that forced commanders to contract expensive civilian aviation maintenance and base security guards while soldier mechanics and infantryman from deployed units remained at their home bases. Trump increased the FML by three thousand and, more important, removed White House restrictions on support to Afghan forces, permitting the resumption of active, or status-based, targeting of the Taliban.

Despite Trump's decision, Mattis did not want to change the FML or the rules of engagement until the president decided on the overall strategy. But he and Tillerson were delaying that decision, mainly by making themselves unavailable for principals committee meetings on the subject. They had other priorities in mind, such as North Korea.

When I pressed Tillerson after a May 31 Haqqani network truck bomb attack in Kabul's diplomatic quarter killed more than 150 people and wounded over 400, he told me, "You might have it all figured out, H.R., but I don't."

I thought to myself, *We might lose a war before you catch up.*

A few days later, I spoke with President Ghani by video in the Situation Room. He stated that Afghans were facing a new level of threat and an urban war with Kabul as the primary battleground. He noted that the physical target of the May 31 attack was the U.S. embassy, but the real objective was to affect decision-making in our policy review.

Postponing meetings was not the only impediment to policy development. Tillerson's review of the department organizations made it difficult for NSC directors even to find State Department officials to participate in policy coordination. Those who did participate usually had no direct line of communication to Tillerson.

Faced with mounting obstruction and false stories quoting unnamed White House, Pentagon, and State Department officials claiming I was trying to convince Trump to send massive U.S. reinforcements to Afghanistan, I asked Vice President Pence to chair future PC meetings on the South Asia strategy. In addition to his authority as VP, Pence had the right personality and demeanor to cut through the obstruction and delaying tactics.

★   ★   ★

MEANWHILE, PYONGYANG'S nuclear and missile programs appeared increasingly dangerous. When Trump heard about the idea of a high-level briefing for the whole Senate on North Korea and the maximum pressure strategy—I did not tell him that Senator McCain had given me the idea at Sedona—he wanted to host the briefing at the White House.

On Wednesday, April 26, Matt Pottinger, Allison Hooker, and I briefed the president on North Korea in advance of the senators' arrival. Trump asked Hooker, our senior director for the Korean Peninsula, how long she had been working on North Korea. "Sixteen years," she answered.

I told Trump that Hooker had been to North Korea more times than all but a few Americans. I hoped he was beginning to understand that he had tremendously dedicated, talented, and experienced professionals working for him on the NSC staff. (A month later, Hooker would have to resign from the State Department so I could convert the position to one of the very few permanent NSC positions because Tillerson had refused to renew her assignment.)

I walked with the president down the steps adjacent to the Oval Office, past several offices, the Navy Mess, and the Situation Room. Trump greeted staffers who had stepped into the hallway hoping to see him. One might imagine that those who worked in the West Wing saw the president often, but Trump rarely deviated from his daily commute from the Residence, through the Rose Garden, and into the Oval Office. We exited the West Wing, walked across the parking lot, and entered the ground floor of the Eisenhower Executive Office Building. Priebus and Bannon were waiting in the greenroom adjacent to the auditorium.

Trump sat in a chair across from them. I sat down to his right. He was in a good mood—maybe reflecting on the Syria strikes, the Xi summit, and the progress made in increasing the pressure on North Korea. He turned to me and said loud enough for Bannon and Priebus to hear, "You know, General, you may be the best hire I ever made. You are doing a great job." The praise was uncharacteristic and unanticipated.

Surprised, I said, "Thank you. It is a privilege to do this job for you, Mr. President."

I introduced Trump to the senators. He made brief remarks and then turned the session over to Tillerson, Mattis, Dunford, Pompeo, and Coats. Trump, Priebus, Bannon, and I walked back to the White House.

It was 3:30 p.m. I went directly to the White House Briefing Room to deliver remarks and answer questions about Trump's first one hundred days in office from a foreign policy and national security perspective. I wondered whether this backgrounder and others were a waste of time; they had little effect on reporting. Headlines over the next few days included "Trump's 100 Days on World Stage: Rallying Some and Repelling Others," "The Entertainment Presidency," and "Trump's 100 Days of Failure?"[1] Many reporters struggled with political bias, compounded by their profound dislike of Trump. Their reporting reinforced Trump's conclusion that the press was biased against him and inspired his more than two thousand insults against reporters as "dishonest," "corrupt," and even "enemies of the people."

It was 4 p.m., but the day was far from over. I met with the Polish president's foreign policy advisor to discuss a future Trump visit to Warsaw. I then joined President Trump at 5 p.m. for an update on the president of Argentina's visit and the work the Commerce Department was doing to increase Argentinian agricultural imports. After discussing avocados, I told Trump that I was about to call South Korea's national security advisor, retired brigadier general Kim Kwan-jin.

The mention of South Korea triggered a rant from Trump on trade and how South Korea, "a very wealthy country," was free riding on U.S. security. Trump described KORUS, the Korea–United States Free Trade Agreement, as the "worst trade deal ever." He said the same of NAFTA.

Some advisors were trying to convince Trump to declare his intention to withdraw from NAFTA prior to his one-hundredth day in office. They were pushing on an open door. Trump believed that merely threatening to act was not as effective as taking action. Peter Navarro had slipped a draft executive order onto Trump's desk directing the U.S. trade representative to "provide to Canada and Mexico a notice of withdrawal of the United States from NAFTA."

Gary Cohn and I, along with Secretary of Commerce Wilbur Ross and Secretary of Agriculture Sonny Perdue, advised the president that he was in a strong position to renegotiate NAFTA without withdrawing.

As we joined Trump in the Roosevelt Room at 6 p.m., Ross assured Trump that the soon-to-be-confirmed U.S. trade representative, Robert Lighthizer, was the very best person to renegotiate NAFTA. "Lighthizer understands your goals," he said.

Trump grumbled, "Lighthizer, Lighthizer, all I hear is 'Wait for Lighthizer.'"

The Senate would confirm Lighthizer two weeks later.

Mexican foreign minister Luis Videgaray somehow knew about the meeting and asked me to call him when it was over. I told him that the earlier phone conversation with President Enrique Peña Nieto had helped, but that it would be important for Mexico to negotiate in good faith. Trump could lose patience at any moment.

After the call to Videgaray, I met with Kevin Harrington, senior director for strategic planning and assessments, and Nadia Schadlow, who had taken on the role of senior assistant to the president for national security strategy. I had made copies of pages from Zbigniew Brzezinski's memoir, *Power and Principle*, in which he describes his effort to develop a "conceptual framework" for the Carter administration's foreign policy. I pointed out a passage in which Brzezinski is candid about the administration's failure "to project effectively to the public the degree to which we were motivated by a coherent and well-thought-out viewpoint."[2] As we discussed organizing the congressionally mandated National Security Strategy around America's core interests, I summarized the discussion on NAFTA to highlight the need for an integrated approach to national security, economic, and trade policy. I asked Harrington and Schadlow to consult with

Navarro and others to help elevate the discussion about trade above tactics like the imposition of tariffs or the withdrawal from trade deals.

When I called Brigadier General Kim, he was eager to get some of the U.S. Terminal High Altitude Area Defense (THAAD) missiles in position before the leftist candidate for president, Moon Jae-in, won the election, so that the new government could not obstruct their deployment. Moon had made statements about reevaluating the deployment of the one-billion-dollar counter missile system, and his comments had incensed Trump, who had told me to "get South Korea to pay for them." My explanation to him—that the system was ours and was protecting our forces and the more than forty thousand U.S. civilians who live in South Korea—was unpersuasive.

Trump's disruptive nature could be advantageous. Many preexisting policies needed to be disrupted. But his impoliteness and capriciousness, in tweets or off-the-cuff comments to the press, were often counterproductive. The White House communications team did an uneven job of coordinating with the NSC staff in advance of Trump's press engagements on foreign policy. During an interview with Reuters on Friday, April 28, Trump had trade and THAAD missiles on his mind, stating that he wanted to "terminate" both NAFTA and KORUS. He also said that South Korea should pay for THAAD. Pottinger told me that Trump's statements had the South Korean government reeling. They had already paid a heavy price for the THAAD deployment as Beijing cut off Chinese tourism and shuttered Republic of Korea department stores in China.

On the drive home, I reflected on a day that had included engagements spanning every aspect of the job and topics ranging from North Korea's nuclear program to Argentinian avocados to trade agreements to missile defense. Our team was doing important work, and we were making progress, but nothing was easy, and everything was harder than it needed to be.

It was about to get even harder.

When I arrived home, I said hello to Katie and went upstairs to the sensitive compartmented information facility, or SCIF, that had been installed in the house, to call Brigadier General Kim to try to allay his concerns about THAAD and KORUS. I told him that "President

Trump would adhere to any existing agreements until they were renegotiated."

On Sunday, as I rode to the Fox News studio just a few blocks from the White House, Priebus called to give me a "heads-up" that the president was "as angry as I have ever seen him," over South Korean press stories that I had contradicted him and affirmed our commitment to THAAD under the current agreement.

The president called me a few minutes later. He was indeed irate. "What the fuck were you thinking, General, contradicting me?"

I let him get it out, and then replied with something like "Come on, Mr. President, why do you believe what is reported in the South Korean press? The government spun the conversation on the eve of the election for their own purposes."

Before I could tell him that I had reinforced his message on trade and burden sharing, he yelled again and slammed down the phone.

I smiled at the Secret Service agents, who could not help but overhear, and said, "That went well."

I shrugged it off. I had an interview to do.

During my appearance on *Fox News Sunday*, anchor Chris Wallace focused mainly on the threat from North Korea, discussing recent ballistic missile tests. I told him that the North Korean regime posed a great danger not only to the United States and our allies, but also to China and others.

Someone must have planted the question of whether I had called my South Korean counterpart and told him we would stick to the original THAAD agreement. I responded that "the last thing I would ever do is contradict the president of the United States. What I told our South Korean counterpart is, until any renegotiation, that the deal is in place; we'll adhere to our word."[3]

While I was being interviewed on Fox, Trump appeared on CBS News's *Face the Nation*. In an interview he had taped a day earlier, he told John Dickerson, "I think we've done very well on foreign policy. I think we've done very, very well with relationships with other leaders. I think we're doing great on trade deals."[4]

I had begun to see Trump as akin to Shakespeare's Othello: his insecurity made him susceptible to manipulation. That play's antagonist, Iago, "poisons Othello's ear," and Trump's insecurities, magnified against the backdrop of the Mueller investigation and the hostility of most of the media, made him an easy mark for the many Iago figures around him. Bannon, Priebus, and others employed the same principal tactic as Iago—impugn competitors with accusations of disloyalty or contradicting Trump. And as with Othello, Trump's insecurity made him vulnerable to tragic results.

★ ★ ★

LEAKS TO the press heightened Trump's insecurity, fomented distrust, and made everyone's job harder. Nine days after he chewed me out on the phone, Trump fired FBI director James Comey. His loss of confidence in Comey was understandable, given the dubious origins of the so-called Russiagate scandal and the unprofessional conduct of some FBI officials prior to Robert Mueller's taking over the investigation.

On May 10, the day after he fired Comey, Trump, on the recommendation of Tillerson, met with Russian foreign minister Sergey Lavrov and Russian ambassador Sergey Kislyak in the Oval Office. During the meeting, Trump disparaged Comey as a "loser" and ranted about the Mueller investigation. Tillerson and I were uncomfortable. For better or worse, I had seen how Trump's inner monologue was made audible for whoever was in the room—in this case, Russian officials. It was unfortunate.

After the meeting, I brought our team together and asked them to ensure we controlled the roster for meetings with POTUS even when the secretary of state requested them. We had made the inexcusable mistake of allowing a Russian photographer into the Oval Office, which had allowed Lavrov to release embarrassing photos of the president laughing with his guests, which fueled the narrative of Trump's alleged collusion with the Kremlin.

I knew the Kremlin would be delighted with the meeting and would use the photos to damage Trump. What I did not anticipate was that someone in the administration would play into the Kremlin's hands.

Per protocol, a member of the NSC staff had attended the meeting and produced a "readout" to be distributed to a small, tightly controlled group of recipients. Someone who received that readout jumped to the conclusion that the president had divulged sensitive information. That person shared his or her concern with others, one of whom leaked to the press the false charge that Trump had compromised intelligence sources and methods. Twenty-four hours later, the *Washington Post* reported the following:

> President Trump revealed highly classified information to the Russian foreign minister and ambassador in a White House meeting last week, according to current and former U.S. officials, who said Trump's disclosures jeopardized a critical source of intelligence on the Islamic State.
>
> The information the president relayed had been provided by a U.S. partner through an intelligence-sharing arrangement considered so sensitive that details have been withheld from allies and tightly restricted even within the U.S. government, officials said.[5]

But the information discussed had been shared already with the Russians through routine channels. Moreover, Trump did not know the sources or methods used to develop the intelligence. In an only-in-Washington perverse twist, it was the leaking "current and former" U.S. officials and the *Washington Post* who divulged that the information had been obtained through "an intelligence-sharing relationship."

Katie and I were on our way to an event at the Kuwaiti embassy when the White House communications team called to ask me to make a statement to correct the *Washington Post* story. I walked out to the "sticks," the collection of microphones that news media had arrayed on stands just outside the North Entrance of the West Wing:

> The story that came out tonight as reported is false. The president and the foreign minister reviewed a range of common threats to our two countries, including threats to civil aviation. At no time were intelligence sources or methods discussed, and the president did not disclose any military operations that were not already publicly known. Two other

senior officials who were present, including the secretary of state, remember the meeting the same and have said so. Their on-the-record account should outweigh those anonymous sources. And I was in the room. It didn't happen.[6]

I addressed the alleged disclosure of sensitive intelligence again on May 16, 2017, in the White House Briefing Room, pointing out that the information Trump had shared with Lavrov was "wholly appropriate" and that U.S. national security is "put at risk by this leak and by leaks like this."

But journalists opposed to Trump could not let go of this story, just as they remained preoccupied with allegations of collusion with Russia during the election. Some connected the two without any factual grounds. The *Washington Post* coverage of my statement in the Briefing Room included a quotation from "a former senior U.S. official who is close to current Administration officials" that "it's all clouded because of this problem he has with Russia."[7]

Reporters sourced story after story to numerous "current and former [unnamed] officials." I was struck by how my reporting of basic facts had been distorted by people inside and outside the White House who had different agendas but were happy to use one another.

Years later, as the FBI recovered boxes of documents from Mar-a-Lago, it would become clear that Trump was reckless with classified information. But this and other false stories meant to disparage him did the Russians' work for them by distracting us from our duties and sowing distrust between the president and members of his staff.

Clarifying what really happened was an easy choice for me but was portrayed as compromising. The journalist Fred Kaplan, who wrote an essay entitled "The Tarnishing of H.R. McMaster," stated that I "had been all but incapable of guile" but was "now soaked in the swamp of deceit in the service of Trump."[8] I was more amused than offended at his hyperbolic criticism.

After our first meeting in February, Kissinger hand-wrote a long letter, the first line of which contained the prescient observation that "you are walking a tightrope with chasms on both sides." Three months later, winds from multiple directions were making the tightrope unstable. Attacks in the media, in pseudo-media news outlets, and on social media came from alt-right Trump loyalists who planted stories describing me as a deep-state globalist who was soft on jihadist terrorist organizations and Iran. Virulently anti-Trump people on the left and the Republican establishment right cast my doing my job and, in the case of the Lavrov matter, telling the truth as compromising my integrity and sense of duty.

As the NSC staff and policy process got going, the secretaries of state and defense generated headwinds. The State Department was even refusing to replace rotating Department of State members of the NSC staff. While analogies to war can be overdone, I thought of von Clausewitz's observation about combat as being consistent with the high-wire act of serving as Trump's national security advisor: "It is difficult for normal efforts to achieve even moderate results."[9] I was determined to keep my head up and my eyes forward. My family, friends, and many of my colleagues would serve as my balancing pole. And when the wind became too great or too erratic, they would serve as my safety harness.

*　　*　　*

ON MAY 10, the same day I attended the Lavrov meeting, I spoke with Dr. Kissinger over lunch in my office. I told him that the first months had been turbulent, but that our team was coming together and helping Trump clarify his foreign policy agenda. I pulled down two memoirs of Kissinger's time in Washington, *The White House Years* and *Years of Upheaval*, and asked him to inscribe them. When I opened *The White House Years* to the title leaf, I saw the inscription from my mother, Marie "Mimi" McMaster, who had given the book to me for my birthday in 1990. I had been moving so fast that I had not registered that May 10 was the fourth anniversary of her death. As I fought back a wave of emotion, I told Kissinger how my mom, a great educator who had taught in underserved communities in Philadelphia for decades, had instilled in my sister and me a desire to serve.

"I miss her," I said, "and I sometimes still feel the impulse to call her." Mimi had a gift of looking at every situation logically and placing events and circumstances in perspective. When faced with adversity, she had displayed a streak of stoicism. But she was positive and optimistic. Her message was that "If you do what is right and do your best, everything will work out for the best." That combination of stoicism and optimism was an approach to life I found helpful in combat and in Washington. I told Kissinger about Mimi and how I was determined to follow her example, to ignore the noise associated with Washington politics and encourage NSC staff to do the same.

Kissinger told me about his own mother's strength of character. "She was the one who made the decision to flee Germany in 1940. I was very fortunate to have her with me for my years in Washington and until her death in 1998, when she passed at the age of ninety-seven. I miss her every day." He signed *The White House Years* on the leaf behind my mother's note.

I stayed in contact with Kissinger, and years later, I spoke with him on Zoom to get his advice before writing this book. I told him that around the time of our lunch together in my office, I realized that I faced a fundamental choice of either fighting off those who were engaged in subterfuge with the president and were weaponizing various media against me or ignoring the noise and doing the best job I could. I chose the latter.

Kissinger told me in his distinctive German accent, "You made the right choice; they would have eaten you alive."

CHAPTER 9

TRAVELS
WITH TRUMP

DONALD TRUMP'S EXCELLENT ABRAHAMIC AD-VENTURE . . . Trump Signals Shift in Middle East Strategy with Symbolic First Stop in Saudi Arabia . . . *The Trump fire hose of news threatens to hobble his presidency* . . . **ON SAU-DI TRIP, TRUMP TASKED WITH MENDING RELA-TIONS** . . . Donald Trump places his bets on Iranian isolation . . . *SAUDIS GIVE TRUMP A RECEPTION FIT FOR A KING* . . . Trump signs 'tremendous' deals with Saudi Arabia on his first day overseas . . . **TRUMP DECLARES 'RARE OPPORTUNITY' FOR PEACE AS OVERSEAS TOUR STOPS IN ISRAEL** . . . President Trump meets with Abbas in Bethlehem, says 'truly hopeful' for peace deal . . . **SHORT ON TIME, YAD VASHEM PACKING EMOTION INTO TRUMP VISIT** . . . President Trump talks terrorism with Pope Francis, climate change with the Vatican . . . **'HE IS SOME-THING': TRUMP VISITS POPE FRANCIS AT THE VAT-ICAN** . . . "To celebrate China's new global influence, Mr. Xi is gathering dozens of state leaders, including President Vladimir V. Putin of Russia, in Beijing" . . . NATO members anxiously hope Trump's visit will bring renewed commitment . . . *TRUMP REMAINS A NATO SKEPTIC* . . . Donald Trump tells NATO allies to pay up at Brussels talks . . . This year's G-7 Summit features 4 new leaders, with very different goals . . . **AMERICA FIRST DOESN'T MEAN AMERICA ALONE**

AS AIR Force One took off, I felt a sense of relief. It would be an arduous trip, but I was happy to leave behind Washington for a while. The Lavrov meeting leak was typical of the destructive behavior too many people in that city were engaged in. Maybe the overseas trip would allow us to focus on the substance of foreign policy.

I shared the four-person office between the galley and the conference room with Cohen, Priebus, and Kushner. They complained about the uncomfortable chairs that did not recline. I assured them that Air Force One was much more comfortable than the C-17 cargo aircraft I was used to taking to the Middle East. I learned on those flights that the key to getting rest was to stake out a comfortable spot on the floor.

The president was in a good mood when he popped into the office. He noted, as he often would on trips abroad, "General, you are always working." And I gave what was becoming my standard answer: "Mr. President, that is what you hired me to do."

Before dinner was served, I briefed the president and First Lady on the first three stops of what would be a nine-day odyssey.

The first stop, Saudi Arabia, had been a strategic partner since President Franklin D. Roosevelt met with King Abdul Aziz Ibn Saud on the deck of a U.S. heavy cruiser in 1945. But our partner had for nearly five decades been the principal funder of mosques and schools that systematically extinguished empathy and taught an ideology that was a gateway to jihadist terrorism. ISIS was using Saudi textbooks to teach children intolerance and hatred for Jews as well as "infidels" and "rejectionists" who did not adhere to their extreme interpretation of Sunni Islam.

I advised Trump against getting involved in internal Saudi politics, especially the power struggle between Crown Prince Mohammed bin Nayef (MBN) and his cousin, and son of the king, Mohammed bin Salman (MBS). Kushner had a close relationship with MBS, and it was clear that a power shift was under way, but I was ambivalent about the crown prince. During a meeting at the Pentagon weeks earlier, the thirty-one-year-old had professed a desire to combat extremist ideology, but his description of the problem was a bit off. At the end of the meeting, the crown prince gave his interpretation of the roots of jihadist terrorism, placing all the blame on Iran. I could not let this pass. "Your Highness, I would just like to point out that none of the hijackers who murdered nearly three thousand people on September 11, 2001, were Iranians."

Despite my doubts about MBS and his power struggle with soon-to-be unseated crown prince Mohammed bin Nayef, I believed that Saudi Arabia was at a turning point. MBS had told the president when he visited Washington weeks earlier that the Saudi king and leaders across the royal family now understood the danger of prose-lytizing hatred and intolerance. Younger generations had not borne witness to the Al-Saud's ("House of Saud's") role in national unifi-cation or in lifting the country out of poverty, illiteracy, low life ex-pectancy, and high infant mortality. The king and soon-to-be crown prince knew that holding together the country's coalitions of tribes, religious scholars, merchants, and technocrats required social and economic reforms. And the kingdom was deeply concerned about Iran's intensification of its proxy wars in Iraq, Yemen, and Syria and its pursuit of nuclear weapons and the development of a long-range missile and drone complex.

King Salman welcomed Trump and the First Lady at the foot of Air Force One. They walked together on a red carpet lined by a mil-itary honor guard. As our motorcade departed King Khalid Interna-tional Airport, it was already clear that our hosts had pulled out all the stops. Billboards welcoming Trump with his smiling image lined the highway on the way to the Murabba Palace. I thought to my-self that they knew exactly how to win Trump's favor. As we turned onto the road leading to the palace gate, over a dozen horses flanked the presidential limousine, their riders carrying alternating Ameri-can and Saudi flags.

Upon entering the Royal Court Palace, a small U.S. party joined King Salman and his top officials for the traditional welcoming drink of Arabic coffee. After a ceremony during which Saudi officials and U.S. heads of defense and other large companies signed letters of intent for over $110 billion in deals and even more over the next ten years, we traveled to the Ritz-Carlton hotel to prepare for dinner at the Murabba Palace.

That's when we learned the billboards and the horses had been only a warm-up. As we turned down the hotel's long driveway, laser lights lit up the building with alternating images of the American and Saudi flags and the faces of President Trump and King Salman. The sword dance that evening, as we arrived at the courtyard of the Murabba Palace, was still to come. I thought about how that palace symbolized the kingdom's long struggle between tradition and modernity. When built by the founder of the kingdom, King Abdulaziz, in the 1930s, the palace showcased the new technologies that conservative clerics rejected, such as automobiles and electricity.

Although press reports dismissed the fanfare as the Saudis playing to Trump's penchant for adulation, Saudi leaders were also signaling their desire to welcome the United States back after the estrangement of the Obama years.

After the dinner at the palace, I went to the president's suite to hear his assessment and to summarize the next day's activities. Trump seemed at home in the ornate, gilded hotel room packed with extravagant floral arrangements, fruit bowls, date trays, and plates of Middle Eastern sweets. The pageantry and the successful meetings seemed to have invigorated him.

Bannon was engaged in his typical combination of sycophancy and agitation, alternating praise for the president with lamentations of how Trump was under assault from the press, the FBI, the deep state, and "globalists." As Gary Cohn and I tried to help Trump focus on the next day's events, Bannon pulled Trump back into his preferred territory: the morass of partisan domestic politics. He must have recognized that his influence depended on Trump's anxiety and sense of beleaguerment. I had begun to see Bannon as a brash yet fawning court jester who "entertained" the president with stories, mainly about those who were out to get him and what he could do to "counterpunch."

I interrupted: "Mr. President, I thought I might give you and the team a quick reminder of the agenda for tomorrow." Then I launched into the first of many quick briefings I would give him on the road. "You will begin with something like speed dating as you meet with the leaders of Bahrain, Qatar, Egypt, and Kuwait for just under thirty minutes each. Later, you will meet with all leaders of Gulf Cooperation Council countries at the conference center, after which you and the First Lady will attend the opening ceremony for the inaugural global summit on combating extremism," I said, referring to what came to be known as the Riyadh Summit. "Many of the fifty world leaders in attendance will want photos with you. I will escort Ashraf Ghani and a few others over to you and then help you break contact and get to the greenroom to relax before your speech, which will be the first after King Salman's. The speech will be historic. Yours, the king's, and other key messages are mutually reinforcing. The final event of the day will be your opening of the Etidal, or the Global Center for Combating Extremism. You were scheduled for a Twitter forum event at the very end of the day, but based on the multiple events and the late hour of the opening ceremony with King Salman, we intend, with your approval, for Ivanka to fill in for you."

"Okay, General. Ivanka will do a great job."

All went accordingly, but the majority of the media was so stuck on covering the administration as if it were a soap opera that the significance of the Saudi Arabia trip was apparent only in retrospect.

Our team had worked with the Treasury and State Departments to develop concrete "deliverables," such as the Etidal, a nonprofit established in Riyadh for combating extremism, and a new center for countering illicit finance. The president's messages promoting solidarity, peace, and humaneness among "people of the book"— Jews, Christians, and Muslims—were ones we would amplify in Jerusalem and Rome. We were sowing seeds for what would become, years later, the Abraham Accords, an agreement that most experts thought impossible, especially under the Trump administration. I wished that more Americans could see beyond their silos of cable news and vitriolic partisanship to understand more fully the good, as well as the bad and the ugly, of the Trump presidency.

★   ★   ★

AIR FORCE One touched down in Israel at 12:15 on Monday, May 22, 2017, the date commemorating the reunification of Jerusalem after the 1967 Six-Day War, in which Israel defeated a coalition of Arab nations and seized, among other territory, the eastern half of the city.

The welcoming ceremony was ornate. After walking the line of troops, the president and First Lady mounted a red carpeted stage equipped with a podium, alongside Israel's president, Reuven Rivlin, and his wife, Nechama Rivlin, and Prime Minister Benjamin Netanyahu and his wife, Sara Ben-Artzi. Rivlin noted that Israel needed a strong United States and that the United States needed a strong Israel. Netanyahu referred to Trump's speech in Saudi Arabia and stated that Israel's hand was extended to all its neighbors in peace. He noted that Trump had traveled from Riyadh to Tel Aviv and hoped that "one day an Israeli prime minister will be able to fly from Tel Aviv to Riyadh."[1]

After the ceremony, we moved to the president's helicopters, which had been transported from the United States for the short sixty-six-kilometer flight to Jerusalem. As we flew north, I pointed out what I had seen several times before, from Israel Defense Forces helicopters—Israel's "narrow waist," the mere 8.7 miles separating the Mediterranean Sea and the West Bank. Israelis view the West Bank, also occupied after the Six-Day War, as critical to their security, because it added thirty miles to their country's "waist." And after leaving the Gaza Strip in 2005, only to see Hamas turn that territory into a terrorist haven for an organization committed to destroying Israel and killing Jews, it was understandable that Israeli leaders were unwilling to end their security presence in the West Bank.

The president and First Lady's trip to the Church of the Holy Sepulcher and the Western Wall was powerfully symbolic. Trump was the first president to visit East Jerusalem, and he was doing so on the fiftieth anniversary of its annexation. I had been to Jerusalem several times before, but one cannot help but feel a strong sense of spirituality transcending day-to-day stresses. Those stresses seem small when the visitor realizes they are following in the footsteps of Jesus or King David.

Above the Western Wall was a site of profound importance to all three Abrahamic religions. Jewish tradition holds that the Temple Mount is where God gathered the dust to create Adam, where Abraham nearly sacrificed his son Isaac, and where King Solomon built the first temple of the Jews, which Babylonian king Nebuchadnezzar destroyed. The Temple Mount was also the place of Jesus's nascent religious study, where he learned from the Old Testament and began forming and demonstrating the values that became the tenets of Christianity. Muslims call the Temple Mount Haram al-Sharif (the Noble Sanctuary) and believe that the Prophet Muhammad ascended to heaven from the site in 1419. This place that perhaps has more historical and theological significance than any other inspires awe and humility.

I had enjoyed the company of Gary Cohn as we followed the president to each site. We knelt down to touch the Rock of Golgotha, where Jesus was crucified, and we walked to the Western Wall together to tuck our prayer notes into its crevices. There, I asked God to give me the ability to do my duty and the fortitude to ignore or overcome the obstacles that might keep me from doing so.

★   ★   ★

REPORTERS AND former officials with experience in the Middle East described Trump's desire to broker the "deal of the century" between Israel and the Palestinians as naïve. But I thought that a touch of naïveté might be necessary to make progress on one of the longest-running and most complex conflicts in the world.

When, nearly three weeks earlier, on May 3, Trump hosted the president of the Palestinian Authority, Mahmoud Abbas, at the White House, he had caused consternation across the Arab world and in Europe and among factions in Israel with the statement "I'm looking at two-state and one-state, and I like the one that both parties like . . . I can live with either one."

In the meeting with Abbas and his party in the Cabinet Room, Trump had used language consistent with a two-state solution, but he was very direct about the need for the Palestinian Authority to reform and to contest the grip that the terrorist groups Hamas and Palestine Islamic Jihad had on Gaza and the inroads they were making into the West Bank.

Trump had also begun to put pressure on Netanyahu by saying to many audiences that he did "not think Bibi wants to make a deal." He was not wrong. Netanyahu and other Israeli leaders had legitimate concerns that a two-state solution would be unviable.

The horrific Hamas terrorist attacks on Israel over six years later, on October 7, 2023, revealed that the viability of a two-state solution depended on ensuring that terrorists cannot control territory on Israel's borders.

The main obstacles to enduring peace had not changed: Did Palestinians have the right to return to land lost since 1948? Should Israeli settlements in the West Bank be dismantled? What is the future of East and West Jerusalem? It remained difficult to imagine answers to those questions that both sides would find acceptable.

The morning after the visit to the Western Wall, I met Stephen Miller on my way to see Trump before we departed for another busy day. I had already worked with Miller to add language to the president's forthcoming speeches at the Palestinian Authority in Bethlehem and at the Israel Museum: the added text would concern a horrible terrorist attack at England's Manchester Arena that had killed twenty-two and injured more than a thousand innocent concertgoers. Miller told me that the president had modified the language slightly, adding his description of terrorists as "losers." The president had also, Miller said, made additions to a speech he would give later in the day, at Yad Vashem, Israel's Holocaust memorial museum, to announce that he had decided to move the U.S. embassy from Tel Aviv to Jerusalem. Finally, Miller informed me the president had seen a film last night at dinner that portrayed Palestinian leaders encouraging terrorist acts against Israelis and rewarding the murder of innocents.

I thanked Miller for filling me in and went to see the president.

As I walked into his room, Trump asked me, "Do you like calling the terrorists 'losers'?"

I responded, "I like it. It is an accurate description for people who murder innocents."

Trump then told me about the film Netanyahu had shown him. I surmised from his description that it had spliced together footage of Abbas to make it appear that he had called for the murder of Israeli children.

I told Trump that Miller had mentioned that he might now announce the move of the U.S. embassy to Jerusalem. I asked him to reconsider that decision so he could hear from his cabinet first and to give us time to develop a plan to maximize the advantages of such a move and mitigate any negative consequences.

He agreed. "Okay, General, you can take it out of the speeches."

The motorcade moved quickly along the cleared roads for the short drive into the West Bank and on to Bethlehem. I rode with Trump. Policemen lined the entire route at intervals of between twenty and fifty yards. Trump stewed about the film from the night before. I assumed that Netanyahu had shown the film not just to undermine Trump's relationship with Mahmoud Abbas, but also to prevent the president from pushing harder for a moratorium on new Israeli West Bank settlements or for a two-state solution unacceptable to the Netanyahu government.

In Bethlehem, Mahmoud Abbas waited for Trump at the Mukataa, the seat of Palestinian government, at the end of a red carpet with two children in biblical-era dress bearing flowers. A band and honor guard stood at attention as Abbas and Trump walked up the red carpet together. Anthems played. Trump and Abbas reviewed the troops. They walked into the Mukataa, to a receiving line of Muslim, Orthodox, and Catholic clerics.

The rest of us went in through a side door, entered a square room, and sat in chairs across from the Palestinian delegation. I leaned over to Kushner and said, "I hope this meeting doesn't blow up. It sounds like Netanyahu ran an operation on the president of the United States last night."

From the outset of the meeting, it was clear the film screening had the desired effect. Trump had a compassionate side, and any abuse or harm to children incensed him. I had seen that side of him when he learned of the murder of children in Syria. His anger boiled over. Now he accused Abbas and others in the room of murder. His tone and his words were threatening. Members of Abbas's party, most of whom had attended the congenial meeting in the White House just two and a half weeks earlier, wore expressions of befuddlement and panic. Tillerson, who was sitting to my left, stared at the floor.

The worst was over. The bilateral meeting broke up, and a stunned Abbas walked with Trump across the courtyard to where both would make short statements. Trump, returning to the terrorist attack at the Manchester Arena, offered his condolences to the families of the fallen, calling the terrorists "evil losers" who must be "driven out from our society forever." On the prospects for enduring peace between Israel and the Palestinians, he stated his desire to do "everything I can . . . to achieve a peace agreement between the Israelis and Palestinians." Abbas also described the Manchester Arena murders as a "horrible terrorist attack."[2]

⁎ ⋆ ⋆

WE DEPARTED Bethlehem and drove to Yad Vashem, the Holocaust memorial museum in Jerusalem. It was my fourth visit, but I experienced again the same waves of emotion that had washed over me during my previous experiences there.

One enters the memorial and is immediately gripped by a sense of foreboding. It is Europe in the early 1930s. The floor slopes downward. Gray granite walls narrow toward the ceiling, squeezing out the light. One descends as humanity did when good men did nothing to stop the mass murder of Jews, prisoners of war, homosexuals, and people with disabilities. Moving forward, we see the Nazis begin to use gas vans, which they first tried out on Russian prisoners in the summer of 1941. They then reversed this approach: instead of bringing the murderers to the victims, they brought the victims to the murderers.

The visitor to Yad Vashem hits the bottom of a ramp as large shipments of German Jews begin on October 15, 1941. At the Wannsee Conference in December of that year, leaders and bureaucrats of government agencies deliberately planned the implementation of the program to kill all the Jews of Europe. My knees were weak from feelings of profound sorrow for those who suffered and for everything each condemned person might have experienced, and what they might have contributed to the world had they lived—weak, too, from the profound disappointment that man has the capacity for evil on a scale that is almost impossible to comprehend.

The deep sorrow and foreboding one experiences in the first half of the museum allow no room for hope. It is when the U.S. Army, alongside British, Canadian, Free French, and Free Polish forces, crossed the English Channel in June 1944 that the floor at the Yad

Vashem memorial begins to slope upward, toward sunlight streaming through the window at the far end of the memorial.

Everyone responds differently to a visit to Yad Vashem, and I wondered what Trump was feeling. The press roundly criticized his hasty inscription in the memorial guestbook, "It is a great honor to be here with all of my friends—so amazing and will never forget!" as remarkable for its "lack of gravity or deep reflection."[3] His self-absorption and insecurities encumbered his ability to demonstrate his feelings, yet I hoped he felt not only the heavy weight of sadness as he descended the central walkway, but also that weight lifting as he ascended toward the light. I wanted him to see Yad Vashem as the most profound argument against those who would have the United States disengage from consequential competitions abroad, such as "the long war" against jihadist terrorists. Evil, if not confronted, only grows, inflicting unspeakable harm on humanity.

Trump's speech after a moving ceremony in the Hall of Remembrance was heartfelt. He noted that the mass murderers of the Holocaust had to be stopped physically. He extolled the strength and resilience of the Jewish people and noted that "As long as we refuse to be silent in the face of evil, as long as we refuse to dim the light of truth in the midst of darkness, as long as we refuse to become bystanders to barbarity, then we know that goodness, peace, and justice will ultimately prevail."

As I worked on a draft of the speech with Stephen Miller, I had thought this the most important line, and I sensed that it resonated with the small group gathered around Trump, including Margot Hershenbaum, the only surviving member of her family. Hershenbaum presented Trump with a replica of her sister Ester Goldstein's personal journal, which contains entries from Ester's deportation from Germany to Latvia, where she was shot to death in a forest.

★ ★ ★

HOURS AFTER the final event in Israel, a speech at the Israel Museum in Jerusalem, we arrived at Villa Taverna, the U.S. ambassador to Italy's residence in Rome.

After the president and First Lady were settled in, I walked onto

April 4, 2017; Washington, D.C. We meet with President Abdel Fattah al-Sisi of Egypt and his team in Washington. I was confident that there was nowhere to go but up in our relationship with Egypt and other Middle Eastern states. *(ZUMA Press, Inc./Alamy Stock Photo)*

June 12, 2017; Cabinet Room, the White House. Secretary of Defense James Mattis and I attend a cabinet meeting. Despite our common backgrounds as military officers, we would struggle to forge a collaborative working relationship. *(AP Photo/Andrew Harnik)*

April 1, 2017. Six weeks into the job, we traveled to the Alisal Ranch in Solvang, California, to celebrate the wedding of our daughter Colleen to Lieutenant Lee Robinson. Her sisters, Katharine and Caragh, were maids of honor. *(Courtesy of Colleen Robinson)*

April 6, 2017; Mar-a-Lago. After dinner with Chairman Xi Jinping, President Trump meets with cabinet officials and senior advisors to review the results of strikes on Syria. *(White House Photo/ Alamy Stock Photo)*

April 9, 2017. Flying back to Washington with Trump after the Mar-a-Lago summit with Xi Jinping. I would spend many hours in the president's Air Force One suite briefing him on upcoming events and staffing him for phone calls with world leaders. *(White House Photo/ Alamy Stock Photo)*

April 16, 2017; Arg Palace, Kabul, Afghanistan. U.S. chargé d'affaires Hugo Llorens and I meet with Afghan president Ashraf Ghani and his cabinet to design a compact in which the Afghan government would implement necessary reforms as a precondition for continued U.S. assistance. *(Photograph from social media)*

April 17, 2017. I meet with Pakistani Army Chief of Staff Qamar Javed Bajwa to communicate that President Trump would end U.S. serial gullibility and pay attention to Pakistani leaders' actions rather than their words.
(Courtesy of the Pakistan Military)

April 18, 2017; Rashtrapati Bhavan, New Delhi, India. Meeting with Prime Minister Narendra Modi on the last leg of the South Asia trip. We discussed deepening cooperation, and I was grateful to receive a blessing from the prime minister.
(PIB/Alamy Stock Photo)

May 23, 2017. I joined Rex Tillerson, Jared Kushner, and Gary Cohn to leave notes at the Western Wall.
(REUTERS/Jonathan Ernst)

May 24, 2017.
We joined President
Trump and the First
Lady for an audience
with Pope Francis.
(AP Photo/Evan Vucci)

**Left: June 20, 2017;
Washington, D.C.** Vice
President Mike Pence and
I convinced Trump to
meet with President Petro
Poroshenko of Ukraine.
Joining us from left to right:
Ukraine's Ambassador
to the U.S. Valeriy Chaly,
Foreign Minister Pavlo
Klimkin, President Petro
Poroshenko, and U.S.
Ambassador to Ukraine
Marie Yovanovitch.
*(Courtesy of the President of
Ukraine)*

July 6, 2017; Hamburg, Germany. Ambassador to the United Nations Christoph Heusgen and I staff Chancellor Angela Merkel and President Trump for their meeting prior to the G20 Summit. The leaders often chided each other. Trump was right to object to Nord Stream 2 and Germany's paltry defense spending. *(BPA/Alamy Stock Photo)*

July 13, 2017; Élysée Palace, Paris, France. Gary Cohn, Reince Priebus, Donald Trump, Joe Dunford, Tom Bossert, Mike Pompeo, and I listened to President Emmanuel Macron and his national security team as he made the case for a sustained joint effort in Syria prior to the parade celebrating Bastille Day and the one-hundredth anniversary of the U.S. entry into WWI. *(Official White House Photo by Shealah Craighead)*

August 11, 2017; Bedminster, New Jersey. An impromptu press briefing with Secretary Rex Tillerson and Ambassador Nikki Haley during which Trump said that he was considering military options for Venezuela.
(Jim Watson/AFP via Getty Images)

July 18, 2017; Roosevelt Room, the White House. I arranged for President Trump and Vice President Pence to have lunch with officers and noncommissioned officers who had extensive experience in Afghanistan prior to the president's decision on the South Asia strategy.
(Official White House Photo by Shealah Craighead)

September 18, 2017; New York. White House Chief of Staff John Kelly and I confer at the United Nations General Assembly meeting at UN headquarters. *(AP Photo / Seth Wenig)*

October 10, 2017. Henry Kissinger and I join in a panel discussion at the Center for Strategic and International Studies to commemorate the seventieth anniversary of the National Security Council. I appreciated Kissinger's sense of humor as well as his counsel. *(Chip Somodevilla / Getty Images)*

November 7, 2017; The Blue House, Seoul, South Korea. During the Asia Odyssey trip, I was most concerned about the visit to South Korea, but the visit affirmed the alliance before we arrived in Beijing. *(Courtesy of Yonhap News)*

November 9, 2017; Great Hall of the People, Beijing, China. I hand Trump materials for his last meeting of the day with Premier Li Keqiang.
(REUTERS/Jonathan Ernst)

November 14, 2017; Manila, Philippines. Rex Tillerson and I accompany Trump as he gives a statement to members of the media before departing from the East Asia Summit at the end of a five-country trip.
(AP Photo/Andrew Harnik)

December 24, 2017. Katie, my West Point classmate Father (Major General) Paul Hurley, and I tour a deserted White House on Christmas Eve.
(Courtesy of the author)

February 2, 2018. I attend Trump's meeting with North Korean escapees, including Ji Seong-ho and Lee Hyeon-seo, prior to the State of the Union address in which he condemned North Korea as "cruel" and "depraved." Trump selected the background portrait of President Andrew Jackson because he saw himself in the tradition of his populist predecessor.
(Zach Gibson/Bloomberg via Getty Images)

April 6, 2018; Oval Office. Katie, family members, and my staff join the vice president and the president in the Oval Office. Trump thanked me for my service and wished me well. We had spoken for some time about my departure, and I left on good terms.
(Courtesy of the author)

April 6, 2018. Katie and I depart the White House on my last day. The National Security Council and the White House staffs surprised us with a "clap out."
(Courtesy of the author)

the villa's back patio and noticed, just outside the seven-acre property, what looked like an apartment building with an unusual number of antennas and satellite dishes on the roof. Our Secret Service detail told me that the surveillance and communications equipment had appeared on the roof soon after the Chinese had purchased the building.

Early the next morning, I dropped off my bags to be loaded onto Air Force One and returned to Villa Taverna to meet with the president. While he got dressed, I briefed him on key intelligence and events over the past several days, from the killing of ISIS's second-in-command in Syria to a new set of sanctions on Iran to the forensics on the WannaCry cyberattack, a ransomware attack on hundreds of thousands of computers across 150 countries using a digital worm from North Korea.

I warned the president that it would be another long day for him and the First Lady, but a consequential one. For me, the first event of the day would be the experience of a lifetime.

I am Catholic. My sister, Letitia, and I attended an excellent Catholic elementary school, Norwood-Fontbonne Academy, in the Chestnut Hill neighborhood of Philadelphia, and our family had gone to Mass at Immaculate Heart of Mary every Sunday. Katie either taught at Catholic high schools or worked in faith formation for Catholic dioceses for many years; and when the option was available, our daughters went to Catholic schools. But what had solidified my faith over the years were experiences in combat that were very difficult to explain except for divine providence. I had borne witness to moral and physical evils that might have shaken anyone's faith. But I had also seen good triumph over those evils in ways that only affirmed my belief in God.

The Vatican expects visitors to observe tradition and is a stickler for protocol. Our motorcade pulled through large gates and into a courtyard. The Swiss Guard opened the doors, and the president and First Lady preceded our party to meet with the pope.

We entered the pope's study and, as instructed, lined up in front of high-backed armchairs facing one another. Pope Francis moved clockwise, opposite Tillerson, White House director of social media Dan Scavino, and me, silently taking each person's hand in his hands.

Pope Francis took my hand, looked me in the eye, and said, "Please pray for me," I smiled and responded, "Holy Father, I hope that *you* will pray for *me*."

I felt a peculiar sense of calm and serenity. I saw in the pope's countenance his understanding of the challenges I would face. In the coming months, I would reflect on this brief but powerful encounter and recall the first few lines of the Serenity Prayer: "God grant me the serenity to accept the things I cannot change, the courage to change the things I can, and the wisdom to know the difference."

Although Pope Francis and Trump had jousted in the media over the border wall, there was no discernable tension between them. The president's gift to him, a box of signed first edition books by Martin Luther King Jr., was appropriate and thoughtful. Pope Francis's gift to Trump, signed copies of three documents, was pointed: the copy of Francis's encyclical on climate change, "Laudato sí," was clearly meant to challenge Trump's skepticism on global warming. Trump promised to read it.

I caught myself smiling, thinking, *It's a good thing Trump isn't Catholic, or he'd have to go to confession for that lie.*

After we left the pope, Tillerson and I met briefly with Cardinal Pietro Parolin, the Vatican secretary of state, and then trailed behind the president and First Lady on tours of the Sistine Chapel and St. Peter's Basilica. Priests and nuns from the United States joined us. Tillerson and I spoke with them as they guided us.

As Rex and I took our first steps down to the Vatican necropolis, walking beneath St. Peter's Baldachin, the bronze canopy on which Bernini labored for nine years, I looked up at the marble canopy's radiant sunburst, meant to evoke the Holy Spirit. Visiting the tomb of Saint Peter, who was crucified upside down nearby, during the Christian persecutions of Roman emperor Nero, made me think that the most prominent theme of Trump's travels, promoting religious tolerance, was a noble but not a novel endeavor.

We descended below the level of the upper grottos that hold papal tombs and entered the dimly lit chamber housing Peter's grave. Rex and I knelt next to each other in prayer. It was a moment of solace in our less-than-harmonious relationship. I allowed myself to hope that he and I might overcome our incompatibility and work together, change the things we could and accept those we couldn't. We looked at each other and nodded before we stood. I wondered if he had the same thought.

We departed the Vatican for the short drive to the Quirinal Palace, where Trump was to meet with Italian president Sergio Mattarella. The main building, which has twelve hundred rooms and has served as the residence for thirty popes, four Italian kings, and twelve presidents of the Italian Republic, is surrounded by a majestic courtyard.

If Trump had experienced inner peace while visiting the Vatican, it was wearing off. He found it difficult to understand why he was meeting with President Mattarella rather than with Prime Minister Paolo Gentiloni, whom he had met in Washington on April 20. I explained that under the Constitution of the Italian Republic, the president is the head of the state and commander in chief of the armed forces, while the prime minister, whom the president appoints and Parliament approves, holds executive power. Trump had little patience for protocol. The pace of events and what he regarded as a superfluous meeting had made him cranky.

After the meeting with Mattarella, I rode with him and Jared on the way back to Villa Taverna, where Trump was scheduled to meet with Gentiloni. He was getting tired and angry. He turned toward Jared and me in the far back and said, "How long is this fucking trip? Whose idea was this?"

I smiled and said, "It was Jared's idea, Mr. President," which prompted a smile from Jared and a scowl from Trump.

Trump rallied, however. The meeting with Gentiloni was cordial, even though each man asked the other to do things that were unlikely to happen: Trump wanted Italy to spend more on defense, and Gentiloni wanted the United States to grant entry to more migrants from the Middle East and North Africa. In a moment of spontaneity typical of Trump, he invited the prime minister to join him in addressing the embassy staff and family members who had gathered outside. After Rex said a few words, I introduced Trump and Gentiloni, who thanked our diplomats, staff, and family members for their service.

★   ★   ★

THE NEXT leg of the trip concerned me the most. Candidate Trump had called Brussels a "hellhole"; had celebrated Brexit, predicting that more countries would follow the United Kingdom's lead and depart the European Union; and had said the NATO alliance was "obsolete," not only pointing out (as other American leaders had done) that many member nations were free riding on U.S. defense, but also suggesting that the United States might not come to the aid of NATO allies if they were attacked. Businessman Trump thought it logical to condition fulfillment of the treaty obligation under Article 5, to treat "an attack on one as an attack on all," on whether the attacked country had met its pledge to invest at least the equivalent of 2 percent of its gross domestic product in defense.

In the months prior to the trip, especially in preparation for White House visits by European leaders and the NATO secretary-general, I had shown the president statistics on military spending by NATO member nations. Trump was right that many countries were not fulfilling their pledge to invest at least 2 percent in defense. But, I told him, Russia wanted nothing more than to divide NATO and the EU countries and fragment the most successful military alliance in history as a precursor to reestablishing control of former Soviet states and dominant influence over the former nations of the Warsaw Pact. On the short flight to Brussels, I suggested to Trump that he press hard to get NATO nations to increase defense spending while not giving Putin what he wanted—a divided alliance.

Cohn gave the president similar advice on trade: to demand changes to EU protectionist and unfair economic practices that disadvantaged American companies and workers, but not to advocate for the disintegration of the European Union. We told Trump that divisions in the transatlantic relationship and within Europe were good not only for Putin, but also for the country that posed the largest economic challenge to the United States—China.

I grew more concerned as we drew closer to Brussels. Watching the news on the flight had put Trump in a bad mood. Being away from home for a long stretch of time, combined with the constant drumbeat of Russiagate coverage, had made him anxious. In the midst of the trip, he had hired a new lawyer to interact with the Mueller Commission. Priebus and Bannon, who advanced their influence through cultivating a bunker mentality and portraying themselves as his most loyal defenders, only stoked Trump's anxiety. I told Gary that I was concerned. Trump needed to lash out—and he might do so against NATO and the European Union in a way that would be a boon to our adversaries.

The motorcade took us directly to the Royal Palace, where the president and First Lady met briefly with King Philippe and Queen Mathilde. It was the first of three meetings in well-appointed rooms that evoked Belgium's troubled history as a territory, principality, and, after 1830, a federal constitutional monarchy. Because Belgium had been so frequently ravaged over history, from the Middle Ages through the world wars of the twentieth century, its leaders were naturally staunch advocates of the European Union and NATO.

But Trump was incurious about Belgian and European history and only vaguely aware of the success of those organizations relative to Winston Churchill's prediction in 1946 that if Europe did not come together to form a "family," it would be condemned to "infinite misery" and "final doom."[4] I hoped Trump might also see Europe as an American success due to the relief effort after World War II; the Marshall Plan, which had reconstructed Western Europe; and the defense of the Continent, which had contributed to victory in the Cold War against the Soviet Union.

But in Trump's mind, the success of Europe had occurred at the expense of the United States. The European Union was an unfair competitor that employed a range of unfair trade and economic practices. There was an element of truth to Trump's perspective, as U.S. trade representative Bob Lighthizer would teach me in the coming months. But Gary Cohn and I tried to help Trump see that we could demand reciprocity in trade and market access while also advocating for a strong Europe.

We sat down across from Belgian prime minister Charles Michel at 5:30 p.m. I could sense that the breakneck schedule of the past week, Trump's anxiety over being abroad, the testimony back home of ex-CIA director John Brennan before the House Intelligence Committee on Russian interference in the 2016 election, and being in the home of international organizations he loathed had him on edge. The conversation with Prime Minister Michel was direct but polite, and mercifully short. I was grateful to get to the hotel after we dropped the president off at the U.S. ambassador's residence, where he would spend the night.

The next morning's meetings with the presidents of the European Commission and the European Council, Jean-Claude Juncker and Donald Tusk, respectively, in the Europa building in Brussels, were benign mainly because Trump and the EU leaders talked past one another. Trump and European Council president Tusk agreed that Russian gas pipelines to Europe were problematic because they fed the Kremlin's ATM and gave Vladimir Putin coercive power.

The meetings were cordial, but most of the press viewed Trump exclusively through the lens of his brash persona, misinterpreting body language and minor comments as indicators of major tensions. Reports on his meetings had become formulaic: Trump was rude and destructive to relationships.

Like his European counterparts, the recently elected president of France, Emmanuel Macron, was wary of Trump. Trump greeted Macron outside the U.S. embassy in Brussels, after which our delegation shook hands with Macron and his entourage. The dining room was perfectly suited for a one-table conversation. Over lunch, Trump and Macron found common ground in their penchant for challenging conventional wisdom and in their skepticism of international organizations. Both had tapped into popular discontent over the failures of government elites and inept bureaucrats to win elections. They shared similar views on migration and border security. I was happy to see them get along, but I soon grew concerned as each fed off the other's skepticism of NATO.

Macron enthusiastically joined Trump in criticizing NATO because, I believed, he calculated that he could use Trump's skepticism of multilateralism in France's favor. With the brash American president's "abandonment" of Europe, the French president could make a case for EU "strategic autonomy" in the form of trade and economic policies that sidestepped geostrategic competitions with Russia and China in ways that benefited France's economy. And because the United States was not *actually* abandoning Europe, France, like Germany, could continue to economize on defense.

Next up: the NATO summit itself.

In a room on the second floor of the U.S. ambassador's residence, I sat next to the president at a round table for a final preparation session. Mattis and Tillerson joined. Stephen Miller was taking notes. Trump, who would give a speech to dedicate the 9/11 memorial at the new NATO Headquarters, wanted to threaten to pull out of NATO if member nations did not "pay their dues" and "pay arrears" for past underpayments to the organization.

I tried to explain—as I had many times before—that the commitment was for NATO nations to spend at least the equivalent of 2 percent of GDP on their own defense capabilities. Talk of "dues" and "arrears" to NATO would only confuse leaders, rather than put pressure on them to own up to their commitments. I tried not to sound exasperated. "Mr. President, the best way to make your point is not for the United States to threaten to renege on its obligation, which would weaken the alliance's ability to deter Russia or other hostile actors, but to get others to live up to theirs under Article Three of the treaty, which obligates member states to 'maintain and develop their individual and collective capacity to resist armed attack.' Threatening to leave NATO would be a gift to Vladimir Putin. And *vacillating* on Article Five while standing in front of a remnant of the North Tower of the World Trade Center at a ceremony commemorating the only time the alliance evoked Article Five after that mass murder attack on your hometown would not be a good look."

Trump relented and went to his quarters to rest before we departed.

Later, as I was packing up for the drive to NATO headquarters, Stephen Miller came to me. He had just been with the president, and I could tell by the look on his face that he was bearing bad news. He started with "I swear I had nothing to do with this. The president called me in and dictated some changes to the speech."

Trump had excised a sentence affirming the United States' commitment to Article 5 of the treaty. I was not worried about that—NATO leaders should not be expected to affirm their intention to uphold a treaty to which they are signatories every time they speak. More concerning, though, was new language in the speech: Trump had followed through on demanding that NATO countries pay "arrears" in their "dues" to NATO. Much worse, he had added that the

United States would not be obligated to come to the defense of countries that were "delinquent" in their "payments."

Miller gave me the news as he departed for NATO Headquarters to load the speech into the teleprompter. I met Tillerson and Mattis at the top of the residence's marble staircase. I needed their help. "Let's all ride with the president so we can explain why that language is offensive and counterproductive."

Mattis replied as we stepped outside: "H.R., I think you can convince him. I'm going to ride with Rex."

I responded, "Would both of you please get in the fucking car?"

They acceded.

On the short drive from the ambassador's residence to NATO Headquarters, I told Trump that the reaction to his comments would focus exclusively on his threat of withdrawal from NATO and not on members' failure to meet their obligations. Tillerson and Mattis reinforced this point.

Finally, about halfway into our twenty-minute drive, Trump said, "Okay, okay, you can take it out, General."

With the issue resolved, I tried to raise Stephen Miller on my cellphone, to tell him to delete the new language from the teleprompter. He was waiting for my call, but the jammers in the motorcade made it difficult to get through. I finally got a broken message to him. He made the change just prior to the president's arrival at NATO Headquarters, the political and administrative center of the North Atlantic Council.

NATO secretary-general Jens Stoltenberg met us out in front of the brand-new structure on Boulevard Leopold III in Haren and walked us through the building complex and to the greenroom. He thought that Trump would be impressed with the new home to the North Atlantic Council, and he was—just not in the way Stoltenberg had hoped. Trump said something about the stupidity and cost of the new building, observing that "one bomb would take out the whole thing." He was right. The new headquarters symbolized the overconfidence of the post–Cold War period.

I exited the building and walked past the 9/11 memorial and the podiums to the U.S. seating area, where I joined Gary Cohn. "How was the ride?" he asked.

"I'll tell you after this statement," I responded.

Later, members of the media criticized Trump for omitting the explicit pledge to adhere to Article 5 of the NATO Charter. The *Washington Post* decried his comments on burden sharing as "confrontational, nationalist rhetoric." But Trump had made the points he wanted to make on burden sharing without emboldening adversaries or creating cracks in the alliance that the Kremlin could easily exploit.

I turned to Gary, "I think that was about as good as we could hope for."

After a flag-raising ceremony at the far side of the headquarters complex, a dinner meeting followed. All twenty-eight heads of state were to speak for a few moments while seated at a massive U-shaped table. As Tillerson, Mattis, and I ate our dinners on our laps seated behind the president, I could see that Trump was losing his patience. I whispered to Mattis, "I don't think he's going to make it."

Trump, disregarding the note cards I had given him, scolded the countries that were failing to "pay what they owe." Then, he abruptly stood up and walked out. Jim Mattis moved up into Trump's chair, and Tillerson and I departed with Trump.

On to Sicily for the G7.

★   ★   ★

THE TRAVEL team was pared down. With Bannon and Priebus gone, Gary and I would staff the president for the G7, with a much smaller group. We landed at Naval Air Station Sigonella and jumped into the convoy for the scenic 78.3-kilometer drive to the beautiful coastal town of Taormina. Once Trump was settled into his accommodation, I checked out the secure communications in my large room. I threw open the curtains to reveal a panorama of the bay, the setting sun illuminating colorful buildings that rose from the harbor in tiers anchored into the steep slope of Mount Etna.

I couldn't help but think that living at the base of an active volcano was an apt metaphor for serving in the Trump White House.

Early the next morning, Gary and I met the president in his

quarters. Trump was in a good mood. Because the G7 was an economic forum, Gary and the National Economic Council had the lead
in preparation. We summarized the remaining areas of disagreement in the draft communiqué issued at the end of the conference
and the key points Trump might consider making during the round-
table discussions with Angela Merkel, Emmanuel Macron, Shinzo
Abe, Paolo Gentiloni, Justin Trudeau, and Theresa May. The president noted that this leg of the trip "seemed a lot easier."

On the way out, I said to Gary, "It does seem a lot easier, and he is
in a much better mood."

Gary replied, "Consider who is not here."

We were experiencing the absence of Priebus and Bannon agitat-
ing Trump.

We made the short drive to the beautiful San Domenico Palace
hotel. The seven leaders sat at a circular table with a single advisor
seated at tables behind them; Gary was in the room for the economic
discussion, and I joined Trump for the foreign policy and security
discussions. When either one of us was not in the room, we used a
small office down the hall to work.

That night, during a stop for gelato on our walk back to the hotel
after dinner, my phone rang. It was NSC legal advisor John Eisenberg. The relative calm that the president, Gary, and I had noticed
earlier in the day had been short-lived. Priebus and Bannon, having returned early to Washington, had apparently decided that with
Gary and me in Sicily, it was time to try again to effect a purge of
NSC staff. I returned to my hotel room to make the first of several
phone calls to Don McGahn and Reince Priebus.

I was angry because of the blatant violation of trust and frustrated
that Bannon and Priebus were more concerned about sabotaging the
organization that was actually delivering for the president than in
advancing his agenda and the interests of the people who had elected
him. I called Eisenberg to apologize for "shooting the messenger" in
my earlier conversation.

I succeeded in blocking another attempt at a baseless mass firing, but I wondered how much longer it would be before the next
attempt. The wolves were always circling, and my absence from
Washington had given them another opportunity.

*   *   *

THE NEXT morning, Gary and I gave a press backgrounder before joining Trump's motorcade to Naval Air Station Sigonella, where the president would address American servicemen and -women and their families before leaving on Air Force One. I worked with Miller to ensure that the speech summarized the purpose and accomplishments of the trip. I also hoped it would help Trump understand better how he could advance his agenda through effective presidential diplomacy and that Gary's and my teams were helping him do so.

Melania introduced the president to those gathered. She described the nine-day trip as a "home run."

I agreed with her assessment.

On Air Force One, Gary and I met with our teams to discuss how to keep the momentum from the trip going. Someone suggested that the two of us author a joint op-ed, so we went to work on an outline and asked our teams for suggestions.

The May 30 op-ed in the *Wall Street Journal* stated that the "world is not a 'global community' but an arena where nations, nongovernmental actors, and businesses engage and compete for advantage." We wrote that "America First" did not mean "America Alone" and that the Trump administration was committed to "protecting and advancing U.S. interests while also fostering cooperation and strengthening relationships with allies and partners."

The reaction to the op-ed demonstrated that Gary and I occupied the space between Trump's virulent base of neo-isolationists and those who hated Trump and saw him as the greatest threat to their idealized international order. Some in the latter category wrote rebuttals that were hysterical in tone and full of ad hominem attacks. Others clung to Russiagate and claimed that all the administration's efforts, even the op-ed, "have no standing." Gary and I were not surprised that serving in the Trump administration subjected us to the vitriol associated with America's severe polarization.

The trip overseas was a success, but everything was much harder than it should have been. I thought of what von Clausewitz had said about the friction of war: "Everything is very simple in war, but the simplest thing is difficult."[5] Fighting a war, he noted, was "like movement in a resistant element."[6] In battle, the enemy is the principal cause of friction. But in the Trump White House, as in American society, we were at war with ourselves. The "circular firing squad" in the White House both reflected and reinforced the us-versus-them mentality in U.S. politics and society.

CHAPTER 10

GUARDING INDEPENDENCE OF JUDGMENT

PRESIDENT TRUMP ANNOUNCES U.S. WITH-DRAWAL FROM THE PARIS CLIMATE ACCORD . . . "I was elected to represent the citizens of Pittsburgh, not Paris" . . . Trump Gives Defense Chief Authority to Set US Troop Levels in Afghanistan . . . *TRUMP REVERSES PIECES OF OBAMA-ERA ENGAGEMENT WITH CUBA . . .* **TRUMP COMMITS UNITED STATES TO DEFENDING NATO NATIONS . . .** McMaster to Valley Forge Military grads: "Humanity needs you to lead and to serve" . . . *UKRAINE PRESIDENT PETRO POROSHENKO IN WASHINGTON TO MEET PRESIDENT TRUMP . . .* Ukrainian leader, a Russian adversary, gets low-key welcome . . . Indian Prime Minister Narendra Modi arrived in Washington D.C. on Sunday carrying a long list of problems affecting US-Indian relations . . . **TRUMP TAKES MORE AGGRESSIVE STANCE WITH U.S. FRIENDS AND FOES IN ASIA . . .** Trump Welcomes South Korean Leader as Options on the North Wane . . . Trump preparing withdrawal from South Korea trade deal, a move opposed by top aides . . . **TRUMP: US PATIENCE WITH THE NORTH KOREAN REGIME 'IS OVER' . . .** *GULF PLUNGED INTO DIPLOMATIC CRISIS AS COUNTRIES CUT TIES WITH QATAR*

ABOUT TEN people had gathered around the small table in the dining room that served as Trump's retreat from the formality of the Oval Office. It was not a calm sanctuary, as Trump is not one for contemplation or introspection, and this meeting, like countless others in that room, had taken on the quality of a free-for-all.

As always, Fox News played on the big screen opposite the president, who sat at the head of the table. We were discussing the speech he was about to give announcing the United States' withdrawal from the Paris Climate Accords.

I had recommended—along with Gary Cohn, Rex Tillerson, and others in the administration—that the United States stay in the agreement. We suggested that Trump use the threat of withdrawal to drive changes consistent with his legitimate concerns, including unfair burdens on the U.S. economy and U.S. industry; financial commitments that amounted to U.S. taxpayers funding carbon-reduction efforts in developing economies; and exposure to lawsuits if U.S. industries did not meet the "voluntary" goals in the agreement. Moreover, Trump saw the agreement—which, like the JCPOA, also known as the Iran nuclear deal, had not been ratified by the Senate—as an infringement on U.S. sovereignty.

I had conceded all those points but recommended that Trump use the threat of getting out as an incentive toward arriving at a future agreement that did not put the United States at a competitive disadvantage while addressing the greatest sources of human-induced global warming: growing carbon emissions from China and India.

In one meeting, I had told Trump, "Mr. President, if we pull out, we join the only other non-signatories, Syria and Nicaragua. It is not a club membership that we ought to seek." In addition to seeing diminished U.S. influence in areas that required multinational support, withdrawing would limit Trump's ability to steer future climate discussions in a productive direction from "within the tent" of the Paris Agreement or to promote solutions based on free-market incentives, such as cheap natural gas (to displace coal-fired power plants) and next-generation nuclear fission.

And if we failed to reform the agreement, Trump could still get out.

Trump was unpersuaded.

Once Trump decided to get out, Gary and I tried to maximize

the positive and mitigate the negative consequences of the decision. Now, in the dining room, I was trying to convince Trump not to add insult to injury. I was fine with the tough stance, but as with the NATO speech, I found language added at the eleventh hour insulting and counterproductive, especially the line "I was elected to represent the citizens of Pittsburgh, not Paris."

I waited for a break in the conversation. "Mr. President, you might consider dropping the one sentence about Pittsburgh and Paris. Macron invested a good deal of his political capital to try to convince you to stay in. The sentence is a gratuitous kick in the nuts."

Pence and I had spoken about this moments before, and he backed me up. "I agree, Mr. President. It is a strong speech without that line."

Bannon chimed in: "It's the strongest line in the speech. Your base will love it."

Trump left it in.

Trump's style often impeded his ability to exploit opportunities, such as connecting reductions in carbon emissions to energy security or the role the U.S. energy sector could play in both. This was similar to his failure to connect border security to immigration reform. "Pittsburgh not Paris," like "I will have Mexico pay for that wall," was an incendiary appeal to his political base, not a statement that advanced his priorities.

Trump's longing for affirmation from his base sometimes sabotaged his wish to advance U.S. interests. But when that longing was aligned with important correctives to unwise policies, his energy and his disdain for convention could be both powerful and positive. I wanted to help him align his urges with the development of sound policy and purposeful engagements with foreign leaders.

*   *   *

WE ACHIEVED such an alignment on Trump's policies toward Cuba and Venezuela. The Obama administration had taken a similar approach to the socialist dictatorships in those countries as it had to the theocratic dictatorship in Iran, assuming that our policies were the problem rather than the nature of these regimes. Key architects of the drive toward accommodation of the dictators in Havana and Caracas had imbibed the New Left interpretation of history at America's top universities, where students learned that the world is divided into oppressors and oppressed and that geopolitics is a choice between socialist revolution and servitude under "capitalist imperialism."

In 2014, President Obama and Cuban leader Raúl Castro had announced the intention to normalize relations between Cuba and the United States. The Obama administration lifted U.S. travel restrictions, reduced limitations on remittances, increased U.S. banks' access to the Cuban financial system, and reopened the U.S. embassy in Havana and the Cuban embassy in Washington. In March 2016, President Obama visited Cuba and even did the wave with Castro at a baseball game to celebrate the agreement.

As the two presidents celebrated, political prisoners languished in Cuban prisons, enduring extended solitary confinement, beatings, forced labor, and denial of medical care. Obama, like Trump, evinced an unseemly affinity for authoritarians, but neither man acknowledged the double standard he applied when criticizing the other.

On June 16, we flew in Marine One from the South Lawn of the White House to Andrews Air Force Base and boarded Air Force One for the flight to Miami. Sen. Marco Rubio and I sat across from the president in his office and briefed him on the "run of show" for the speech he would deliver at the Manuel Artime Theater, a former church that takes its name from a member of Fidel Castro's rebel Army who later became political leader of Brigade 2506 forces in the aborted Bay of Pigs invasion in 1961.

Rubio's staff had helped frame the new policy. The senator and the president chatted amicably. Despite their animus for each other during the Republican primary election of 2016, they seemed to have moved on.

Trump's speech summarized the new policy. Our long-term goal would be to encourage a shift away from an Army-dominated dictatorship and toward representative government that respected the rights of the Cuban people. We would financially starve the Cuban regime while supporting the emergence of *cuentapropistas*, entrepreneurs who comprised Cuba's growing middle class.

I stayed in the greenroom for the speech, but I could hear the cheers and applause from the mainly Cuban American audience.

*   *   *

BACK IN Washington, the visit of the president of Romania, Klaus Iohannis, gave Trump an opportunity to mature his understanding of the threat from Russia. It was also an opportunity for me to help Trump continue his call for burden sharing in NATO while allaying concerns about his commitment to mutual defense under Article 5.

June 9 was a packed day as I rushed back to the White House from the Cathedral of St. Matthew after paying my respects at the funeral Mass for former national security advisor Zbigniew Brzezinski. Brzezinski had been very gracious to me, and I regretted that I would no longer have the opportunity to consult with this man of strong conviction who had served during the 1970s, a period of turbulence and polarization analogous to the present.

After I briefed him, Trump looked up from the map I had slid onto his desk, glanced around the room, and asked, "What questions do you think I will get?" He meant questions from the press after the short statements the leaders would make in the Rose Garden after the meeting.

"Mr. President, you will certainly get a question about whether you are committed to Article Five of the NATO treaty."

Bannon interjected, "I don't think anyone will ask that."

I told Trump, "You are going to be asked that question. An unambiguous 'yes' is worth two Army divisions in Europe."

The first question from the press, as predicted, was whether Trump stood by Article 5. Trump answered clunkily, but unwaveringly, "I'm committing the United States—and have committed—but I'm committing the United States to Article Five."

The New York Times, the paper to which someone had leaked the twenty-seven-word affirmation of Article 5 that Trump had excised from the NATO speech in Belgium, ran an article with the headline "Trump Commits United States to Defending NATO Nations." I was relieved, but I knew that Putin and his useful idiots on social media and in the pseudo-media in the United States would continue to stoke Trump's skepticism about the alliance.

In one meeting in the Oval Office, Bannon hit all of the Kremlin's talking points: the futility of the wars in Afghanistan, Syria, and Iraq; the trillions of dollars wasted; how our allies are screwing us on trade as they free ride on American security; the weakness of NATO; corruption in Ukraine; how unfair we had been to Russia in enlarging NATO and in the imposition of sanctions.

When he finished, I asked, "Steve, why are you an apologist for the Kremlin?"

He replied, "I am not an apologist for the Kremlin," then quickly changed the subject.

When I suggested that Trump host the president of Ukraine, Petro Poroshenko, in the Oval Office for a drop-by meeting, Bannon, predictably, recommended that he not do so because the meeting might "anger Putin" and because the Ukrainian government was "rife with corruption." I conceded the point on corruption: Poroshenko was no angel. He had campaigned on transparency and reform, but the Panama Papers leak in 2016 revealed that he had set up an offshore company in the British Virgin Islands a few months before he became president. Pence and I told Trump that the meeting would be an opportunity to encourage Poroshenko to reform his government and to hear his perspective on Russia and the war in Ukraine. Trump would not commit.

On Tuesday, June 20, I joined Poroshenko and his party in Vice President Pence's office, along with Tillerson, Ross, Secretary of Energy Rick Perry, and U.S. ambassador to Ukraine Marie Yovanovitch. It was a positive meeting. Pence and I finally convinced Trump to host Poroshenko for a drop-in.

Yovanovitch—whom Trump would later undermine, disparage, and then fire after allowing his personal lawyer Rudy Giuliani to run a shadow diplomatic effort in Ukraine to gather compromising information about Joe Biden and his son Hunter's shady business dealings and influence peddling—remembered the drop-in meeting as "awkward and disconcerting." But I thought that Trump connected with fellow businessman Poroshenko and that his typically direct style was effective.

Trump cited "a Ukrainian American friend of mine" who had told him that Ukraine was a corrupt country and that Crimea was Russian. It was the kind of direct comment that shocked the uninitiated, but Trump's bluntness was more often helpful than not. Poroshenko needed to hear that message. The meeting was important because the conversation, like Trump's conversation with President Iohannis of Romania, counter-balanced the Russian and alt-right narratives and the false justification for Russia's 2014 invasion of Ukraine.

In an interview at the end of May, Trump said, "I have been told by many, many people that I was doing a great job in terms of foreign policy." He was, but it took a constant effort to help him focus his disruptive energy on positive outcomes, especially when others were instigating presidential words and actions to tear down relationships and alliances critical to advancing American interests.

★   ★   ★

TRUMP HOSTED many other leaders in June, but the top-priority visits occurred back-to-back at the end of the month: Prime Minister Modi of India on June 25–26 and President Moon of South Korea on June 29–30.

I wanted both visits to be special. The White House ranking system for foreign leader visits included three levels—state visit, official visit, and working visit. Both Modi and Moon were on official visits, and both would experience firsts for the Trump White House. Modi would be the first head of state the president and First Lady hosted for dinner in the Blue Room, an oval state parlor with a magnificent view of the White House Portico, the South Lawn, and the Washington Monument. The first for President Moon and his wife would be dinner in the State Dining Room.

A challenge for the Modi and Moon visits would be how to advance Trump's trade agenda in a sensible way without undermining important relationships. India's lack of reciprocity in market access incensed Trump. And the Korea–United States, or KORUS, Free Trade Agreement continued to inspire Trumpian rants that rivaled those on NAFTA. KORUS was a "horror show" and a "Hillary Clinton special" that had "given" 250,000 American jobs to South Korea.

The number was probably made up, but it was true that the agreement had not lived up to what the Obama administration had promised. During a June 6 meeting on trade in the Roosevelt Room, I observed that we were "discussing tactics, but what we need is a strategy." I suggested a simple problem statement like "How to respond to China's overcapacity and unfair economic practices to reduce risks to national security, promote fair/reciprocal trade, and foster U.S. economic growth."

It was a constant struggle to elevate the discussion and focus on objectives. As with NAFTA, Gary and I responded to Navarro and Bannon's inciting Trump over KORUS with the argument that getting out of KORUS rather than renegotiating the agreement would undermine U.S. objectives. Their response was to label us "globalists" and end-run the decision-making process.

I joked with Gary that we were taking turns jumping on the "grenades" Bannon and Navarro were rolling into the Oval Office. These grenades sometimes arrived in the form of a draft KORUS withdrawal letter slid onto the president's desk or charts mounted on cork boards that listed unfair trade practices across the top and the offending countries down the left side. South Korea had the distinction of receiving the most check marks across those boxes.

Contrary to accusations that Gary and I obstructed Trump's trade agenda, we did our best to advance it. U.S. trade representative Lighthizer had been confirmed on May 11. He was prioritizing NAFTA, so the initial effort to renegotiate KORUS fell to Cohn and our very competent special assistant to the president for trade, Clete Willems. Gary and I coordinated his conversations with the trade minister of South Korea, Kim Hyun-chong, and my conversations with National Security Advisor Chung Eui-yong. Our consistent message was "There are problems with KORUS that the president directed us to fix, and we need to show him that you are willing to give on critical issues." Over the next year, Lighthizer, ably assisted by Willems, would deliver a renegotiated agreement that addressed Trump's concerns, including improved market access for U.S. automobiles.

The trade battles were exhausting and kept pulling me back in because of national security implications. Tariffs on steel and aluminum imports came up several times a month. Each time, I told

Trump that we risked losing focus on the real issue, which was Chinese overcapacity, overproduction, dumping, and trans-shipment of steel and aluminum.

I often used a simple, blunt metaphor: "Mr. President, if we shoot our allies to get China, China wins."

It worked—at least until March 2018, when he began to impose heavy tariffs that would affect many U.S. allies, including Japan, the European Union, and Canada.

★ ★ ★

DESPITE TRUMP'S frustration with India's protectionist policies, I was less concerned about the Modi visit than the Moon visit. Trump often seized on an anecdote that illustrated unfair trade and economic practices. On India, it was tariffs on motorcycle components that disadvantaged the iconic American company Harley-Davidson. Although the president often exaggerated the numbers—India's 39 percent tariffs became 200 percent tariffs—it was a good example of India's self-defeating protectionist policies. Three years later, Harley-Davidson would stop manufacturing in India, at a time when Modi was hoping to lure more foreign manufacturers to the country.

We huddled in the Oval Office for a few moments between the meeting with Modi's delegation in the Cabinet Room and the statements and question-and-answer session in the Rose Garden. I warned Trump that the prime minister was a hugger and, based on how well the visit was going, would probably hug Trump after their statements. Although Trump was known to hug the occasional American flag onstage, he was not a big hugger of people.

The hug was delivered and reciprocated in a way that was not too awkward. Success.

Modi departed on June 27, just two days before Moon's arrival.

★ ★ ★

AT 6:30 p.m., on Thursday, June 29, I sat down next to my South Korean counterpart, Chung Eui-yong, at the long rectangular table in the State Dining Room, the room President Thomas Jefferson had used as his office and cabinet room. Although the dinner party was large, and the room has a high ceiling, we could easily hear the banter between President Trump, President Moon, and the two First Ladies. The dinner was the first time the two leaders were meeting in person. Chung and I hoped the conversation would remain light and set a good tone for the substantive conversations to follow the next day.

When Chung and I met at nine o'clock that morning, I had warned him that any reluctance to complete the emplacement of additional THAAD missile systems would appear to Trump as ingratitude for the U.S. commitment to defend South Korea from the growing threat of North Korean missiles. "Please tell President Moon not to repeat his recent statement that the THAAD deployment would depend on an environmental assessment. Trump is already not a fan of THAAD, and as a real estate developer, he really hates environmental assessments." South Korea was proceeding with a plan that I had drawn on a paper napkin after dinner at my home two weeks earlier: to place the remaining THAAD systems in an approved smaller area while the environmental assessment progressed.

As the White House stewards served kabocha squash consommé, Trump brought up defense burden sharing and his responsibility to get the American people a "better deal on trade." Moon communicated his team's willingness to work with the administration to accomplish both. I wrote a note on the back of my White House menu and passed it to Chung: "All the hard questions are out of the way."

When Moon indicated that he was okay with the deployment of the remaining THAAD missiles, I wrote, referring to the plan that Chung and I had sketched out, "The napkin is working so far."

As the stewards served Dover sole, however, Moon qualified that statement with the need for an "environmental assessment." Trump, predictably, harrumphed, vociferating about how environmental assessments "are a waste of time." Still, the conversation remained civil. As the white peach and raspberry terrine arrived, I wrote a final note on the back of the menu: "I think we are in the clear and can move forward tomorrow."

But staying aligned with the Moon government would require a sustained effort. In the joint statement, our South Korean counterparts insisted on language that held out the prospect of negotiation with North Korea at some point and an acknowledgment that Seoul would take the lead role in any effort to talk with the North Korean regime. In turn, Pottinger, Hooker, and I insisted on language emphasizing sanctions enforcement as essential for convincing Kim Jong-un that denuclearization was in his best interest.

After the press event in the Rose Garden, I joined Vice President Pence with Moon and his delegation in the vice president's ceremonial office in the Eisenhower Executive Office Building. Moon said that, just like Saddam Hussein and Muammar Khadafi, Kim believed that he needed nuclear weapons for defense. Pence asked Moon, "Why does Kim Jong-un need nukes when he has conventional artillery in range of Seoul? We have to consider the possibility that Kim wants the weapons for offensive purposes." That difference of opinion about what drove Kim Jong-un was bound to create tension and disagreement that Pence, Pottinger, Hooker, and I would try to resolve in the coming months.

★   ★   ★

I WAS happy to manage friction with allies as well as adversaries; it was part of the job description. But self-generated internal friction was galling.

Case in point: the Fourth of July holiday. Our youngest daughter, Caragh, was home from law school, so all three daughters, son-in-law Lee, and future son-in-law Alex were in Washington. On Saturday evening, we went to dinner at the Peking Gourmet Inn, an iconic restaurant frequented by presidents and other celebrities that serves delicious Peking duck family style. It was a fun moment with family at the start of what I thought would be a relatively relaxing next few days with just a few presidential phone calls and a light workday on Monday. The president was at his golf club in Bedminster, New Jersey, where I hoped he was relaxing, too.

On Sunday, I got up early to read in the SCIF before we went to Mass at Saint Joseph's on Capitol Hill. In the middle of the liturgy, the head of the Secret Service detail, Brent, tapped me on the shoulder: "Sir, I am sorry to interrupt you, but the president would like to speak with you now."

I walked down the church steps, crossed the street, got into the backseat of the Suburban parked there, and picked up the secure phone. Before connecting me, the Situation Room advised me that the president was calling on an unsecured line from the golf course.

"Good morning, Mr. President."

He was angry. "What the fuck are you doing to me, General? I already have phone calls tonight, and now I have more phone calls this afternoon."

"Mr. President, I know about the phone calls that you approved for tonight, but I am not aware of any calls this afternoon."

Trump hung up.

I discovered that Tillerson had bypassed the system and gone directly to the president's scheduler to add three calls that afternoon, to Mohamed bin Zayed (MBZ) of the UAE, King Salman of Saudi Arabia, and Emir Tamim of Qatar. The topic was the so-called Gulf crisis, an embargo of Qatar that Saudi Arabia, the UAE, Egypt, Bahrain, and the Maldives had put in place and that included the severing of diplomatic relations and land, sea, and air links. I could not blame Trump for being angry.

Trump had previously told reporters that Qatar permitted the funding of terrorist organizations "at a very high level." I was based there from 2003 to 2004, at Central Command's forward headquarters, where the United States served as the "big dog" on the tiny but wealthy country's "front porch." And it was true that Qatari leaders gave tacit approval to so-called charities that funded terrorist and extremist organizations. Moreover, Qatar hosted members of many terrorist and extremist groups, allowing them to engage in incitement, recruiting, and fund-raising. (More people would become aware of Qatar's duplicity years later, as Hamas leaders lounged in five-star hotels in Doha while terrorists under their command murdered, tortured, raped, and kidnapped civilians in Israel on October 7, 2023.)

I tried to align our response across the departments and agencies, but Tillerson and Mattis, rightfully concerned about access to and support for the largest U.S. military base in the Middle East, Al

Udeid, were eager to defuse the crisis. Both had long relationships with the Qatari royal family—Tillerson as CEO of ExxonMobil, and Mattis as commander of CENTCOM. They were not as concerned as Trump and I were about the ruling family's deceitful behavior.

Mattis, Tillerson, and I needed to reconcile our positions so we could send consistent messages and act in accordance with the president's guidance. In mid-June, our team coordinated a draft of common objectives and talking points consistent with Trump's guidance to use the crisis to convince Qatari leaders to restrict terrorist and extremist financing. Tillerson, however, had decided to pursue his own plan while largely ignoring the president's guidance. As with the phone calls he scheduled for Trump, he was making everything harder than it needed to be.

Before I rejoined the Mass, I phoned the secretary of state. "Why did you bypass the NSC system for head-of-state calls?" He replied that the calls were "urgent" because he was planning a trip to the Gulf for the following week to try to resolve the crisis. I explained that his end run was more than a process foul; it was unfair to the president, who was with his family and already had other phone calls scheduled. And I warned that the calls would prove counterproductive: Trump had told me in no uncertain terms not to schedule a prep session.

"Rex," I said, "you are going to get the opposite of what you want."

After Mass, which ended just as I returned from Tillerson's call, I took the family on a tour of the White House. Later, alone in my West Wing office, I listened in on the president's phone calls. When MBZ and Trump were connected, Tillerson urged de-escalation.

Trump, cutting in, summarized the "two camps" in his own administration. He was clearly not in Tillerson's camp. The president evoked the May 22 mass murder attack in Manchester, England, that had killed 22 and injured 1,017 at a concert by American pop star Ariana Grande. I heard anger well up in his voice. "I am tired of it. People are tired of it. It has to stop."

MBZ sensed an opportunity and asked for more time.

Trump asked, "Rex, your feelings?" Tillerson got in only a few words about the exaggerated claims of Qatari financing of terrorists when Trump cut him off: "I don't give a damn. Just get it stopped."

The president then broadened the discussion to Saudi financing of terrorists: "Everyone tells me Qatar, Qatar, Qatar . . . It is Saudi Arabia, too?"

MBZ noted that Saudi funding was no longer sanctioned by the state, but he acknowledged that funds flowed to terrorist and extremist organizations from individuals and organizations.

Trump was done. "The Gulf crisis may get ugly, but not as ugly as blowing up the World Trade Center . . . not as ugly as Manchester . . . So, Mohamed you need time. My attitude is, keep a lot of pressure on Qatar. We have to starve the beast . . . Rex, give it time. If it gets nasty, okay."

The call with King Salman, with his son MBS listening in, was more of the same. By the time he spoke with Tamim of Qatar, Trump was angrier and more impatient. He told the Qatari emir to stop funding and harboring terrorists.

It was a predictable outcome. I never told Trump that Tillerson had bypassed the NSC system. I did not want to create more angst for either one of them. The only beneficiaries of obvious divisions in the administration would be Washington lobbying firms representing the Saudis, the Emiratis, and the Qataris—who, in the coming months, would get paid money for nothing.

I hoped that the counterproductive calls might convince Tillerson to collaborate and let me help him. But during his trip to Kuwait, Qatar, and Saudi Arabia, Tillerson was essentially incommunicado. He presented Gulf State leaders with proposals inconsistent with Trump's guidance, which they largely ignored. The difficult relationship with Tillerson was becoming more than unpleasant; it was clearly an impediment to a cohesive U.S. foreign policy.

★　　★　　★

MY PROBLEMS with the secretary of state continued as we prepared for Trump's impending trip to Poland, which would be followed by a stop in Hamburg for the Group of 20 (G20) conference. I hosted a secure videoconference with the Quint—our "club" of national security advisors for France, Germany, Italy, the United Kingdom, and the United States—to affirm the common objectives.

What I did not share with my counterparts was my concern about Trump's first meeting with Vladimir Putin, to take place on the sidelines of the conference. Tillerson had insisted that the additional attendees be limited to the "plus-ones" of him and Lavrov. Tillerson had first met Putin in 1999, when ExxonMobil struck a deal with Russian state-owned oil giant Rosneft. In 2013, Putin awarded him the Order of Friendship, one of the highest honors Russia gives to foreign citizens. Tillerson is a patriot and a man of integrity, but that wouldn't matter to certain members of the press. Wouldn't having me in the room help counter the perception that Trump and Tillerson were unduly sympathetic to the dictator?

The president would no doubt continue to be the object of the Russiagate narrative. But for Tillerson, maintaining personal control over the conduct of foreign policy was more important than blunting inevitable criticism.

We are all, to some extent, prisoners of our experiences. For over ten years, Tillerson had served as CEO of ExxonMobil, where he and his fellow top executives occupied the "God Pod," a twenty-thousand-square-foot suite, separated from their employees. It was not surprising, then, that collaboration was not Tillerson's strong suit. He was trying to pull control of foreign policy over to Foggy Bottom.

Tillerson was freelancing based on what he thought was good for the country. I was trying to guard the elected president's independence of judgment and fit his ideas into coherent avenues of implementation.

CHAPTER 11

WINNING FRIENDS
AND
INFLUENCING FOES

U.S. CONFIRMS NORTH KOREA FIRED INTER-CONTINENTAL BALLISTIC MISSILE . . . North Korean Missile Test Marks Direct Challenge to Trump Administration . . . Trump Has Picked America's Enemies in Russia Over Its Friends in Europe . . . Donald Trump's Poland visit sparks fears of widening divisions in Europe . . . Trump says Western civilization at stake in Warsaw speech . . . Trump, showered in Polish praise, backs NATO's Article 5 . . . *THOUSANDS PROTEST IN HAMBURG AS TRUMP MEETS WITH MERKEL BEFORE G-20* . . . **G20: TRUMP AND PUTIN HOLD FIRST FACE-TO-FACE TALKS** . . . President Erdoğan, Trump hold surprise meeting at G-20 . . . Trump had undisclosed second meeting with Putin, White House confirms . . . Death of U.S. soldier in Afghanistan highlights the evolving role of conventional combat troops there . . . Trump continued to pressure China for help with North Korea . . . **TRUMP AND MACRON CEMENT UNLIKELY FRIENDSHIP IN BASTILLE DAY VISIT** . . . For France, Trump at Bastille Day was Deeply Symbolic . . . Zbigniew Brzezinski, National Security Adviser to Jimmy Carter, Dies at 89 . . . *WASHINGTON REMEMBERS BRZEZINSKI, AND A VERY DIFFERENT ERA*

NOTHING RUINS a Fourth of July holiday quite like a North Korean ballistic missile test. Dan Coats called me before midnight on the third to share indicators of an impending launch. Matt Pottinger called at 3:06 a.m. to tell me that a launch had occurred. It appeared to be an unprecedented intercontinental ballistic missile.

I spoke with Secretary Mattis for ten minutes around 5:30 to coordinate a principals committee meeting, obtain his guidance, and share the instructions I had given Pottinger. The Policy Coordinating Committee, comprising Pottinger and the assistant secretaries of relevant departments and agencies, would draft options by early afternoon and get them to the principals by 3 p.m. I jumped into the Suburban for the short ride to the White House.

As soon as I arrived, I made a series of phone calls to coordinate our response. At 7:20 a.m., Matt, Allison, and I outlined the purpose of the principals meeting to ensure a common understanding of the launch, clarify objectives, and ensure that our response advanced our overarching policy goals. At 7:36, Secretary Mattis affirmed the time line and our approach. At 8:03 p.m., I checked in with Chung Eui-yong in Seoul, after his national security council meeting in the "Blue House," the Republic of Korea presidential residence. He told me that the Moon government was not ready to call the missile an ICBM. I responded, "Eui-yong, just because you don't call it an ICBM doesn't mean it's not an ICBM."

At 8:19, I called Trump to brief him on the launch, get his approval on the objectives, and hear his guidance. He told me he wanted us at "maximum pressure" and to use this as an opportunity to further restrict resources available to Kim's regime. He agreed with our recommendation that Tillerson put out the official statement, which noted that "Global action is required to stop a global threat." The statement affirmed that the United States "will never accept a nuclear-armed North Korea."[1]

Even though Trump had agreed that Tillerson should issue the statement, the president could not resist responding personally to Kim Jong-un, tweeting:

Donald J. Trump ✔
@realDonaldTrump   ...

North Korea has just launched another missile. Does this guy have anything better to do with his life? Hard to believe that South Korea.....

7:19 PM · Jul 3, 2017

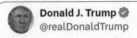

Donald J. Trump ✔
@realDonaldTrump   ...

....and Japan will put up with this much longer. Perhaps China will put a heavy move on North Korea and end this nonsense once and for all!

7:24 PM · Jul 3, 2017

It was another example of an unconventional tweet reinforcing policy. It was all there: maximum pressure, allies, burden sharing, and Beijing's ability to coerce Pyongyang.

At 10:07, I hosted a principals call to convey the president's guidance. Noting the president's order to "get to maximum pressure" on Pyongyang, I suggested that it was time to employ secondary sanctions on Chinese and other banks involved in illicit financial flows to the Kim regime. Treasury had actions ready, but Tillerson had slowed them down. The actions included sixteen targets related to the evasion of DPRK sanctions, the most significant of which was the designation of the Bank of Dandong as an institution of "primary money laundering concession" under Section 311 of the USA Patriot Act.

By the early afternoon, the Policy Coordinating Committee, an interagency group that NSC senior directors convene at the assistant secretary level, had sent out a matrix with objectives and the critical actions each department was to take. I checked in with Mattis at 2:34 p.m., and then with Pompeo at 2:42, before we assembled the principals committee for final approval and coordination of the response. I chaired the meeting in the Situation Room with those able to attend. Others joined by video.

When Nikki Haley summarized her efforts to pursue additional UN Security Council sanctions, Tillerson was unenthusiastic and dismissive. Rather than propose actions such as interdiction of DPRK ships engaged in smuggling, Mattis spoke only of diplomatic pressure. He and Tillerson feared that escalating tension with North Korea might lead to war. But we had all agreed that maximum pressure was necessary for Kim to conclude that he was safer without the weapons than he was with them.

This was all following a familiar pattern. Tillerson and Mattis's actions to reduce tensions with North Korea rather than ratchet up the pressure on Pyongyang were bound to further strain my relationship with them. Their actions were also at odds with what Trump wanted. We should have been working together to convince other nations to increase the pressure on North Korea, and we would have an opportunity to do so during the trip to Europe and the G20 conference. But the energy it took to keep our own team aligned would remain a distraction.

★   ★   ★

THE NEXT day, I got to the White House at around 5 a.m. to drop off my bag and read intelligence prior to the short helicopter flight with the president to Andrews Air Force Base. As Air Force One took off, I joined Trump for a call with President Abdel Fattah al-Sisi of Egypt to discuss the Gulf crisis. Despite the interruptions of his Independence Day weekend, Trump was in good spirits. I told him he would have an enthusiastic crowd for his major speech at the Warsaw Uprising Monument at Krasinski Square. After Gary and I reviewed the trip with him, he walked to the midsection of the plane to mingle with the staff.

As we arrived at the Royal Castle (Zamek Królewski) in Warsaw, I thought of Poland's tortured history. The castle, like Poland itself, was severely damaged in 1939, in the Nazi and Soviet invasions. It was almost completely destroyed in the cataclysmic battles between German forces and their erstwhile Soviet co-conspirators in 1945. Unlike the vast majority of European nations that had largely disarmed under the assumption that Russia was no longer a threat, the Poles had strong memories of brutal attacks, dismemberment, and traumatic occupation at the hands of the Nazis and the Soviets during World

War II and subjugation to the USSR during the Cold War. The Poles understood the importance of a strong defense.

As the crowd assembled for Trump's speech, our delegation met with Polish president Andrzej Duda and his team in the castle's Knight's room. In their discussion, Duda focused on the threat from Russia, reinforcing what Trump had heard from Presidents Sauli Niinistö (Finland), Iohannis, and Poroshenko. He took out a map to highlight the threat from Russian forces in the city of Kaliningrad and requested that U.S. troops be permanently stationed on Polish soil. He raised the prospect of joint U.S.-Polish battalions with long-range precision strike capabilities—the U.S. HIMARS rockets that would, years later, prove invaluable to Ukraine's defense.

I had told Trump how Poles had been disappointed in 2012 when President Obama denied missile defenses for Poland in an effort to reassure Putin. A little more than a year later, Putin invaded Ukraine. Now was the time, I told him, to deepen defense cooperation with Warsaw, as a way to deter further Russian aggression. Duda and other leaders helped disabuse Trump of the idea that Vladimir Putin was a misunderstood leader who would abandon his revanchist agenda if only he were reassured.

We then walked with Duda to the Great Assembly Hall, where Trump greeted other Polish leaders and the leaders of Bulgaria, Croatia, Estonia, Hungary, Latvia, Lithuania, Romania, Slovakia, and Slovenia, who were in Warsaw to attend the second summit of the Three Seas Initiative. Trump shook hands, taking in the room's columns, chandeliers, and mirrors as he sat down to applause.

"Thank you. I greatly appreciate it. This is a beautiful room, I must say. I love beautiful rooms, and this is one of them."

His prepared remarks expressed U.S. support for "a new future for open, fair, and affordable energy markets that bring greater security and prosperity to all of our citizens." Alluding to the need to break Russia's stranglehold over the Three Seas nations, he urged the assembled leaders to "continue to diversify your energy sources, suppliers, and routes" and "ensure that your infrastructure, like your commitment to freedom and rule of law, binds you to all of Europe and, indeed, to the West." Trump portrayed the United States as a critical part of the solution to energy insecurity and overdependence on Moscow, pledging to support "a commonsense approach to protecting natural resources—one that responsibly balances economic growth, job creation, and energy security." In retrospect, after Russia's massive reinvasion of Ukraine in 2022, it is obvious that Trump's counsel was prescient and should have been heeded with a greater sense of urgency.

As we entered Krasinski Square, I thought that the speech Trump was about to deliver was well suited to the moment. He warned Russia to stop its global destabilizing activities and affirmed U.S. commitment to Article 5 of the NATO treaty. The lines that I fought hardest to get into the speech were meant to strengthen the transatlantic relationship and allay concerns that Trump viewed the European Union as a competitor that should be broken up: "A strong Europe is a blessing to the West and to the world. One hundred years after the entry of American forces into World War I, the transatlantic bond between the United States and Europe is as strong as ever." The speech went on to celebrate the cultures and principles that bind the United States to Poland, the rest of Europe, and the West.

It was a clear celebration of universal values and rights that transcended geography or ethnicity, but Trump's critics could not resist the urge to cast his speech as "racist" and "an alt-right manifesto." It was predictable but disappointing that a speech echoing President John F. Kennedy's 1963 "Ich bin ein Berliner" speech or Ronald Reagan's 1987 "Tear down this wall" speech became, for these critics, when delivered by Trump, "a dog whistle for white nationalists."[2]

If Putin was momentarily concerned about Trump's strong counter to his claim that Russian illiberal nationalism was the best defense of the West, he could find comfort in the vitriol and divisions apparent in those criticisms.

★   ★   ★

SOON AFTER we arrived in Hamburg, we traveled to the Hotel Atlantic Kempinski for a meeting with Angela Merkel and her team. Despite claims to the contrary in the press, Merkel and Trump had a good rapport and seemed to enjoy chiding each other.

Trump said something like "Clearly you think NATO is fantastic, so why aren't you paying up?"

And Merkel responded with something like "You are the world superpower, that should make you proud. China wants to be the superpower and will become that if you vacate your position."

Trump then turned to me and asked, "How many troops do we have in Germany?"

"About thirty-five thousand, Mr. President, plus rotational troops in Europe as part of the European Defense Initiative."

He then asked Merkel pointedly, "Why are we defending you against Russia when you are not paying and [when you're] burning gas that is giving cash to the Kremlin?"

Trump was right to chide the chancellor. She had assumed that Putin could be placated. Trump was also correct when he told Merkel that her economic model of exporting goods manufactured with low-cost energy from Russia was "unsustainable."

Merkel and Trump both used the perception of tension in their relationship to appeal to their political supporters. After the meeting in Hamburg, Merkel indirectly chided him: "Whoever believes the problems of the world can be solved by isolationism and protectionism is making a tremendous error."

After we returned home from Hamburg, Merkel would let me know that comments aimed partly at me and an op-ed I had coauthored in the *New York Times* had been necessary to appeal to her political supporters and the many Germans who disliked President Trump. I understood completely. If she needed to criticize me to help herself in the forthcoming election, "it was a service I was happy to provide." I was more concerned about what she and Trump seemed to have in common: the assumption that a close relationship with Vladimir Putin could forestall future Russian aggression.

★   ★   ★

ON TO the G20. Trump attended the initial plenary session and then had others—including, controversially, Ivanka—sit in for him while he conducted meetings. Turkish president Recep Tayyip Erdoğan insisted on an unscheduled meeting, during which he ranted about "140 trucks supplying the mainly Kurdish SDF in northeast Syria."

But the most anticipated moment—by the press and by Trump—was the meeting with Putin. To prepare the reflexively contrarian president, I told him several times over the previous weeks what Putin wanted out of the meeting and what Putin wanted Trump to say:

- Putin wanted sanctions relief; he would hold out the prospect of economic and trade opportunities.
- Putin wanted the United States to abandon Ukraine; he would portray Ukraine as corrupt and unworthy of support while claiming that it had always been part of Russia.
- Putin wanted the United States and our allies out of Syria and Afghanistan; he would say that we were wasting money and perpetuating wars.
- Putin wanted to divide Americans further and drain the remaining confidence in our democratic institutions and processes; he wanted Trump to make statements indicating that he believed Putin and disbelieved the U.S. intelligence community, to perpetuate Russiagate and amplify the vitriolic discourse in American politics.

My basic message during the final prep meeting at the Hamburg Messe convention center was "Do not be a chump."

I told Trump how Putin had duped Presidents George W. Bush and Barack Obama. "Mr. President, he is the best liar in the world." I suggested that Putin was confident he could "play" Trump and get what he wanted—sanctions relief and the United States out of Syria and Afghanistan on the cheap—by manipulating Trump with ambiguous promises of a "better relationship." He would offer cooperation on counterterrorism, cybersecurity, and arms control.

I could tell that Trump was getting impatient with my "negative vibe." I said what I needed to say. If he was going to be contrary, I hoped he would be contrary to the Russian dictator, not to me. I left the room as Putin and Lavrov arrived.

The readout from the meeting revealed the string of lies and deceptions I had anticipated from Putin. Unsurprisingly, he claimed that Ukraine had been a part of Russia since the sixteenth century; that he had to protect Russian speakers in the east from Ukraine's campaign of ethnic cleansing. He also played down North Korea's ICBM test, claiming that Pyongyang was not close to developing a nuclear weapon or an ICBM. We should not worry about Kim, Putin advised, because the regime would resolve itself if we just opened the border and got the North Korean economy going. I took this deception as a positive sign that maximum pressure was working. Putin was concerned about potential U.S. and allied military action against Pyongyang—especially after our strikes on Syria three months earlier.

On Syria, the Russian leader went beyond false promises on Iran and safe zones to predict that Assad would transition out of power. Beyond offering a "cyber working group," Putin gave Trump "his word" that he had never looked at any of the classified information Edward Snowden, an American citizen he was harboring in Russia, had stolen and given to WikiLeaks. As Tillerson and Trump told me about portions of the meeting, I wondered how either of them had been able to keep a straight face.

To appeal to Trump's optimistic interpretation of the U.S.-Soviet alliance during World War II, Putin showed Trump a video of Russia's Northern Fleet salvaging the USS *Thomas Donaldson*, a 7,200-ton Lend-Lease ship that a German U-boat had sunk in the arctic in 1945, before it could deliver its cargo of Sherman tanks. The idea was to evoke the memory of the United States and the Soviet Union as allies during World War II and to keep alive the pipe dream of conciliation with Putin's Kremlin as the best way to advance both countries' interests.

Putin used his time with Trump to launch a sophisticated and sustained campaign to manipulate him. Profilers and psychological operations officers at Russia's intelligence services must have been working overtime. Even as the meeting stretched into its second hour, Putin did not run out of material. To suggest moral equivalence between U.S. interventions in Latin America and the Russian invasion of Ukraine, Putin cited the "Roosevelt Corollary" to the Monroe Doctrine, a foreign policy declaration by U.S. president Theodore Roosevelt in 1904–5 stating that the United States could intervene in a country's internal affairs if that country were engaged in chronic wrongdoing.

At the dinner later that evening, as the two leaders squared off for a long conversation, Putin handed Trump a list of ideas for collaboration, including the development of an amusement park near Moscow. I wondered if Putin hoped the list would leak, or if he planned to leak it later, to revive stories of Trump's failed pursuit of business deals in Russia, feed the Russian collusion narrative, weaken Trump, and divide Americans further.

Putin got the desired effect from the meeting and the dinner. The press focused almost exclusively on whether Trump had raised the issue of Russia's attacks on the 2016 U.S. election. But Trump had encouraged the media's preoccupation with the subject. At a news conference in Poland a day earlier, when asked if he would state unequivocally that Russia had meddled in the election, Trump said that "other countries" could be to blame and "nobody knows for sure." When reports emerged of his long conversation with Putin at dinner, it fed the collusion narrative further.

I wished that Trump could separate the issue of Russian election meddling from the legitimacy of his presidency. He could have said, "Yes, they attacked the election. But Russia doesn't care who wins our elections. What they want is to pit Americans against one another and reduce our confidence in our democratic institutions and processes." He might also have pointed out that those who fed the "not my president" and Russia collusion narratives were doing Putin's work for him.

But Trump was caught in a vortex created by the interaction of those narratives with the fragility of his ego and his deep sense of aggrievement.

★   ★   ★

ON DAY two of the G20, we filed into the meeting room and sat across from our Chinese counterparts. Trump asked Xi Jinping to begin. Like Putin, Xi seemed worried that Trump might act against the growing threat from Pyongyang's nuclear and missile programs. Xi was also fearful of a Kim regime collapse that could result in the loss of a "buffer state" between U.S. allies and his border. To justify his hedging on sanctions, Xi warned against "excessive pressure" and "long-arm jurisdiction"—his phrase for U.S. secondary sanctions on Chinese banks involved in circumventing sanctions.

But then he contradicted that argument with a metaphor: "Those who are barefooted do not fear people with good shoes." He wanted us to conclude that the North Korean people were so accustomed to deprivation that sanctions were futile. He urged no chaos and no wars while communicating his desire to keep North Korea intact with the observation that China had lost 190,000 men during the Korean War to ensure there was not a hostile power on the China-Korea border. He then made a token promise to support more pressure on North Korea after the next provocation.

It was obvious that Putin and Xi had coordinated their efforts to downplay the threat and portray maximum pressure as ineffective or dangerous.

Trump countered Xi's effort to obfuscate and delay a reckoning by again observing that China could solve the North Korea problem if Xi decided to do so. Trump reminded Xi of the danger of proliferation. What if Japan, South Korea, and others concluded that they needed nukes, too?

As we boarded Air Force One at the end of the summit, Gary Cohn and I compared notes. On balance, the trip was a success. Although the reaction to our op-ed after the G7 had been mixed, Gary and I drafted (with our staffs) another essay, this time for the *New York Times*. In it, we emphasized the need to take advantage of opportunities associated with "vast supplies of affordable energy" and "untapped markets that can be opened to new commerce." Critics accused us of cloaking irrational Trump policies in coherent language. But we were helping Trump direct his disruptive nature toward what needed to be disrupted.

★   ★   ★

WE HAD only three days back in Washington before another trip to Europe—this time to Paris, for Bastille Day and to commemorate the one-hundredth anniversary of the United States' entry into World War I.

Upon arrival in Paris, we went directly to the ambassador's residence, the Hotel de Pontalba, one of the most magnificent homes on one of the most storied streets in the city. Its sixty thousand square feet easily accommodated the president and his immediate staff. After lunch, we departed for a reception in honor of the president and First Lady at the Hôtel des Invalides, the seventeenth-century complex constructed under Louis XIV for the care and housing of disabled veterans and as a place of worship. After the band performed and troops passed in review, our party trailed the presidents and First Ladies through the Musée de l'Armée, the military museum of the Army of France. I smiled when President Trump remarked that he did not know France had such a rich military history.

We drove to the Élysée Palace for a small group meeting with Macron; his chief diplomatic advisor, Philippe Etienne; and his economic advisor. Gary and I greeted Macron and our counterparts and took our seats next to Trump.

Trump explained his rationale for withdrawing from the Paris Climate Accords. He told Macron that "Ivanka and my whole family wanted me to stay in, but the people who voted for me wanted me out." He then aired his grievances about the lack of reciprocity in trade and market access in the European Union.

We walked downstairs for a joint press conference. Even in Paris, Trump could not escape questions about Russiagate and, in particular, Donald Trump Jr.'s meeting with a Russian attorney to hear damaging information about Hillary Clinton.

Nobody loves a show like Donald Trump, and the Bastille Day parade is quite a show. We sat in the bleachers with the presidents and the First Ladies, front and center. The parade had it all—marching troops, mounted cavalry, vintage tanks and armored cars, modern combat vehicles, an overflight of fighters and bombers, and even a military band on horseback.

On the return flight, Trump told me, "Tell Mattis I want to have a similar parade on the next Veterans Day or Fourth of July."

Although I was not one to shirk a responsibility, I was happy the parade issue fell clearly in Mattis's area of responsibility.

★ ★ ★

IN HIS last tweet before he passed away, Zbigniew Brzezinski wrote, "Sophisticated U.S. leadership is the sine qua non of a stable world order. However, we lack the former while the latter is getting worse."[3] Despite the friction, we were helping Trump win friends, influence foes, and exert U.S. leadership internationally. Battles within the administration, I had come to realize, would be a permanent feature of Trump's presidency. I had to work harder to minimize the effect of those battles on the development of sound policy. The stakes were too high not to, as North Korea's ICBM, China's reluctance to pressure Pyongyang, and Putin's unrelenting efforts to manipulate Trump and divide Americans further attested.

CHAPTER 12

KNIVES OUT

THE KNIVES ARE OUT FOR LT. GEN. H.R. MCMASTER . . . Reince Priebus Is Ousted Amid Stormy Days for White House . . . *TRUMP NAMES HOMELAND SECURITY SECRETARY JOHN F. KELLY NEW WHITE HOUSE CHIEF OF STAFF* . . . **MCMASTER ADDS MUSCLE TO KUSHNER'S MIDDLE EAST PEACE EFFORT** . . . Sean Spicer Resigns as White House Press Secretary . . . *ANTHONY SCARAMUCCI: FIRED FROM THE WHITE HOUSE AFTER 10 DAYS* . . . **FORMER FBI AGENT SAYS RUSSIAN TWITTER BOTS WERE BEHIND PUSH FOR MCMASTER FIRING** . . . Right Wing Media Declares War on National Security Advisor H.R. McMaster . . . Trump and Kushner Push Back on Right-Wing Campaign to Fire McMaster, for Now . . . **NSA MCMASTER ON CHARLOTTESVILLE: 'OF COURSE IT WAS TERRORISM'** . . . Charlottesville residents recall horror of car attack: 'Bodies writhing, blood everywhere' . . . *TRUMP DEFENDS WHITE-NATIONALIST PROTESTERS: 'SOME VERY FINE PEOPLE ON BOTH SIDES'* . . . Stephen Bannon Out At The White House After Turbulent Run . . . **TRUMP ALARMS VENEZUELA WITH TALK OF A 'MILITARY OPTION'**

I THOUGHT that August would be a quiet time in Washington. Congress is in recess. Many locals go away on vacation to escape the capital's heat and humidity. I planned to review long-term projects like the national security, counterterrorism, cyber, and space strategies; the nuclear Posture Review; and various integrated strategies under development.

After five months on the job, I should have known better. It may have been hot and humid outside, but inside, the cauldron of the Trump White House was about to bubble over.

I got word that Trump was going to fire his chief of staff. What would become a familiar process was already under way at the end of July: leaks predicting impending departure, fervent denials by the White House communications team, and, ultimately, a tweet.

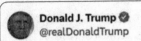

Donald J. Trump ✓
@realDonaldTrump

···

I am pleased to inform you that I have just named General/Secretary John F Kelly as White House Chief of Staff. He is a Great American....

1:49 PM · Jul 28, 2017

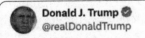

Donald J. Trump ✓
@realDonaldTrump

···

...and a Great Leader. John has also done a spectacular job at Homeland Security. He has been a true star of my Administration

1:54 PM · Jul 28, 2017

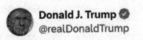

Donald J. Trump ✓
@realDonaldTrump

···

I would like to thank Reince Priebus for his service and dedication to his country. We accomplished a lot together and I am proud of him!

2:00 PM · Jul 28, 2017

I spoke with Kelly on the phone the day before the tweet. He asked me whether he should take the job. He was reluctant to leave the Department of Homeland Security, where he had a degree of autonomy, to enter the fray in the White House. I told him, "I know what it was like leaving command for a staff job"—something no military officer would ever want to do—"but we need you over here, and you can make a difference."

I warned him that the toxicity of the White House was the biggest impediment to serving the president. Priebus "is not a bad person," I explained. "He had this pact with Bannon in an effort to protect himself, and he enabled much of the dysfunction." I pledged the support of the NSC staff and predicted that the vast majority of well-motivated people in the White House would welcome Kelly with open arms.

Kelly brought with him his chief of staff from the Department of Homeland Security, Kirstjen Nielsen. I met with them on their first day and handed them a binder containing the National Security staff vision, mission, goals, key tasks, priority national security challenges, and a description of our process for framing complex challenges and developing options for the president. I told him that, despite efforts to disrupt the process, we were achieving good outcomes.

Later that day, Kelly stopped by an NSC staff all-hands meeting in the EEOB auditorium. I saw him enter through a side door. I introduced him and asked if he would like to say a few words. He walked to the front of the room, put his arm around me, and announced, "I love this guy, and the president does, too."

Our team applauded as Kelly departed. After he left, I summarized his bio and predicted that he would pull the White House team together and help us better serve the president.

Kelly would struggle to get his bearings, as would have anyone taking that job in the Trump White House.

Just before Kelly arrived, Sean Spicer resigned as White House communications director, as Anthony Scaramucci, a financier and entrepreneur with a degree from Harvard Business School, took over the job. I first met "the Mooch" on Wednesday, July 26, in my office. His candor was refreshing, and I felt his sense of humor might lighten things up in the West Wing. I invited him to join me and some of our colleagues at my home for a welcome dinner the following week.

But on July 30, while staffing the president for a late-night phone call with Japanese prime minister Shinzo Abe, Trump told me that Kelly planned to fire Scaramucci the next day, in the wake of an embarrassing *New Yorker* article. The Mooch had not told the reporter that their conversation was off the record—a rookie mistake. The transcript and tape of the conversation contained expletives and uncouth descriptions of Bannon and Priebus.

Shaking his head, Trump said, "I thought I hired *Harvard* Anthony, not *Long Island* Anthony."

We laughed.

"What do you think, General?" Trump asked.

I told him that I had a good first impression of Scaramucci and believed he could overcome his mistake.

"Call Kelly and tell him that, would you?"

Kelly was unpersuaded. I saw Anthony in the West Wing the next day, the day before the welcome dinner at my house. I said, "Sorry you got fired, but please join us tomorrow for what will now be your farewell dinner."

The irrepressible Mooch showed up sporting blue-tinted sunglasses. He apologized to Katie and Colleen, who were on their way out for a separate dinner, for his "potty mouth."

The Mooch's eleven-day tenure in the White House would become a unit of measurement for service in the Trump administration. In case you're wondering, I served for 41.3 Scaramuccis.

We had a fun and relaxing evening. But it was the calm before the storm.

★   ★   ★

AS KELLY arrived, Bannon and his small staff with unclear portfolios were under duress. Priebus was no longer there to protect them, and Kelly was determined to clarify everyone's role. Scaramucci's direct criticisms in *The New Yorker* had further exposed Bannon's self-serving agenda. Many in the White House and beyond were certain he was the source of leaks designed to derail the policy process on Afghanistan, take credit for the president's policy decisions, and undercut his colleagues. Bannon had exposed himself as a malicious, untrustworthy grifter, and he was about to be hoist with his own petard.

Bannon and his acolytes betrayed tactics similar to those employed by the three witches, or "weird sisters," in Shakespeare's *Macbeth*. The witches use equivocating prophecies to manipulate the Scottish general Macbeth. Bannon and his people used false information delivered through social media and pseudo-media, including Bannon's old tabloid website, Breitbart News, to manipulate Donald Trump and turn him against those who might impede their amorphous "alt-right" agenda. But Bannon and his associates were less subtle than the weird sisters.

I had been the target of the weird sisters' campaign of slander and disinformation for weeks, but the attacks on me and the NSC staff intensified after the White House released a statement on August 2 that I had replaced a senior director on the NSC staff with a more experienced official who was better suited for the work ahead of us.

The far-right American news and opinion website for which Bannon had served as executive chairman portrayed the personnel change as a systematic effort to purge the NSC staff of Trump loyalists.

Breitbart connected my decision with the departure of other NSC officials, including Rick Waddell's firing of a staffer whom I had never met. That staffer had, in his first days on the job, composed a conspiratorial "manifesto" calling for political warfare against Democrats, establishment Republicans, and what he described as a cabal of leftists, cultural Marxists, Islamists, and others.

I had nothing against any of those whom Rick and I had replaced. Personnel changes were meant to ensure that the president had the best staffers available, people who understood their roles and responsibilities. But Bannon and his allies saw me as an impediment to their nativist and neo-isolationist agendas. Stories planted in the pseudo-media quickly crossed over into social media and ballooned into what the Atlantic Council's Digital Forensic Research Lab described at the time as the most well-organized campaign against an individual by the alt-right and the Russians.[1]

Consistent with the witches' line in Macbeth's first act, "Fair is foul and foul is fair," the tsunami of attacks under the FireMcMaster campaign accumulated an array of baseless and often contradictory charges all designed to estrange me from Trump. A total of 136,292 posts on social media using the #FireMcMaster appeared between August 3 and 6, with two thirds posted between August 3 and 4. Stories laden with disinformation from the sites Circa News, Breitbart, Liberty Writers News, the Daily Caller, and Young Conservatives garnered 126,000 engagements on a single social media platform alone. Years later, a study of the campaign confirmed an extremely high level of botlike actors and coordinated right-wing cohost activity around three main narratives: McMaster works for the deep state; McMaster is targetting Trump loyalists; and McMaster is "Deeply hostile to Israel."

Alt-right and Russian cohosts began to reinforce one another after a few influential social media personalities made the connection. Conspiracy theorist Alex Jones invited an ultranationalist Russian political philosopher on his show to call for my removal. Paid Russian agent Lee Stranahan, founder of Populist.TV and cohost of a show on the Russian government media outlet Sputnik News, also jumped in. Then internet bots and trolls controlled by Russian intelligence, the so-called Internet Research Agency, amplified the #FireMcMaster campaign. Soon, Fox News personalities Sean Hannity and Laura Ingraham joined in the effort.

While Bannon rallied some members of the far-right-wing Jewish-American organizations supporting him to falsely portray me as anti-Israel, this was quickly debunked when others rallied to defend me from such charges.[2] Even Israeli prime minister Netanyahu and Israeli minister of defense Avigdor Lieberman offered their support. Many Republican leaders called to ask how they might help. Senator McCain described the attacks as "disgraceful."[3] Jared Kushner released a statement: "General McMaster is a true public servant and a tremendous asset for the president and the administration."[4] He included with his tweets a photo of a dinner I had hosted at my home for senior Israeli officials. And under the headline "Israeli Officials Say Under-fire McMaster a Great Friend of Israel," the *Times of Israel* ran a story with supportive quotations from Israeli officials who "were constantly impressed by how pro-Israeli the U.S. national security adviser is."[5]

The smear campaign was not a surprise. Attacks from Bannon and his allies were not new and a government agency had warned me of an impending Kremlin effort designed to diminish my influence and separate me from Trump. But I had anticipated neither the scale of the operation nor the degree to which the Russians and the alt-right would reinforce one another's efforts. As former FBI agent Clint Watts said at the time, the alt-right campaign provided an opportunity for the Kremlin to sow "chaos and disunity among the American government."[6]

While I focused on my job, my comms director, Michael Anton, who understood the alt-right ecosystem well, led the defensive effort. Josh Raffel, senior communications advisor to Jared and Ivanka, volunteered to assist. I had decided to ignore the attacks on me, but it was hard for family members to look away from the sustained effort to defame me, and it was difficult for me to see the attacks on members of my staff, some of whom received threats of physical harm.

Over dinner at my home on August 4, Rupert Murdoch shared his perspective: "Only Trump's opinion matters," he told me. "Try not to worry about what these people are saying. You are doing a great job for the president."

Trump did not fall for the falsehoods. On August 5, he released a statement: "General McMaster and I are working very well together. He is a good man and very pro-Israel. I am grateful for the work he continues to do serving our country."

I saw Trump at Bedminster on August 7, when I had lunch with Mike Pompeo and two senior intelligence officials with whom I had served in Afghanistan. He echoed Murdoch: "Remember General, only my opinion matters, and I think you are doing a great job."

But the "witches" were unrelenting. After the President supported me publicly, Breitbart accused Trump of defying his base in defending the "globalist general."

I appreciated Trump's reassuring words, but I also knew he was attuned to the views of those who would continue to attack me and many members of our team on the NSC staff. Trump had thrown cold water into the cauldron, but Bannon and his allies would continue to roil and boil.

★ ★ ★

FIVE DAYS after my lunch at Bedminster with Pompeo, a "Unite the Right" rally in Charlottesville, Virginia, turned deadly when a twenty-year-old Ohio man accelerated his car into a crowd of counterprotesters, killing thirty-two-year-old Heather Heyer and injuring approximately thirty others, five critically.

Trump equivocated during a press conference in Trump Tower during which he intended to talk about infrastructure. When asked about Charlottesville, he told reporters, "I think there is blame on both sides." He went on to say, "You had some very bad people in that group," referring to the white nationalist groups rallying against removal of a Robert E. Lee statue. "But you also had people that were very fine people, on both sides."

Later in the day at Bedminster, he seemed to recover from that bout of moral equivalence, condemning "in the strongest possible terms this egregious display of hatred, bigotry, and violence." But he added, "On many sides, on many sides."

Much of his statement was irrefutably positive, such as "We have to come together as Americans with love for our nation and true affection." But as often was the case, his obsession with avoiding any offense to a political base that included a racist fringe undermined his ability to lead the country through a difficult and divisive experience. Some of the same groups that received only tepid condemnation for the violence at Charlottesville were those whom Trump and his supporters would mobilize under the false claims of widespread fraud during the 2020 presidential election.[7]

The day after the Unite the Right violence, I appeared on two Sunday news shows, on ABC and NBC. My intention was to clarify the president's policy on North Korea, but I knew that the first questions would be about Charlottesville. When George Stephanopoulos asked if the violence was terrorism, I answered unequivocally, "Of course it was terrorism."

Then, on *Meet the Press*, Chuck Todd asked about attacks against me and about my relationship with Bannon. After noting, "You've had your own run-ins with the alt-right," he cited a tweet asserting that "McMaster's media allies who he leaks to are trying to frame

Bannon for #Charlottesville." Todd then asked, "Um, what is going on inside this White House with you and Mr. Bannon?"

I responded, "Well, this is just a lot of noise, from my perspective."

I tried to turn it back to North Korea as Todd raised Bannon again, interjecting brusquely, "Can you and Steve Bannon still work together in this White House or not?"

I responded, "I get to work together with a broad range of talented people, and it is a privilege every day to enable the national security team."

Todd told me that I hadn't answered the question. I replied that I was "ready to work with anybody who would help advance the president's agenda and advance the security and prosperity of the American people."

Todd still wasn't finished and asked if I believed that Bannon was working to accomplish those same outcomes.

I ended the interview by responding that "I believe that everyone who works in the White House who has the privilege, the great privilege every day, of serving their nation should be motivated by that goal."

As I walked out, I thought that Todd had been right to push me on those questions. As I saw it, Bannon and his allies were not in the White House to serve their nation. They were there to advance their own agenda, at all costs, even if it meant undermining the Constitution we were all sworn to "support and defend."

The next day, Bannon was out. As with Lady Macbeth, his demise came as a consequence of his own ambition. As with Lady Macbeth, his sociopathy was a kind of political suicide. Out of the White House, he would continue to grift among his supporters. Two years later, he would be arrested and charged with fraud over an online fund-raising scheme to build a wall on the Mexico border. Bannon used flattery and dissembling to work his way back into Trump's good graces in time to help instigate the January 6 assault on the U.S. Capitol and secure a presidential pardon for himself. In 2023, his podcast earned the dubious distinction of having the highest percentage of unsubstantiated and false claims of the seventy-nine political podcasts studied.[8]

★   ★   ★

AS THE August humidity reminded me that Washington really is a stifling swamp, I split time between the capital and Bedminster, staying for a few days at a time in a small guest room on the grounds of the club adjacent to the pool and gym and across from the president's and First Lady's residences.

Bedminster provided an opportunity to engage with Trump away from the hectic pace and many distractions of Washington. After the August 7 lunch with Pompeo and officials from his agency, we had an informal meeting with Trump to discuss Afghanistan. The intelligence officers stressed the importance of their mission. They described how they had foiled attacks against Americans and prevented jihadist terrorist organizations from becoming more dangerous. Trump asked questions, and the discussion helped him revise his assessment of the situation. It also helped him understand the vital role the U.S. and Afghan militaries played in our counterterrorist efforts. It was clear that a proposal to privatize support for Afghan armed forces would still require significant Defense Department infrastructure. The discussion also revealed that an "over-the-horizon" approach to counterterrorism would have little effect on terrorist organizations.

Trump was relaxed. He was away from people who agitated him or constantly vied to curry favor. I often visited his apartment in the morning and in the evening to prepare him for and listen in on his phone calls with heads of state. I began the succinct briefings with "Mr. President, the purpose of this call is . . ." I then gave him a card. "Here are the points you may want to make." After summarizing what he might hear from that head of state, I asked the Situation Room to connect the call. During the call, I would occasionally pass him notes with pertinent information or recommended points.

But agitation sometimes visited Bedminster, too. On August 11, Tillerson, Haley, Kelly, and I met with Trump in a small conference room to discuss the implementation of the maximum pressure strategy for North Korea. When Tillerson expressed hope that "we will get to negotiations with North Korea through China," I pointed out that using Beijing's offices was "inconsistent with the strategy that the president had approved and a bad idea because it would dissipate pressure on the North, drive a rapprochement between Pyongyang

and Beijing, and put China in the driver's seat." I was concerned
that China was already reverting to form and continuing to use the
DPRK and its nuclear and missile programs as a means to maintain
its geographical buffer and drive a wedge between the United States
and its South Korean and Japanese allies.

To reinforce the point that we needed more pressure on Pyongyang, not diplomatic help from Beijing, I mentioned the great work
that Ambassador Haley had done in securing stronger UN Security
Council sanctions, including bans on North Korean exports of coal,
iron, lead, and seafood. If enforced, the sanctions would reduce
North Korea's annual export revenue by more than a third.

My comments apparently triggered Tillerson's disdain for Nikki
Haley. He denigrated her work at the United Nations in impolite
terms. As the conversation got heated, Kelly suggested that we move
on to a press event he had arranged, in part, to demonstrate unity
among this disunified segment of Trump's foreign policy team. We
were to follow the president through a portico and onto a small lawn
where Trump, flanked by Tillerson, Haley, and me, would take questions.

Before we left the room, Tillerson said, "Mr. President, please
don't say anything about military options for Venezuela." As we
walked past the swimming pool on the way to the press pool, I said,
"Rex, you know that he is a contrarian, and now the first thing he is
going to say about Venezuela is that we are considering military options." Sure enough, when a reporter asked Trump about Venezuela,
he said, "Venezuela is not very far away, and the people are suffering,
and they're dying. We have many options for Venezuela, including a
possible military option, if necessary." Asked if it would be a U.S.-led
military operation, Trump said, "We don't talk about it, but a military operation, a military option is certainly something that we could
pursue."[9] (There were no military options under consideration.) This
was another slightly amusing example of how it would have been
much easier on all of us if we had collaborated more closely.

Yet Tillerson and Mattis continued to prioritize control over collaboration, even after a series of failures ranging from the phone
calls to Gulf leaders to the president's Venezuela comments. There
were many examples of this, including a meeting at the end of July

in the Pentagon intended to convince Trump of the value of allies and American military presence abroad. I was on a short vacation in California, and Mattis and Tillerson had cut me out of the planning. The meeting was an utter disaster, ending with Trump berating all those present. It quickly devolved into a Trump rant in which allies were "trade abusers" and all present were "stupid people" who had been duped by those abusers. Someone leaked to the press that Tillerson, after the disastrous meeting, had called Trump "a moron." The estrangement between him and Trump grew after he refused to deny that he had done so.

It was past time for us to work better together.

The president, who was always game for gossip, intrigue, and infighting, often asked leading questions to see if I might criticize Tillerson or Mattis. I never did. And I never would. And I told Mattis and Tillerson, "Whenever you are ready to expand your club of two to a club of three, I am embarrassingly free."

There were glimmers of cooperation with Mattis but he and Tillerson continued to play bureaucratic power games. On June 19, Senior Director for Asia Matt Pottinger told me that he was not welcome at a security dialogue with Chinese officials that the State Department was hosting the following day. I called Rex, who simply said, "I am hosting the meeting, and Pottinger is not welcome."

I told him, "That doesn't make sense. Pottinger is the president's senior advisor on Asia." I then called Mattis and explained the situation. I said I would rather not bother the president with this and then asked him to talk to Tillerson. Mattis called back. He had talked to Rex: Pottinger would be admitted. I thanked him.

After Tillerson tried to exclude Pottinger, I went to the vice president for advice. I could deal with Tillerson's hostile demeanor, but I was concerned about its effect on our ability to serve the president. I told him that, in addition to excluding NSC personnel from meetings, the State Department was withholding personnel from normal rotation to the NSC staff. I mentioned that I had asked Tillerson for a one-on-one meeting. I suspect Pence encouraged him to agree to it. I regretted having to ask the vice president to act like a vice principal of a high school, but it was the only option short of bringing the deterioration in the relationship to Trump.

Tillerson arrived for our June 30 meeting with his chief of staff, Margaret Peterlin. A meeting on the National Security Strategy was just breaking up, so I asked Nadia Schadlow, who had the lead for the strategy, to stay for what became a two-on-two meeting. The grievances Tillerson aired were ones we had already acted upon and rectified. He was not getting read-aheads on time; I told him that we sent them out at least three days in advance but that, in the future, would send them directly to him and Peterlin. He wanted more long-range predictability; I showed him the "horse blanket" calendar with events, presidential travel, principals committee meetings, and backward planning milestones for all the above. He raised "implementation by the White House;" I reminded him that every case to which he had objected had been at the behest of or approved by people in his department. He raised "inappropriate communications" by Nikki Haley, in particular, a speech she had given on Iran. I told him that I could not find any daylight between Haley's statements and the president's positions, while promising to send draft talking points for all key issues to him for approval before distributing them to the rest of the cabinet.

The sit-down wasn't going well. I emphasized the purpose of the NSC and used 9/11 as an example of the dangers associated with a lack of coordination among agencies. Tillerson's centralization in the department, combined with his inaccessibility, was slowing everything down. He was sabotaging the process by telling assistant secretaries not to attend White House meetings and withholding personnel. I explained that this behavior was not hurting me; it was hurting the president's ability to set his foreign policy agenda and make timely decisions.

"Rex, you wanted fewer in-person PCs, but you are not replying to paper PCs on time," I said. "And we send our coordinated materials in advance, but then you 'table-drop' briefings, so no one has an opportunity to read them in advance, and remote stations cannot access them at all."

"I want it that way," he responded.

We were clearly getting nowhere. The most productive agreement that emerged from our discussion was that to improve coordination among key cabinet officials, we would conduct brief phone conferences every Tuesday and Friday morning.

But I knew that the real problem was not lack of coordination or read-aheads or too many meetings or the planning horizon. The problem was, Tillerson and Mattis had decided to run foreign and defense policy. They viewed the president's disruptive tendencies as dangerous.

Mattis had started saying he was determined to ensure that "reason triumphs over impulse." It was clear that he and Tillerson were playing the role of reason and that Trump had been cast as impulse. That is why I did not take personal offense to their obstructionist or even their occasionally rude and petty behavior. They seemed to have concluded that Trump was an emergency and that anyone abetting him was an adversary. While Bannon had viewed my efforts to give Trump options as constraining the president from the alt-right agenda that he and many Trump voters wanted to advance, Mattis and Tillerson viewed my efforts as enabling a president who was a danger to the Constitution.

Trump's denial of the 2020 presidential election results and his encouragement of the January 6, 2021, assault on the Capitol Building might be invoked as an *ex post facto* justification for their behavior. But in August 2017, I was just trying to help the elected president set his own course for foreign policy and national security. I saw many of Trump's disruptions as opportunities to challenge and reverse what I believed were failing policy approaches, from the Middle East to South Asia, from the Indo-Pacific to Northeast Asia. Besides, the only person who had been elected was Trump, and he had the right to make disruptive decisions consistent with his authorities under Article II of the Constitution.

A secondary explanation for Tillerson's and Mattis's behavior may have been as simple as proximity. The NSC staff and the national security advisor are close to the Oval Office. Cabinet secretaries are farther away. Normally, the Departments of State and Defense are at loggerheads. But because Mattis and Tillerson were playing a competitive game of influence, they had aligned closely with each other, in part to compensate for the disadvantage of distance. I tried and failed to convince them that I was not in competition with them. I worked every day to give them greater access and to amplify rather than mute their voices. Whenever the president asked, "What do you think, General?" on questions that had policy implications, I would say something like "Let me consult with your cabinet and some experts and get back to you" or "We should have a discussion with Secretary Tillerson and Secretary Mattis on that."

Finally, Tillerson and Mattis may have bought into Washington bureaucratic cultural folklore in which the NSC staff and the national security advisor appear as the usurpers of departments' authority and prerogatives. Tillerson—like me, new to Washington—had been warned about the dangers of an overbearing NSA. Both men were close with Bob Gates, former secretary of defense, CIA director, and deputy national security advisor, who had shared his frustrations with an Obama administration NSC staff that grew to 450 people, lamenting, "It was that micromanaging that drove me crazy."[10]

But ours was not the Susan Rice NSC staff, and no one was trying to run an operation out of the EEOB.

The tragedy is that Mattis and Tillerson were playing a zero-sum power game. Sometimes their actions seemed petty, but they were designed to put the NSC staff and me in our place. Mattis's assistance with Tillerson was a temporary phenomenon. As I came under attack from the alt-right and the Russians, Mattis arranged a call with me that I thought might be an offer of assistance or encouragement. Instead, he informed me that he had decided that all military personnel detailed to the White House would have to wear their uniforms while on duty. If I wanted any exceptions, I could send a memo to a colonel on his staff.

I responded, "Mr. Secretary, you cannot be serious. Do you even know what I am dealing with over here?" Mattis knew that officers detailed to the NSC staff wear civilian clothes so people in the U.S. government and foreign counterparts do not confuse their military rank with their position. He did not raise the subject again.

Mattis and Tillerson seemed to believe that undermining me, the NSC process, or the NSC staff would garner more influence for them. But the more independent of the president and the White House they became, the less effective they would be. And the more they impeded coordination, the more difficult it would be to sustain a consistent approach to the nation's most important challenges to security and prosperity. As a senior State Department official observed years later, "I didn't understand why the Secretary [Tillerson] had to pick fights with the White House . . . I mean with H.R. in particular. . . . It undermined his own effectiveness as the primary formulator, implementer of foreign policy."[11]

I had tried everything I could think of to improve the relationship. I am sure I made mistakes. I remained calm and respectful in our interactions, but I am terrible at masking emotion. I might have complained directly to the president, but I really did want Tillerson and Mattis to maintain a good relationship with Trump and help the president develop and implement his foreign policy and defense agenda.

Moreover, I had realized that Trump was not a team builder. He enjoyed and contributed to interpersonal drama in the White House and across the administration.

CHAPTER 13

MOVEMENT IN A RESISTANT ELEMENT

Deadly Barcelona attack is worst in a day of violence in Spain . . . **PRESIDENT UNVEILS NEW AFGHANISTAN, SOUTH ASIA STRATEGY** . . . Trump is expected to deploy about **4,000 more troops to Afghanistan** and try to tighten expectations on its government and that of neighboring Pakistan . . . Trump says U.S. can't afford 'hasty' withdrawal from Afghanistan . . . *'WE ARE NOT NATION-BUILDING AGAIN,' TRUMP SAYS WHILE UNVEILING AFGHANISTAN STRATEGY* . . . former Afghan president Hamid Karzai [denounced] Trump's strategy as "a clear message of killing, killing, killing" . . . Afghanistan endorses Trump's revised strategy; Taliban warns of 'graveyard' . . . **"OUR TROOPS WILL FIGHT TO WIN," TRUMP SAID** . . . *TRUMP'S AFGHANISTAN WAR STRATEGY: USE MILITARY TO FORCE PEACE TALKS WITH TALIBAN* . . . The Pentagon has described the war as a "stalemate" . . . **TRUMP'S AFGHANISTAN STRATEGY TURNS UP THE HEAT ON PAKISTAN** . . . *PUTIN, RESPONDING TO SANCTIONS, ORDERS U.S. TO CUT DIPLOMATIC STAFF BY 755* . . . **U.S. RETALIATES AGAINST RUSSIA, ORDERS CLOSURE OF CONSULATE, ANNEXES** . . . Trump mulling withdrawal from Korea trade deal . . . **NORTH KOREAN NUCLEAR TEST DRAWS U.S. WARNING OF 'MASSIVE MILITARY RESPONSE'** . . . *POSSIBLE TWO-STAGE HYDROGEN BOMB SEEN 'GAME CHANGER' FOR NORTH KOREA* . . . Trump Moves Closer to Decertification of Iran Nuclear Deal . . . **TILLERSON, MATTIS, MCMASTER PRESENT IRAN PLAN TO TRUMP** . . . *DONALD TRUMP DENOUNCES IRAN OVER NUCLEAR DEAL*

FRIDAY, AUGUST 18, 2017, would be the second time that Trump used Camp David. Trump, who favored resorts that bore his name, had been pleasantly surprised by the 125-acre presidential retreat in Maryland. Navy Seabees do a phenomenal job maintaining the grounds and the structures, which include guest cabins, a chapel, Aspen Lodge (the president's guest house), and Laurel Lodge (a meeting and conference facility).

I stayed home that morning. White House Military Office couriers delivered the PDB book. I read it in the SCIF. ISIS terrorist attacks in Barcelona on Thursday had killed 13 people and injured at least 130 others. I locked the book in its bag and placed it in the safe before joining several conference calls.

Just before noon, I walked out of Quarters 13, past the old officers' club, and to the edge of the large lawn on the north side of Roosevelt Hall that serves as the helicopter landing zone for Fort McNair. I joined my colleagues there in time to recommend that they turn their backs to the U.S. Marine Corps Osprey tilt-rotor aircraft as they hovered and landed, buffeting us with the rotor wash. As we walked up the ramps and sat facing each other along the bulkheads, I wondered how our NSC meeting with the president at Camp David would end.

I reflected on what had become the saga of the South Asia strategy. The first obstacle had been the State and Defense Departments' unwillingness to abandon flawed assumptions and develop options other than the withdrawal strategy that was leading to slow failure.

In our first principals committee meeting, on July 16, Tillerson had table-dropped a briefing coordinated with Defense that started with three premises: a tougher approach to Pakistan is unlikely to lead to improvements in the Pakistani Army's behavior; an Afghan military victory over the Taliban is unattainable; and there is a viable political path to a negotiated agreement with the Taliban. It was as if all the work the NSC had coordinated since May had been discarded.

It had been equally difficult to convince Trump to consider alternatives to withdrawal. The alt-right and isolationists had been in his ear, as had those lobbying to turn the war over to private security contractors. Members of the White House staff had fed the press disinformation to portray me as tricking Trump into abandoning his promise to withdraw. Despite my best efforts to get the president into a good frame of mind for the first NSC meeting on the South Asia strategy on July 19, that meeting had been a disaster. Trump immediately went into harassment mode, railing against the "stupid people" who had "wasted trillions of dollars." Would the second NSC meeting on the South Asia strategy, at Camp David, be any different?

After the first meeting, we had regrouped. Pence exhorted the principals to show Trump "what winning looks like." I directed our staff to develop two alternatives to the status quo: withdrawal and sustained commitment with a more effective approach to helping Afghan forces fight the Taliban. But most important, I worked to expose Trump to a wider range of perspectives, including the intelligence officers he had met at Bedminster. At the suggestion of Pence, I called General Dunford to coordinate lunch in the Roosevelt Room with military officers and noncommissioned officers who had completed multiple and recent tours in Afghanistan. Before Trump's meeting with them, I had welcomed the three Army noncommissioned officers and an Air Force officer into my office. I told Master Sgt. Henry Adames, Maj. Eric Birch, Master Sgt. Zachary Bannon, and First Sgt. Michael Wagner that the president had a lot of people in his ear and that he needed to hear from those who had been fighting the war. "There are no right or wrong answers to his questions. Just answer honestly and stick to what you know."

We walked to the Roosevelt Room. After introductions, the president asked the press pool to come in for some photos. As lunch was served, I asked each service member to introduce himself and describe his experience in Afghanistan. As the vice president excused himself for another meeting, Trump asked them, referring to Afghanistan, "Do you want to go back?"

They answered all together: "Yes, Mr. President."

Trump was puzzled. "Why?" he asked.

Master Sergeant Bannon answered, "Mr. President, we want to finish the job [against the enemy] so our children and grandchildren don't have to go there."

Trump then asked what we needed to do differently.

They described, with examples, the inconsistent short-term approach to the war, the restrictions on the use of force against the

Taliban, the lack of assets such as surveillance platforms and close air support, the troop caps that had forced them to break up teams, and the terrorist haven in Pakistan. They were honest and direct about corruption among Afghan forces: the diversion of assistance and money and the "ghost" soldiers on the rolls.

But contrary to the content of Tillerson's table-dropped briefing of the following day, the soldiers and airman told Trump that, with the proper authorities, sufficient assets, and adequate numbers of special operations forces as advisors, the Afghans could win. They then asked Trump to lift restrictive rules of engagement, asking why the rules were more restrictive in Afghanistan than they were in Syria. When Trump asked why the war was important, the service members were adamant that our operations in Afghanistan in support of Afghan forces were preventing attacks in the United States.

The meeting went well. I could see that our servicemen had challenged Trump's prejudices. But in the months that followed, the president would revise his memory of that meeting to realign with those prejudices. Trump would claim that the soldiers had criticized their commanders. They had not. They had merely noted that some NATO officers on the staff were not familiar with the U.S.-only counterterrorism fight.

In multiple conversations with Trump over the weeks prior to the Camp David meeting, I told him, "You are right to be frustrated over the war. All of us who served in Afghanistan are frustrated. We have been fighting under a withdrawal strategy for eight years. Maybe that has something to do with the lack of progress. We told the Taliban we are leaving and then tried to negotiate a deal with them. How the hell is any of that going to work? Let us give you options, and after we do, if you decide to get out, we will get out." Pence and Kelly had reinforced that message.

As I looked out the window as our aircraft paralleled the Potomac River into Maryland and then turned north toward Catoctin Mountain, I wondered if I had violated the Scowcroft model and become more of a policy advocate on South Asia than an "honest broker." But I had fought to give the president a choice beyond the status quo, what I saw as a slow, painful path to failure in Afghanistan.

★   ★   ★

UPON ARRIVAL at Camp David, we joined the president for lunch around the long rectangular table in the Laurel Lodge dining area. The president was in a good mood, and the conversation was relaxed. After lunch, we moved into the large conference room. The president sat at the center of one of the table's longer sides, rather than at the head. I sat to his left. Ricky Waddell sat across from us. Members of the NSC and Lisa Curtis, senior director for South and Central Asia, and John Eisenberg filled out the table. My chief of staff, Ylli, sat behind me.

I had decided that it would be more effective for Ricky to narrate the courses of action, after which the president would hear from his advisors. Leaks and disinformation associated with our previous deliberations had portrayed me as an advocate for a much larger commitment of troops than any of the options under consideration called for. I did not want the messenger to taint the message.

I gave only a brief introduction: "Good afternoon, Mr. President. The purpose of this meeting is to obtain your decision on the South Asia strategy. After General Waddell summarizes the courses of action, you will hear the assessments and recommendations of your National Security Council."

Ricky's delivery was clear and succinct. Trump listened attentively to the courses of action and the recommendations of all his advisors. Each offered their endorsement of the recommended South Asia strategy, which included expanding the strategic relationship with India, removing the time limit on U.S. military support for the Afghan armed forces, lifting restrictions on U.S. forces, and ending the delusion that Pakistan was an ally in that fight. Sessions was candid about his reluctance to recommend a sustained commitment but said that after hearing the cost and consequences of withdrawal, he believed that the new approach could accomplish the mission at acceptable cost and risk.

After everyone spoke, Trump turned to me and said, "What do you think, General?"

"Mr. President, it won't surprise you that I believe that the recommended option is the best way to secure America's vital interests.

You would establish a sound policy for the region and the first long-term, sustainable strategy to win in Afghanistan."

Trump approved the recommended South Asia strategy.

Before we departed, Kelly asked all of us to pose for a photo as Trump signed the presidential decision memorandum directing implementation. The president would announce the decision and explain the strategy on Monday in a speech at Fort Myer, Virginia. Over the weekend, we would finalize our communications rollout and plan to inform key allies and members of Congress. Kelly told everyone that he expected that there would be no leaks. With Bannon gone, there were none.

★   ★   ★

AS WE lined up for cars, several cabinet members thanked me for running a process that gave all of them a voice and resulted in the best available outcome. I thanked them in return. In the midst of attacks on the NSC staff and me, the Charlottesville controversy, and multiple personnel changes, including a new White House chief of staff, we had helped Trump challenge assumptions, understand a complex problem set, consider multiple options, and make a sound decision. The collaborative process had worked under duress and delivered. The long saga of the South Asia strategy demonstrated that Trump did not need to be controlled or fed carefully selected information. He needed a wide range of perspectives and multiple options.

On Monday evening, I walked through the Rose Garden to the Residence and then up the steps to join the president and First Lady; their son, Barron; Jared and Ivanka; Stephen Miller; and Trump's longtime bodyguard, former New York City police officer Keith Schiller, in the living room. When Miller and I had reviewed the speech with Trump earlier in the day, he seemed to take full ownership of it and the strategy it announced. The president had taken out one of his medium-point Sharpies and partly written, partly dictated the following paragraph:

> My original instinct was to pull out—and, historically, I like
> following my instincts. But all my life I've heard that decisions

are much different when you sit behind the desk in the Oval
Office; in other words, when you're President of the United
States. So I studied Afghanistan in great detail and from every
conceivable angle. After many meetings, over many months,
we held our final meeting last Friday at Camp David, with my
Cabinet and generals, to complete our strategy.[1]

But now, as I sat across from him on one of the white couches just
hours after he had written those words and approved a speech that
contained a commitment to "fight to win" through "attacking our
enemies, obliterating ISIS, crushing al-Qaeda, preventing the Taliban from taking over Afghanistan, and stopping mass terror attacks
against America before they emerge," Trump was wavering. Like a
groom getting cold feet on his wedding day, he turned to his "best
man," Schiller, and asked, "What do you think? Am I doing the right
thing?"

Schiller, like many Americans, had imbibed the "graveyard of
empires" argument regarding Afghanistan. He thought that the
United States was doomed to fail there, just as the British and the
Soviets had failed before us. Schiller also echoed the criticism that
the United States and our allies were wasting money and resources
trying to remake Afghanistan in an alien, Western image.

As Trump looked back at me, I expressed respect for Keith and his
views, but reminded the president that he had heard similar opinions many times over the past six months. His speech would make
clear that Afghans were "fighting to defend and secure *their* country
against the same enemies who threaten us." We were not in Afghanistan to fulfill imperial ambitions; we were helping Afghans "build
their own nation and define their own future."

I went on: "Mr. President, your speech rejects the use of 'American military might to construct democracies in faraway lands or try
to rebuild other countries in our own image.' As you have heard me
say many times, Afghanistan does not need to be Denmark for this
strategy to succeed."

With a look of resignation, he responded, "Okay, General, let's go."

As we stood, he said what I would hear many times over the coming months: "I am doing this for you."

And I responded as I did every time: "Mr. President, you made the right decision for our nation. You should never do anything for me."

As our motorcade passed Arlington National Cemetery and entered the gates of Fort Myer, I thought of our servicemen and -women and especially the Gold Star families of those who had made the ultimate sacrifice in Afghanistan—including the Kelly family, whose son Robert was killed in action in Helmand Province, Afghanistan, on November 9, 2010. Much of the president's speech that day was dedicated to them: "Now we must secure the cause for which they gave their lives. We must unite to defend America from its enemies abroad. We must restore the bonds of loyalty among our citizens at home, and we must achieve an honorable and enduring outcome worthy of the enormous price that so many have paid."

When Trump delivered those lines and ended the speech with "Thank you. May God bless our military. And may God bless the United States of America," the audience of mainly servicemen and -women gave him a round of applause much louder than the pro forma ovations expected for a commander in chief.

In the speech, Trump outlined the dramatic changes in the strategy, including "a shift from a time-based approach to one based on conditions." The United States would "not talk about numbers of troops or our plans for further military activities." The strategy would emphasize "the integration of all instruments of American power—diplomatic, economic, and military—toward a successful outcome."

I had drafted a few lines so Trump could deliver an unambiguous message to a Pentagon that had resisted earlier efforts to lift restrictions and ensure that troops had the authorities and the assets necessary to accomplish the mission:

> . . . the brave defenders of the American people, will have the necessary tools and rules of engagement to make this strategy work, and work effectively and work quickly.
>
> I have already lifted restrictions the previous administration placed on our warfighters that prevented the Secretary of Defense and our commanders in the field from fully and swiftly waging battle against the enemy. That's why we will

also expand authority for American armed forces to target the terrorist and criminal networks that sow violence and chaos throughout Afghanistan.

On negotiations, Trump made clear that military gains were necessary to get to an acceptable agreement: "Someday, after an effective military effort, perhaps it will be possible to have a political settlement that includes elements of the Taliban in Afghanistan, but nobody knows if or when that will ever happen." Despite that clear guidance, the State Department would continue to pursue negotiations with the Taliban while the Defense Department clung to the perverse rationale that an intensified military effort against them might impede rather than incentivize negotiations.

The message to Pakistani leaders was unambiguous: "We can no longer be silent about Pakistan's safe havens for terrorist organizations, the Taliban, and other groups that pose a threat to the region and beyond." Trump noted that "we have been paying Pakistan billions and billions of dollars at the same time they are housing the very terrorists that we are fighting. But that will have to change, and that will change immediately. No partnership can survive a country's harboring of militants and terrorists who target U.S. service members and officials." It would also remain a struggle to get State and Defense to stop providing aid to the Pakistanis.

The *Washington Post* reported that former Afghan president Hamid Karzai and Pakistani leaders were unhappy with the South Asia speech. I considered those reactions a positive sign. At home, the reaction to the speech was mainly positive, even in a mainstream media environment generally hostile to everything Donald Trump did.

The president made a good decision and a courageous one, having been aware that elements of his base were calling for "ending endless wars." But I was concerned: Trump was already wavering. Implementation of the strategy would be critical. The best way to allay his concerns over his base would be to demonstrate success in Afghanistan and across the region.

★   ★   ★

AT THE end of August, I planned to focus on two important integrated strategies: Russia and Iran. Both were ready to go to the president. Trump had gained a greater appreciation for the threat from Russia, which was now demanding that the United States reduce the staff in our Moscow embassy by 755 personnel. In response, Trump had approved the closure of the consulate general and official residence in San Francisco and of trade mission offices in New York and Washington. The closures dealt a significant blow to Russia's intelligence network in the United States, which was integral to its sustained campaigns of political subversion and information warfare. Although Trump still clung to his forlorn hope for a game-changing entente with Putin, his penchant for reciprocity overcame his reluctance to take strong action.

We scheduled an NSC meeting on Iran for September 8 and one on Russia for later in the month. Labor Day Weekend, I thought, would give me an opportunity to review both strategies. But Labor Day was a holiday, and spoiling holidays is what Kim Jung-un does.

As I prepared Trump for a September 1 phone call with President Moon, he wanted to discuss trade with South Korea rather than the threat from North Korea. Navarro had renewed calls for the president to withdraw from KORUS *before* attempting to renegotiate it. Given the importance of staying aligned with South Korea on the maximum pressure strategy, I recommended renegotiation. I told Trump that I had just met in San Francisco with my South Korean and Japanese counterparts and that Seoul was ready to share more of the defense burden and renegotiate KORUS. Shouldn't we demonstrate unity with South Korea as we confronted the threat from North Korea's missile and nuclear programs? Trump agreed to talk to Moon about renegotiating rather than withdrawing from KORUS.

The phone call started well. Trump reinforced his expectation that Moon appear strong. It was time "to stick out our chest and see if we can get it [denuclearization] done." Trump stressed that "it is not time to talk." He also reiterated his expectation of "reciprocal" trade, but he did not say that he intended to pull out of KORUS. In the coming days, Navarro would try, even in the wake of a North Korea nuclear test, to push Trump's buttons with phrases like it "looks strong to get out [of KORUS]." But Trump responded that while "we need to get a better deal at some point, we need to play it cool."

Thirty-six hours separated the conversation with Moon from a phone call I received at home around 11 p.m. North Korea had conducted its sixth nuclear test, what Pyongyang claimed was a hydrogen bomb.

I staffed the president for a flurry of phone calls over the next several days—with Moon, Abe, Xi, Merkel, and Prime Minister Malcolm Turnbull of Australia. Trump stressed the urgency of the situation and the need for greater efforts to maximize pressure on the Kim regime. He pushed Xi to cut off aviation fuel and finished petroleum products while conveying his expectation that China support additional UN Security Council sanctions. But Xi resurrected some of the old language of moral equivalence, calling for "a balanced approach to all parties."

I wondered if Xi was pushing back on maximum pressure due to the belief that Tillerson and Mattis's "peaceful pressure" language indicated that Trump was not serious about a military option. But it was actually worse: in contravention to the strategy, Tillerson and the State Department were continuing to pursue talks with North Korea and asking China to be an interlocutor.

Xi might have also been encouraged to go back to "a balanced approach" by Trump's stated belief that U.S. military exercises were "provocative" and an unnecessary expense. Trump's reluctance to apply the military dimension of pressure on the North could create space for China to advocate for another "freeze-for-freeze" agreement.

★   ★   ★

WHILE THE friction in implementation of the North Korea strategy came from within the administration, the main resistance to developing a sound Iran strategy originated from outside. European allies had come to regard the Iran nuclear deal, the JCPOA, as an article of faith and were trying to convince Trump to stay in it. Many in the Republican Party had come to see getting out as an end in itself.

I was sympathetic to the statement that candidate Trump had made many times in 2016 when he described the JCPOA as "the worst deal ever." The Obama administration had wanted to separate the deal from Iran's proxy wars, but the deal gave the regime a cash payment of $1.7 billion up front and a subsequent payout of approximately $100 billion in unfrozen assets. As cash flowed to the regime, Iran used the windfall to intensify its proxy wars and expand sectarian conflicts in the region. In the words of former CENTCOM commander Gen. Joseph Votel, Iran grew "more aggressive in the days [after] the agreement."

Although President Trump was eager to get out of the "terrible deal," I wanted to give him comprehensive options and to consider the effects. Staying in the JCPOA in the near term, despite common knowledge of his inclination to get out, would create leverage for us to isolate the Iranian regime diplomatically as well as economically. Trump could use that leverage to get others to support fixing the deal's flaws.

The effort to give Trump options for an overall Iran strategy into which the JCPOA decisions fit, instead of viewing "stay or get out" in isolation, created more tension with Mattis and Tillerson and with Trump supporters who had concluded that getting out fast was an unmitigated good. Tillerson and Mattis were in favor of staying in the agreement, but after a principals framing session in May, they dragged their feet on the development of options for an overall Iran strategy while Trump got more impatient.

We finally held our NSC Iran meeting on September 8, Jim Mattis's birthday; Dina Powell brought cupcakes. The meeting had obviously leaked. A flurry of op-eds advocating for staying in the Iran deal or getting out appeared as foreign leaders called to try to make one final argument to stay in. In the days prior to the meeting, I tried to elevate the discussion and focus on the overall policy. I briefed Trump in the Oval Office, emphasizing the ideology that drove the Iran regime's "permanent hostility to the United States, Israel, and its Arab neighbors." I handed Trump a note card with goals he had already approved: Iran's malign influence and power neutralized; a durable balance of power in the region restored; a cessation to Iran's hostility to the United States and our allies. The NSC meeting went smoothly. Trump was very clear that he wanted "maximum sanctions on Iran and North Korea."

Time is an important dimension of strategy. Tillerson and Mattis's delay of the South Asia strategy turned out to be fortuitous, because it gave Trump the time he needed to evolve his understanding of the nature of the war, the enemies we were fighting, and what was at stake for the American people and our nation's vital interests. On Iran, however, the lack of clarity due to multiple delays gave space to the president's critics and those focused on the narrow issue of staying in or getting out of the nuclear agreement. Much of the tension with Mattis, Tillerson, and me was over how hard I was pressing to get options in front of the president for the South Asia strategy, Iran, and Russia. Soon, tensions over the implementation of decisions the president had already made would surpass those associated with getting new policies in place.

Even when the tensions from the power game resulted in personal insults, I instructed our team to ignore them. For example, on one occasion, I departed early from a widely attended conference call following a DPRK missile test to staff the president for a call with a foreign leader. Secretary Mattis was unaware that my deputy, Ricky Waddell, and Director for Korea Allison Hooker had remained in my office to listen to the rest of the call on speaker. When Tillerson complained that I was pushing too hard to develop contingencies for North Korea, Mattis expressed sympathy by describing me as an "unstable asshole." When Ricky told me this, he said he was shocked and did not know what to do. He apologized for not interjecting to defend me. I told him that he did the right thing. It was best to ignore the insult.

Despite the friction from inside and outside the White House, however, our team was making progress on a range of strategic documents important for communicating and implementing the president's agenda, including the National Security Strategy, the Nuclear Posture Review, and the Space Strategy.

The national security decision-making process had been stress-tested and had delivered results in the form of sound policies oriented on priority national security challenges from actors ranging from Russia to North Korea, to Iran, to South Asia and the war in

Afghanistan, to Venezuela and Cuba, to China and a comprehensive framework for the Indo-Pacific region.

My personal efforts to form a more collaborative relationship with Tillerson and Mattis were not succeeding, but our senior directors had cultivated very positive relationships across all the departments and agencies. Our two deputies, Ricky and Dina, worked very well with their counterparts at State and Defense. Consistent with the saying that you can get a lot done if you don't care who gets the credit, our senior directors and deputies had coordinated in advance many of the documents that Tillerson and Mattis received from their internal policy offices.

Moreover, I had high hopes that General Kelly would help reduce the friction with Tillerson and Mattis. But by the fall of 2017, I had concluded that the compounding power games inside the White House and between the White House and the State and Defense Departments would be like friction in war—a permanent condition. And it was unlikely that the acrimonious political and media environments would improve. We were moving in a resistant element, but we were moving.

Of course, the main judge of my effectiveness was down the hall, in the Oval Office. Trump had stood by me when I was under full-scale assault. But with Bannon ejected from the White House, those who wanted me out of my job would expand their avenues of attack.

CHAPTER 14

CONTRADICTION
AND CONTENTION

TRUMP TAKES AGENDA OF CHANGE TO THE UNITED NATIONS . . . In first visit, Trump urges reform so U.N. can meet full potential . . . *A BLUNT, FEARFUL RANT: TRUMP'S UN SPEECH LEFT PRESIDENTIAL NORMS IN THE DUST* . . . With Combative Style and Epithets, Trump Takes America First to the U.N. . . . Mr. Trump promised to **"CRUSH LOSER TERRORISTS,"** mocked North Korea's leader as **"ROCKET MAN"** and declared that parts of the world **"ARE GOING TO HELL"** . . . At U.N., Trump Singles Out 'Rogue' Nations North Korea and Iran . . . Trump says democracy must be restored in Venezuela soon . . . *FRANCE'S PRESIDENT DEFIES TRUMP AT THE UN* . . . **TRUMP GIVES THE U.N. HIS VISION OF A WORLD GOVERNED BY SELF-INTEREST** . . . Hurricane Maria strikes US territory of Puerto Rico . . . *IRAQI KURDS SET TO VOTE ON INDEPENDENCE, PANICKING NEIGHBORS AND WASHINGTON* . . . Iraqi Kurds decisively back independence in referendum . . . **WHAT THE HELL HAPPENED IN NIGER?** . . . **U.S. MILITARY RE-EVALUATES MISSION IN NIGER AFTER DEADLY ATTACK** . . . *Islamic State ambush killed four elite U.S. soldiers* . . . President Trump on Sunday said Rex Tillerson is "wasting his time" by trying to negotiate with North Korean leader Kim Jong Un . . . Turkish troops enter northern Syria in new operation . . . **REX TILLERSON AT THE BREAKING POINT**

ON THE anniversary of the mass murder attacks of September 11, 2001, I walked through the Diplomatic Reception Room and out the South Portico. I remembered how the 9/11 attacks had united Americans, and I lamented the growing discord in the country across the sixteen years since. I allowed myself to hope that the memory of 9/11 might help Americans prioritize what we had in common rather than what divided us. The terrorists on 9/11 did not discriminate based on race, ethnicity, religion, political affiliation, or any other identity category. For us White House staffers, I hoped that the ceremony might inspire us to prioritize our solemn duty to our fellow citizens over the backstabbing and political infighting with which some had been preoccupied.

The president and First Lady walked out of the Residence just before 8:46, the time that American Airlines Flight 11 struck the North Tower of the World Trade Center. A hush fell over us. After a moment of silence, an Army bugler played the twenty-four mournful notes that comprise taps.

As staffers walked quietly back to their offices, I joined the president's motorcade for the short drive to the Pentagon. Upon arrival, we walked into the two-acre outdoor memorial honoring the 184 people, including 59 jetliner crew and passengers, whose lives were lost there at 9:37 a.m. on that infamous day.

Trump's speech was meant to promote resilience, rejuvenation, and unity. He promised "resolve to do whatever we must to keep our people safe," including sustaining the fight against jihadist terrorists and ensuring that "they never again have a safe haven to launch attacks against our country." Trump, referring to "that hour of darkness" in 2001, noted that Americans "came together with renewed purpose. Our differences never looked so small; our common bonds never felt so strong."

After Charlottesville, I had worked with speechwriters Ross Worthington and Vince Haley to include those messages of unity. But as was too often the case, while Trump's words were strong, his commitment to them was weak. In 2019, I would watch with incredulity and revulsion as he directed an envoy to negotiate U.S. withdrawal with the Taliban, invited members of that terrorist organization to Camp David on the anniversary of 9/11, and then canceled via tweet what would have been a humiliating scene after expressing shock that the Taliban had murdered more people in Kabul. He tweeted, "What kind of people would kill so many in order to seemingly strengthen their bargaining position?"

The answer lay in the speech he had given at the Pentagon: "savage killers" whom he had vowed to pursue relentlessly and destroy.

Maybe I should have seen all that coming. I had fought to guard Trump's independence of judgment, and he was making, from my perspective, good decisions. But helping him stick to those decisions required constant engagement, as he was no longer questioning only Obama's policies. He was beginning to challenge his own decisions.

★　　★　　★

BUT IN autumn 2017, I still believed that Trump's unconventional nature held promise for deterring adversaries and improving America's ability to advance our security and economic interests. It was my intention to help him do that during part of the UN General Assembly meeting in New York City from Monday, September 18, through Thursday, September 21.

Metaphors for the three-week long UNGA meeting include diplomatic circus, political speed-dating, a cocktail party where everyone talks but no one listens, and the world's most expensive open mic night. But the UNGA presents an opportunity for the American president to advance foreign policy objectives. And Trump could do so from the comfort of his penthouse in Trump Tower without the travel anxiety he experiences on long trips.

The main event at the UNGA is a general debate, but the most important work occurs on the sidelines of the assembly, in bilateral and multilateral meetings with counterparts. Our overall goal for this General Assembly was to foster unity of effort behind weakening the rogue authoritarian regimes of North Korea, Iran, and Venezuela and to increase pressure on their key sponsors, China and Russia.

On September 18, the fast-paced four days began with an early morning phone call with Xi Jinping, who was skipping the UNGA, from the president's penthouse apartment on the sixty-sixth floor of Trump Tower.

It was my first visit to Trump's New York home, whose Louis XIV–style décor makes Mar-a-Lago look understated. I reminded Trump that the main purpose of the call was to give advance notice of sanctions on any foreign financial institutions facilitating "any significant transaction in connection with trade with North Korea."

Xi would no doubt object. Moreover, he was eager to appear strong going into the Communist Party Congress scheduled for October, so the time to push was right. Trump assured Xi that he would not take any actions that might spoil the vibe prior to the Congress. And Xi urged Trump to finalize the date for what he promised would be a very special state visit in Beijing.

The call went long, and the window for our coordinated motorcade was closing. The UNGA snarls Manhattan traffic, and if we missed the motorcade window, there could be riots in Midtown. We got to UN Headquarters just in time to join UN secretary-general António Guterres and Ambassador Haley for a session that Haley had organized.

Guterres, like Stoltenberg at NATO, used Trump's criticisms to galvanize reforms. Trump stated that the United Nations was in "an unhealthy state" while urging Guterres and the delegates to "start the healing process."

I returned to my makeshift office at the Lotte New York Palace Hotel, on Fiftieth and Madison, to review with Stephen Miller the speech the president would give the following day. The hook would be the seventieth anniversary of the Marshall Plan to highlight America's role in helping Europe and the world rebuild after the most destructive war in history. The speech would call for reform of international organizations while galvanizing pressure on rogue authoritarian regimes and their sponsors.

The speech was solid. Trump's speeches were sometimes too long, too strident, and overburdened with patriotic clichés and flowery language. But the main themes were straightforward, such as the call to confront and deter aggression from "Ukraine to the South China Sea."

Miller and I had labored to reconcile contradictions in Trump's worldview. Some of these were confounding:

Trump believed in American exceptionalism and that the United States was a force for good in the world, but he often manifested moral equivalence.

He was viscerally opposed to communist and socialist dictatorships but was ambivalent at best about the dictators of Russia and China.

He was skeptical about long-term military commitments overseas, but he believed in peace through strength and recognized the need to defeat jihadist terrorists who threatened the homeland or U.S. citizens abroad.

He abhorred democracy promotion abroad but understood that autocrats that bandwagon with Russia and China diminished American power and influence.

He wanted alliances and international organizations to share security and development burdens but viewed multilateral organizations as threats to U.S. sovereignty and their member nations as free riders on American largesse.

He found it difficult even to utter the phrase "human rights" but became impassioned when he witnessed cruelty, such as the serial episodes of mass murder in Syria.

He wanted fair and reciprocal trade and economic relationships but was biased against trade agreements that might advance those objectives.

The UNGA speech was an effort to resolve Trump's paradoxes and lay a conceptual foundation for his foreign policy. One overall mechanism to do so, previewed in the July 6, 2017, speech in Warsaw, was the need to safeguard the sovereignty of nations in which citizens enjoyed liberty and had a say in how they were governed. In New York, Trump would receive applause for the line "We do not expect diverse countries to share the same cultures, traditions, or even systems of government," though he went on to state that "we do expect all nations to uphold these two core sovereign duties: to respect the interests of their own people and the rights of every other sovereign nation."

To clarify Trump's view of America's role in the world, and counter those who accused the United States of imperialist designs, the speech cited the Marshall Plan as evidence that "the United States of America has been among the greatest forces for good in the history of the world, and the greatest defenders of sovereignty, security, and prosperity for all."

Much of the speech was about human rights without using the phrase directly. He singled out the regimes of Cuba, Venezuela, Iran, Syria, and North Korea, noting that "wherever true socialism or communism has been adopted, it has delivered anguish and devastation and failure."

In retrospect, we had crafted a coherent statement of policy while remaining true to Trump's agendas on sharing burdens, reforming international organizations, and demanding fair and reciprocal trade. There was a warning that America "can no longer be taken advantage of or enter into a one-sided deal where the United States gets nothing in return" and an expectation that member nations bear more of the United Nations' costs and "take a greater role in promoting secure and prosperous societies in their own regions."

Most important for the audience to hear was that the United States was not disengaging, but would pursue policies "rooted in shared goals, interests, and values." Trump closed with the observation that "making a better life for our people also requires us to work together in close harmony and unity to create a more safe [*sic*] and peaceful future for all people."

I put the speech aside and thanked Miller for his and his team's collaborative work. We had agreed to a label for our effort to make sense of Trump's paradoxes: "principled realism."

★   ★   ★

THE PRESIDENT arrived at the hotel just as Miller and I finished the final review of the speech. He joined Kelly, Tillerson, and me in a makeshift office and conference room down the hall from the formal meeting rooms into which the White House staff would, over the next three days, rotate the flags of Israel, France, Qatar, the United Kingdom, Egypt, Jordan, South Korea, Japan, Ukraine, Turkey, and Afghanistan as he met with their countries' leaders.

For each of those meetings, we prepared cards that I used to brief Trump verbally just prior to each meeting. The first card covered talking points for the press "pool spray" that normally preceded each meeting. The second listed objectives for the meeting and points he might make to advance those objectives. The third predicted what he would likely hear from his counterpart and his recommended responses.

Trump hated formal preparation, so we readied him under the guise of other discussions. The UNGA was more than an opportunity for him to clarify his agenda. It also allowed our delegation to understand better the perspectives of other world leaders. Much of what I heard was concerning.

*   *   *

MEETINGS WITH Netanyahu and Macron on the first afternoon of the UNGA convinced me that we were behind on Iran and Syria policies. Macron practically begged for clarity in U.S. policy, noting that Russia and Iran were testing us in Syria. He was right.

Lack of clarity in policy encourages a myopic focus on discrete decisions rather than on objectives and the concept for accomplishing those objectives. On Iran, Macron focused narrowly on the JCPOA, suggesting that, instead of killing it, we should try to strengthen it. Trump responded, "I like killing it." And he noted that "Everywhere I see trouble, there is Iran." He was making the important point that any decision on the JCPOA must also address Iran's proxy wars.

Trump's conversation with Netanyahu reinforced that ambiguity in our Syria policy had created opportunities for Putin, Assad, and Iran's supreme leader, Ali Khamenei. I grew convinced that our Israeli friends were falling for Putin's subterfuge. Several weeks earlier, during a dinner with senior Israeli officials in my home, I had told the director of Mossad, Yossi Cohen, a wise and imminently knowledgeable person, that I feared that he and his colleagues were falling for what I had begun to call "Putin's Potemkin Peace Plan."

Putin poured fuel on the flames of war and supported the murderous Assad regime while whispering to Israeli and Arab leaders that he promised to, over time, help diminish the influence of Iran in a post–civil war Syria. But Assad was far more reliant on the Iranians than on the Russians. Iran wanted Syria as part of the "land bridge" that would allow them to put a proxy Army on Israel's border. Putin would never cut Iran out, and Assad would never let the Iranians go.

Netanyahu would not abandon his delusional view of Putin's intentions until after the horrific Hamas terrorist attacks of October 7, 2023. Putin seemed to view the spree of mass murders, rape, infanticide, torture, and kidnapping as a present for his seventy-first birthday. He ramped up violence in Ukraine while supporting Hamas diplomatically and in its information war. Putin seemed to have a propaganda campaign ready to go as Moscow curried favor with other nations with a "pro-Palestinian" stance after having supported Hamas, the organization that diverted international assistance into terrorism, provoked a war that they knew would bring death and destruction to Gaza, and used the Palestinian people as human shields.

In subsequent meetings with Prime Minister May, President al-Sisi, and King Abdullah, Trump would be clear about the threat from Iran and the need to confront its use of terrorist organizations and proxy forces across the Middle East. He told May that the theocratic dictators in Iran "have religious fervor, want to hit Israel and reach the Mediterranean." We finally had a clear but not-yet-announced policy on Iran, and Trump had internalized it.

A working dinner with Latin American leaders followed the meetings with Netanyahu and Macron. The main topic was the "growing crisis" in Venezuela. Trump observed that Venezuela "is collapsing; their democratic institutions are being destroyed." He asked directly, "Why should we not do a military operation in Venezuela?"

Colombian president Juan Manuel Santos answered, reviewing (as I had with Trump) the "bad history" of U.S. interventions in Latin America. Panamanian president Juan Carlos Varela highlighted the potential costs.

Trump joked, "You could be next."
The attendees did not find the joke funny.

*   *   *

THE MOST contentious moment of the next day would likely be a
trade discussion with Prime Minister Trudeau of Canada, concerning NAFTA renegotiation. There was also a developing dispute
over proposed 300 percent tariffs on Canadian airline manufacturer
Bombardier, in response to a complaint from U.S. aircraft manufacturer Boeing. Trudeau was livid about the tariffs. How could it be
a bad day when the most contentious discussion would be with our
nearest (and politest) ally?

I jumped into the motorcade to pick up the president on the way
to UN Headquarters. As my car was trailing his, I intended, once we
arrived at the UN General Assembly Building, to give him an update
on Hurricane Maria, which was devastating the northeastern Carib-
bean and bearing down on Puerto Rico.

When I got out of the car, I saw that "it's not my fault" look on
Stephen Miller's face. As we walked into the foyer, Miller told me
the president had called him to dictate an addition to the speech that
included the text "The United States has great strength and patience,
but if it is forced to defend itself or its allies, we will have no choice
but to totally destroy North Korea. Rocket Man is on a suicide mission for himself and for his regime."

"Okay," I said to Miller. "We just need some time with the president." Fortunately, there was prep time scheduled in the greenroom.
Once we were there, I said, "Mr. President, I saw the changes you
made in the speech. Rocket Man *is* an accurate nickname, but it and
the threat to 'totally destroy' North Korea will drown out every
other important message in your speech."

Before he could respond, the UN officer in charge of stage-
managing leaders appeared in a panicked state and said, "We need
President Trump now."

And off he went.

Several Rocket Man tweets and news cycles later, the rest of
Trump's speech received little coverage.

★ ★ ★

I THEN accompanied Trump to the Secretary-General's Leaders' Lunch. *The UN protocol officer must be a prankster*, I thought, as the ninety-three-year-old Zimbabwean dictator Robert Mugabe was helped into the seat to my left. Over lunch, Mugabe nodded off in between bites of salad. I did not take it personally; four decades of tyrannical rule would make anyone tired. The scene elicited smiles from Prime Minister Hailemariam Desalegn of Ethiopia and President al-Sisi of Egypt as I leaned to my right and said, "I guess I am not a very interesting lunch partner."

On UNGA day three, Trump hosted his own lunch with the leaders of Côte d'Ivoire, Ethiopia, Ghana, Guinea, Namibia, Nigeria, Senegal, South Africa, and Uganda. I introduced Trump. He made a short statement during which he decided, as he often did, to ad-lib, saying, "So many of my friends are going to your countries trying to get rich." He was perhaps not aware of how his comment might draw attention to business deals that had done little to improve the lot of average African people in the postcolonial period. The intention of his remarks was to do the opposite; to cast U.S. investment as an antidote to China's extraction of raw materials and agricultural products in a way that favored a tiny elite and perpetuated cronyism, clientelism, and authoritarian rule.

I cringed only slightly. I suppose I was getting desensitized.

After his statement, Trump asked for the other leaders' "advice on how we can better work together toward a future of peace and prosperity for Americans, for Africans, and for people all over the world." Several leaders expressed concern over growing Chinese influence in Africa and their desire for greater investment from the United States and Europe. President Yoweri Museveni of Uganda said that the United States was missing opportunities. He noted that we all speak English but do business with China. President Alassane Ouattara of Côte d'Ivoire thanked Trump, stating that it was the first time African leaders had a luncheon in which they did all the talking. Guinean president Alpha Condé, at the end, said he had heard that Trump did not have a strategy for Africa, but he saw now that he did, and he thanked Trump for his pragmatic approach to the continent.

Tillerson and I had hoped that the meeting would inspire Trump to give a higher priority to Africa, a continent with a total land area of thirty million square kilometers representing 20 percent of the earth's habitable surface and 1.37 billion people, 17.4 percent of the world's population—which could reach 25 percent by 2050.[1] I got the impression from the leaders gathered that we were pushing on an open door.

Our team would work with the State Department to take advantage of the opportunity. Despite opposition from budget hawks, the Trump administration would continue the very successful U.S. President's Emergency Plan for AIDS Relief (PEPFAR) initiated under President George W. Bush, which accelerates progress toward achieving HIV/AIDS pandemic control in more than fifty countries as well as offering other health security assistance. We would develop and implement a Prosper Africa initiative to incentivize U.S. investments and trade with the fifty-nine countries on the continent. The director of the U.S. Agency for International Development, Mark Green, and Ray Washburne, president of the Overseas Private Investment Corporation, made significant progress in shifting the development model away from direct aid to investments that fostered sustainable economic growth.

Sadly, much of the goodwill Trump developed during the first meeting with the African leaders would evaporate when, less than four months later, someone leaked that he had referred to African nations as "shithole" countries during a meeting with members of Congress on immigration. It was another example of how Trump's disruptive nature created opportunity while his character and prejudices rendered him unable to take advantage of it.

Just days into his presidency, Trump had approved what was in retrospect an ill-conceived counterterrorism raid in Yemen during which U.S. Navy SEAL William "Ryan" Owens was killed, two others were wounded, and an Osprey aircraft was destroyed. The raid had also resulted in the deaths of sixteen civilians. In early May, when I called to tell him that another SEAL, Kyle Milliken, was killed about forty miles west of Mogadishu, Somalia, during a fight with al-Shabaab militants, Trump asked me, "What the hell are we doing in Africa?" He had apparently put me on speaker, and the voice of the First Lady answered his question: "General, aren't we there to fight terrorists so they do not have the opportunity to plan attacks against us?" That was the answer, but Trump remained skeptical, and some of his skepticism was warranted.

When, just weeks after the UN General Assembly, four U.S. soldiers—Staff Sgt. Bryan Black, Staff Sgt. Jeremiah Johnson, Sgt. La David Johnson, and Staff Sgt. Dustin Wright—were killed in an Islamic State ambush in Niger, Trump told me to "tell Mattis to get the hell out of Africa." I called Mattis to suggest an assessment of all counterterrorism missions and recommend that every casualty report have appended to it the mission and its importance to vital U.S. interests.

★   ★   ★

UNGA DAY four meetings with Ashraf Ghani of Afghanistan and Petro Poroshenko of Ukraine were important, I believed, to help Trump understand how sustained support for both countries was in U.S. interests. I met with President Ghani at his hotel the evening before. I emphasized Trump's impatience and that he expected results under the new strategy. The Afghan government had to reduce corruption, prevent so-called green-on-blue attacks (i.e., attacks on U.S. troops by Taliban infiltrators of Afghan forces), and reduce reliance on U.S. forces.

Ghani told me that he was happy to see Trump's strong language in the UNGA address and confident in his ability and the coalition's to meet Trump's expectations under the new strategy. But he expressed concern that the rules of engagement had not been relaxed, despite the president's clear statements in the General Assembly that he had "totally changed the rules of engagement in our fight against the Taliban and other terrorist groups."

I made a note to follow up with Mattis when I got back to Washington.

I was most concerned about the meeting with Poroshenko. Although Trump had recently approved his Russia strategy, which included providing and selling defensive capabilities such as Javelin antitank missiles to Ukraine, he was reluctant to sign the order to do so. I was sure that Putin had told Trump during the G20 dinner that providing weapons to Ukraine would be provocative and that Poroshenko's government was hopelessly corrupt.

Poroshenko highlighted business opportunities in Ukraine rather than the need for assistance. But as I walked out with him after the meeting, he told me that the weapons were needed to deter further Russian aggression. I nodded and stressed the need to take on corruption in his country, to strengthen the state and remove Putin's main talking point on Ukraine.

*   *   *

TRUMP'S NEXT meeting was with President Moon of South Korea, before a trilateral lunch with Moon and Japanese prime minister Abe. Foreign ministers and national security advisors from each country also joined.

Trump set the tone with the announcement of "a new executive order I just signed that significantly expands our authorities to target individuals, companies, financial institutions that finance and facilitate trade with North Korea."

Abe thanked Trump for his leadership on the North Korea problem and emphasized the "unity and solidarity" demonstrated in the meeting.

Toward the end of the meeting, Trump asked me if there was anything I would like to say. I noted that it would be important that "both North Korea and China see every North Korean provocation as pushing us closer together."

The last meeting was with Turkish president Erdoğan. Predictably, he pounded the narrative that the mainly-Kurdish YPG-based militia fighting ISIS in Syria was a PKK (Kurdistan Workers' Party) terrorist Army that posed an intolerable threat to Turkey. Trump looked at me and said, "General McMaster will look into it."

Again, Trump asked Erdoğan to release Chaplain Andrew Brunson "for the Christians."

Erdoğan made it clear that he expected the extradition of Gülen in return. "You have a pastor; we have a pastor."

I was concerned that Trump's deferential treatment of Erdoğan and the ambiguity of our policy in Syria would embolden Erdoğan against the Kurds. Three weeks later, Turkey would launch a major incursion into Syria.

At a dinner that Ambassador Haley hosted for some of us that evening, we all breathed a sigh of relief. We judged the week to be productive, and effective in advancing the objectives we had established at the outset. We had helped Trump use his skepticism of international organizations and his disruptive nature to the United States' advantage.

I joked, "We could have done without the 'Rocket Man' line, but I'll take it."

*　　*　　*

THE NEXT morning, on the way to the airport, I stopped by for coffee with Henry Kissinger at his River House apartment. We sat at the center of his spacious living room facing a large fireplace, our backs to the bay windows overlooking the East River. Our discussion, as usual, was wide-ranging, but the main topic was China.

I reviewed objectives for Trump's upcoming trip to Asia, including the state visit in Beijing.

Kissinger, who more than four decades earlier had driven President Richard Nixon's opening to China, agreed that the strategy of cooperation and engagement with China had failed, but he was reluctant to relinquish hope for an eventual entente with Xi and CCP leadership. He told me that during his last visit to Beijing, the director of the Office of the Central Leading Group for Financial and Economic Affairs, Liu He, who "has never steered me wrong, wants to host you in Beijing prior to Trump's visit."

I thanked him and told him that when Chinese state councilor Yang Jiechi visited Washington, he had also invited me, consistent with the normal practice of national security advisors preceding their presidents to Beijing. But we had decided that Tillerson would visit Beijing instead, in the following week.

I did not tell Kissinger that Tillerson had adamantly opposed my traveling to China, and given the tension in our relationship, I judged it a battle not worth fighting. Even as I deferred to him, however, Tillerson was making it hard to foster the cooperation necessary to support the president.

Although I shared none of that with him, Kissinger was very perceptive. He asked how I was getting along with Tillerson. I told him that I was working on the relationship and hoped that John Kelly might help pull everyone together. But my hopes that Kelly would foster teamwork were already fading. He had clearly bought into the "only one secretary of state" mantra from Tillerson.

Of course, there was only one secretary of state, but the corollary to that phrase was the belief that the national security decision-making process and, by connection, the president should have only a secondary role in the formulation of foreign policy.

During the UNGA, Secretary of State Tillerson had reached out to representatives of the Islamic Republic of Iran in the hope of arranging a confidential meeting with Trump. Although Tillerson and Kelly chose not to inform me about what was certain to be a failed effort, the president, as one would expect, discussed the overture with me.

As usual, I told him what he did not want to hear. Even if representatives of that government who were in New York for the UNGA did speak with Trump, they were powerless to act on what was said and would be terrified of saying anything without the prior approval of Iran's supreme leader Ayatollah Khamenei. Moreover, Trump had just approved an Iran strategy that called for isolating the regime and constraining its resources through sanctions and financial actions. If we wanted allies and partners to join that effort, talking with the Iranians could only confuse the issue.

I remained determined to worry about only what I could control and issues that had a direct effect on U.S. interests or the president's ability to lead. I knew from history that the relationship between the secretary of state and the national security advisor had only rarely been harmonious. I could live without harmony, but the lack of teamwork was consequential.

★   ★   ★

THINGS GOT worse. We returned to Washington as a mini crisis was developing in Iraq over a September 25 referendum on independence organized by the Kurdistan Regional Government there. The referendum, and the violence and chaos that were likely to follow, could empower a candidate like former prime minister Nouri al-Maliki, whose sectarian policies had helped resurrect al-Qaeda as it morphed into ISIS.

On October 2, I asked our team to convene a short telephone meeting with principals. Tillerson interrupted at the outset of it: "I don't even know why we're even having this call." I told him that it was an opportunity for all of us to hear his thoughts, questions, and guidance so we could align our efforts. "But," I said, "if you think it's a waste of your time, you should feel free to drop off."

Tillerson had just returned from the trip to Beijing. I imagined he was tired and frustrated. A statement he had made in Beijing—that he was using "lines of communication" with North Korea—had prompted Trump to tweet, "I told Rex Tillerson, our wonderful Secretary of State, that he is wasting his time trying to negotiate with Little Rocket Man . . ."[2] Although it is never good to see public disagreement between a secretary of state and a president, Trump's tweet was in line with our agreed strategy of maximum pressure. Tillerson's statement was not.

Previously Tillerson had been criticized in the press for parroting Chinese Communist Party language, including that U.S.-China relations should be built on "nonconfrontation, no conflict, mutual respect, and always searching for win-win solutions." Countries subjected to Chinese coercion might have read Tillerson's effort to curry favor with CCP leaders as an endorsement of their message to those countries that they had no option other than servitude to Beijing.

Days later, I sat in the Oval Office for Tillerson's debrief to Trump on the trip to Beijing. He told Trump that he had taken "H.R.'s protocol person" with him. I had to interject: "Rex, Leah Bray is a U.S. Navy commander and former attaché posted in Beijing who knows more about China than all of us combined." Had he made time to listen to her, Tillerson might have benefited from Bray's advice and avoided the semantic traps set for him in Beijing.

I had no option but to try to work through the tensions with Tillerson. As Gary Cohn and I shared a car on the short drive to Foggy Bottom for a meeting with the secretary of state on the president's trip to Asia, I thought there was nowhere to go but up. I was wrong. I was met with what seemed to be deep hostility as I showed Tillerson draft objectives for the trip that had already been fully coordinated with his policy office and the assistant secretary for East Asian and Pacific affairs. At one point, I noted that I had served in the Army for thirty-three years and had never encountered anyone as difficult as him. I suggested that he "might try being nicer and more collaborative."

He responded, "Only my mother and my wife can talk to me that way."

"You should listen to them more," I suggested.

In the coming months, I would continue to try to help Trump reconcile his contradictory predispositions and reduce the contention with Tillerson and Mattis. Not to spoil the story, but the results would be mixed.

CHAPTER 15

ASIAN ODYSSEY (20K MILES WITH TRUMP)

H.R. MCMASTER: IRAN NUKE DEAL IS 'FUNDAMEN-TALLY FLAWED' . . . McMaster pointed to Iran efforts to perpetuate violence across the Middle East . . . *LAS VEGAS SHOOTING: 59 KILLED AND MORE THAN 500 HURT NEAR MANDALAY BAY* . . . Saudi Arabia agrees to buy Russian S-400 air defence system . . . **DONALD TRUMP'S ASIA ADVENTURE: SHOW ME THE LOVE** . . . Trump arrives in Japan, first in five-country Asian tour . . . *In Visit To South Korea, Trump Continues Theme Of Security And Trade* . . . **'I WANT PEACE THROUGH STRENGTH,' TRUMP SAYS IN SOUTH KOREA** . . . *THE ART OF FLATTERY: ASIA WOOS TRUMP WITH SHOW OF PAG-EANTRY* . . . China's plan for influencing Trump: lavish dinners and grand gestures . . . Trump Touts 'Great Chemistry' With China's Xi As Leaders Agree To Closer Ties . . . **"HOW TO PLAY TRUMP": THE DONALD GETS ROLLED IN CHINA** . . . Trump's Visit to China Provides a Propaganda Bonanza . . . *TRUMP GIVES GLIMPSE OF 'INDO-PACIFIC' STRATEGY TO COUNTER CHINA* . . . Trump attacks countries 'cheating' America at APEC summit . . . Trump Heads for Hanoi, Meetings With Vietnam's Leaders . . . **IN DANANG, VIETNAM, TRUMP MAKES A FRIEND-LIER AMERICAN LANDING** . . . Trump insults 'short and fat' (and nuclear-armed) Kim Jong Un . . . **TRUMP AND DUTERTE: A BUDDING BROMANCE** . . . As Trump Meets Duterte in Philippines, Issue of Rights Comes Up 'Briefly' . . . *TRUMP LAUDS 'GREAT RELATION-SHIP' WITH DUTERTE IN MANILA* . . . Trump Asia trip shows president is jealous of despots and their power . . . **TRUMP WRAPPING UP ASIA TOUR DOMINATED BY NORTH KOREA, TRADE** . . . *RECORD 2017 HUR-RICANE SEASON COST $370B, HUNDREDS OF LIVES*

ON FRIDAY, October 6, 2017, two days after the most recent contentious meeting with Tillerson, I sat next to Kelly in the Oval Office for a phone call with President Macron. Trump was in a disagreeable mood. Macron was calling to urge Trump to stay in the Iran nuclear deal, a topic Trump did not want to discuss. The president had been short with me during the preparation for the call and then was rude to Macron during it. Midway through, he started to alternate between giving Macron and me a hard time and occasionally covering the handset and saying something nasty to me.

It was clear that I was serving no productive role for the president during the call. I looked over at Kelly and said, "You have this. I am out of here." I left the Oval Office.

It might be time to end this, I thought. If Trump treated me disrespectfully, how could I represent him credibly with the cabinet? And if he treated our allies disrespectfully, how could I help him achieve unity of effort on critical issues? I wrote out my resignation letter on a legal pad.

Kelly came to my office after the call. He said, "You can't leave, pal. Who is going to do this job?" He had brought with him a copy of *Dereliction of Duty*. "You wrote this book. It is your duty to stay."

I knew from combat in Iraq that exhaustion can creep up on you. During the first week of October, I had recognized some of the symptoms in myself and others. The job was fast paced, and the days were long. I was used to that. But I had grown weary of the unnecessary friction and drama in the White House and with obdurate colleagues in the Defense and State Departments. I had lost my patience with Tillerson and with Trump. I either had to go or redouble my efforts to remain stoic and, consistent with the Serenity Prayer, accept the things I could not change and focus on what I could.

Kelly's appeal was convincing. He was a fellow officer, and I could see that the job was wearing on him, too. He was with the president all day and then struggled to keep up with planning and directing the staff. And in addition to the drumbeat of the Mueller investigation and Trump's anger over it, there was always a crisis. Another hurricane hit the Gulf Coast in early October, but even worse, a deranged gunman murdered sixty and wounded more than four hundred concertgoers in Las Vegas. Trump and Kelly had visited Las Vegas on

Wednesday. Whenever I found my job frustrating, I thought of what it was like to be Trump's chief of staff.

Trump was getting worn down, too. I could see it in his face. The night before the phone call, after returning from Las Vegas, he and the First Lady had hosted a dinner that Katie and I attended with Mattis, the Joint Chiefs, the combatant commanders, and their spouses. It had been an emotional sixteen-hour day, and the president had to be "on" the whole time.

★   ★   ★

DESPITE THE frictions I was encountering, we were helping Trump make sound decisions. I would stay as long as I could fulfill my duties to the president and the nation. I gave Ylli the handwritten resignation letter and asked him to hold on to it just in case I needed it at a later date.

Then I threw myself back into what I could control.

Trump's long-planned eleven-day trip to Asia would take him to Honolulu, Tokyo, Seoul, Beijing, Danang (for the Asia-Pacific Economic Cooperation conference), Hanoi, and Manila (for the ASEAN Summit). Kelly thought the trip was too long and recommended cutting Danang and Manila. I agreed that the trip was long but explained that the APEC and ASEAN gatherings were essential for advancing the Indo-Pacific framework that would serve as the foundation for U.S. policy in the region.

Months before, Gary Cohn and I had proposed dividing the trip into two. Trump could attend APEC and ASEAN first, return home, and then visit Japan, South Korea, and China later in the year. Priebus, who wanted Trump in Washington to advance the domestic agenda, including a deal with Congress on tax reform and a sweeping overhaul of the nation's infrastructure, pushed for one long trip. I recounted for Kelly a meeting in the Oval Office during which Trump approved Priebus's recommendation and I said, "Okay, Mr. President. Please remember when you get grumpy at the end of this trip that it was Reince's idea."

I now told Kelly that with Reince gone, I was prepared to take the blame for the long trip. Xi was already going to try to make Trump's visit to Beijing look like "Trump paying tribute to the Great Emperor," and Trump's absence at APEC and ASEAN right after a visit to Beijing would only reinforce that narrative. It took a few days and a few conversations with Trump, but the trip remained as planned.

It was a nice fall day in Washington. I took a seat with Pottinger, Hooker, Schadlow, Everett Eissenstat (who had replaced Ken Juster as deputy assistant to the president for international economic affairs), and Willems at the picnic table in the First Lady's vegetable garden on the South Lawn. Our purpose was to align Trump's speeches and engagements with the objectives of the trip. Pottinger, who combined skill as a journalist with deep knowledge of Asian history and culture, gave the speechwriters compelling material. We would use the major speeches of the trip to introduce the main themes of the draft National Security Strategy to Trump as well as to the audiences he would address. The fresh air, good company, and opportunity to advance key initiatives in Asia reassured me that I had made the right decision to stay on the job.

Subsequent events further boosted my morale. That evening, I had dinner at the Bombay Club with my Canadian counterpart, Daniel Jean, to prepare for Prime Minister Trudeau's visit the following week. Daniel always provided valuable insights on topics ranging from the dictatorships in Cuba and Venezuela to the nature of the Kim family regime in North Korea. On Saturday, I hosted Chung Eui-yong for breakfast at Quarters 13 to discuss Trump's visit to the Republic of Korea. And on Sunday, I got a rare full day off to attend the Philadelphia Eagles football game with Aunt Nan; my sister, Letitia; my cousin Danny McCormick; and friends I had known for many years. Danny throws a killer tailgate party, and everyone welcomed our Secret Service detail as family. And the Eagles dominated the Arizona Cardinals, winning the game 34–7.

Knowing that others had encountered frictions similar to those I was experiencing was reassuring. On Tuesday, October 10, I met with Dr. Kissinger in advance of an event that the Center for Strategic and International Studies hosted to commemorate the seventieth anniversary of the National Security Council. CSIS president John Hamre facilitated the discussion among former national security advisors Kissinger, Stephen Hadley, James Jones, and me. Brent

Scowcroft, Bud McFarlane, John Poindexter, and Tom Donilon were in the audience and would attend the dinner that followed. Hadley highlighted the role of the NSC as ensuring, "once the president makes a decision and sets a policy, that the departments and agencies are implementing that policy effectively." This would be the major source of tension for Tillerson, Mattis, and me in the coming months.

The last major task before the Asia trip was Trump's speech on the Iran strategy. On October 13, I hosted a conference call with conservative journalists and think tanks previewing his policy. I explained that the policy was not all about the nuclear deal. What they would hear in the speech was a comprehensive strategy designed not only to block Iran's path to a nuclear weapon, but also to counter its missile and asymmetric threats, deny the Islamic Revolutionary Guard Corps funding, and neutralize the IRGC's destabilizing behavior. The idea was, in the short term, to impose strong sanctions outside the deal while trying to convince Iran to renegotiate. If that failed, the president could get out whenever he wanted. The long-term objective was to encourage a change in the nature of the Iranian regime such that it ended its permanent hostility toward the United States, Israel, and its Arab neighbors.

But for those who viewed getting out of the nuclear deal as an end in itself, my words, and Trump's explanation in the speech, fell on deaf ears.

Gary Cohn, Stephen Miller, and I met with Trump in the Oval Office just before the speech. Because the president had gone back and forth so many times on staying in the deal or getting out, I had two versions of the speech prepared and two versions of guidance for statements to the press and conversations with allies and partners. Trump had heard from May, Macron, and Merkel, whose countries were part of the negotiations that had led to the JCPOA. I told him that our allies had blinders on and had come to view the agreement as an article of faith. But those allies were starting to come around to our view that the Iranian regime must be forced either to change its behavior and end its hostility or suffer economic and financial isolation. I told Trump that "No matter what you decide on the nuclear deal, we are prepared to execute the decision and would fit that decision into the overall strategy. Why not at least see if we could convince our allies to help us force the Iranian regime to either enter a better agreement that addresses the full range of Iran's malign behavior or suffer economic and financial isolation?"

"Okay, General, let's try it," he said, but I knew we would not have much time to do so.

After his speech, Trump asked me, "How did I do?"

I told him that it had gone well. "You just announced another radical, but long overdue, shift in foreign policy. Congratulations, Mr. President." Regardless of Trump's ultimate decision on the JCPOA (he would announce the U.S. withdrawal from it in May 2018), we continued to strengthen the sanctions. In 2018, Iranian GDP would fall from 3.7 percent growth per annum to 3.9 percent contraction. Crude oil exports, 2.3 million barrels in 2018, fell to 1.1 million barrels a day by March 2019. Inflation in Iran rose from 9 to 40 percent.[1]

Meanwhile, the power games with Tillerson and Mattis continued. Trump was frustrated that King Salman of Saudi Arabia had announced the purchase of a sophisticated Russian air defense system during a visit to Moscow. He told me to ask the king "Why are we defending you at tremendous cost? While you are there, why not ask Russia to defend you?" I told Trump that King Salman and MBS may have been using the purchase of the Russian weapons to expedite arms sales being held up in Congress.

When I looked into the matter, I discovered that Tillerson, in contravention of what Trump wanted, had asked Senate Foreign Relations Committee chair Sen. Bob Corker to delay those arms sales to encourage Saudi Arabia to lift the blockade on Qatar. Cabinet secretaries are supposed to advance the president's policies and decisions on Capitol Hill, not frustrate them. I knew that Trump would be livid if he knew. I asked Tillerson and Corker to lift the hold.

On October 30, Mattis tried to exclude me from an Oval Office meeting concerning, in part, the nominations of senior military officers. Instead, I walked right in and sat down next to him. After the meeting, I asked Mattis, "Is it true you didn't want me in this meeting?" He didn't answer. I said, "You know he's going to ask me what I think anyway. Why don't we just work together?"

Trump had already asked me about Mattis's nominee for a critical four-star position, and I had told him the officer was among the very best I had ever known. I wrote Kelly a memo arguing that Trump deserved multiple nominations for every four-star position and the opportunity to interview the candidates.

Just prior to the Asia trip, Kelly and I had attended a dinner in the Capitol with Senate Majority Leader Mitch McConnell, House Speaker Paul Ryan, and Mattis. On the way there, I told the chief of staff, "State and Defense are undermining the interagency process." I mentioned examples of foot-dragging on contingency plans, slowing down the development of policy options, and using the Senate to slow down one of Trump's priorities. I told Kelly, "I want to work through this and improve our collaboration, but those two are making it hard."

★   ★   ★

NINE A.M., November 3. Wheels up on Air Force One for a ten-hour flight. Thirteen days and twenty thousand miles with a president who hated long trips and who was preoccupied with his domestic political agenda and Russiagate.

What could go wrong?

I hoped that Trump would appreciate the opportunity to advance his three major policy initiatives in Asia: transparent competition with China, maximum pressure on North Korea, and promotion of fair and reciprocal trade. I planned to keep my interactions with him brief and focused on those objectives.

First stop: Hawaii. We landed at 1 p.m. local time. The drive to Indo-Pacific Command headquarters evoked historical memory of World War II and the advent of the U.S. dominance in the Pacific. Adm. Harry Harris met us outside the Nimitz-MacArthur Pacific Command Center, named for Adm. Chester W. Nimitz and Gen. Douglas MacArthur, who, after Japan's surprise attacks on Pearl Harbor and the Philippines, led the counterattack across the Pacific and accepted the formal Japanese surrender aboard the USS *Missouri* on September 2, 1945.

I thought of historical parallels between that period and the present. Seventy-six years after Imperial Japan's surprise attack, the

People's Republic of China slogans of "Asia for Asians" and "community of common destiny" were disconcertingly similar to Imperial Japan's promise of a "Greater East Asia Co-prosperity Sphere," a term first used by Japanese minister for foreign affairs Hachirō Arita in 1940.

The panoramic view of Pearl Harbor evoked the past as Admiral Harris displayed charts to explain today's growing threat from China's military. The briefing showed the burgeoning numbers of People's Liberation Army ships, aircraft, and missiles relative to U.S. forces. Trump was incredulous that the United States had allowed China to conduct such a massive buildup unanswered. He would keep the charts mounted on a corkboard in the dining room adjacent to the Oval Office.

That evening, our party joined the president and First Lady on the admiral's skiff for a tour of Pearl Harbor and a visit to the USS *Arizona* Memorial. We observed a moment of silence as we looked down at the remains of the ship, which is also the site where 1,177 men lost their lives. U.S. armed forces would lose 109,071 in the Pacific War and see 407,316 killed and 671,278 wounded in World War II overall.[2]

Trump had approved Ronald Reagan's phrase "peace through strength" as one of the four pillars in the draft National Security Strategy, but even the president's proposed military budget, which represented a 10 percent real increase, was inadequate, I believed, to deter conflict in the Indo-Pacific region and beyond.[3] I hoped that the history of this place would help Trump understand the deterrent value of forces deployed forward and that fighting to gain "readmission" to the Pacific after leaving would require enormous sacrifice.

I thanked Harris for the compelling case he had made. His briefing was an example of why Trump needed greater access to senior military commanders. Admiral Harris would soon retire from active duty, and Trump would appoint him ambassador to South Korea.

The opportunity to be with fellow officers, and an early morning swim in the ocean, left me recharged and ready for the journey to Japan.

★   ★   ★

JAPAN WAS the first stop in Asia to symbolize the importance of the alliance. Prime Minister Abe was the world leader most adept at forging a positive relationship with Trump. When the two first golfed together at Trump International Golf Club in West Palm Beach in February, the golf pro Ernie Els had joined them. Soon after Air Force One landed in Tokyo, Trump joined Abe and Japanese golf pro Hideki Matsuyama at the Kasumigaseki Country Club for a round of eighteen holes followed by another Trump favorite, a hamburger. Abe ensured that the burger was made of U.S. beef, as a subtle parry to Trump's complaints that Japan was unfairly restricting market access for U.S. goods. He also provided white baseball caps bearing the message "Donald and Shinzo Make Alliance Even Greater."

After dinner with Japanese national security advisor Yachi Shotaro and our staffs, I passed on an invitation to join White House staffers for late-night karaoke. I needed to conserve energy for the journey ahead. Also, hearing me sing might have resulted in complaints of a hostile work environment.

Every item on our agenda had a purpose. Trump's visit with the families of Japanese abducted by North Korea was a gesture of support for the Japanese people and a message to both Pyongyang and Seoul that the United States would not paper over the many atrocities the Kim regime committed against its neighbors and its own population. A final lunch with Abe and his team provided the right atmosphere for candid discussion. After chiding Abe on market access, Trump turned to defense burden sharing. He described the U.S.-Japan defense treaty first signed in 1951 and revised in 1960, under Abe's grandfather, as "unfair." He asked why Japan did not have to defend the United States if we were attacked but the United States had to defend Japan. He said, "We might as well put Japanese flags on our aircraft." Abe seemed to understand that Trump was generating leverage for negotiations on trade and defense burden sharing.

On defense, Trump was pushing on an open door. Abe had already achieved a vast change in Japan's policy through a historic reinterpretation of the Japanese constitution to permit collective self-defense, end the ban on arms exports, and change other self-limiting practices that derived from the pacifist identity many Japanese across the postwar generations had embraced. Japan was already on the path to develop a range of new defense capabilities, such as long-range precision missiles, that would allow the country to better defend itself and integrate more closely with U.S. forces.

I had urged Trump to push Abe on trade and defense in private rather than in public, because Abe could proceed only at a pace the Japanese society could bear. I told Trump the story of Abe's grandfather Nobusuke Kishi, who signed the revised defense pact in 1960 and was forced to step down as prime minister after a massive public outcry. In 2020, on the sixtieth anniversary of his grandfather's change to the defense pact, Abe would state, "We have elevated the relationship to one in which each of us, the U.S. and Japan, protects the other, thereby giving further force to the alliance."

There would be progress on trade as well. In 2019, Lighthizer finished negotiations on two agreements: the U.S.-Japan Trade Agreement, which included tariff reductions and quota expansions to improve market access, and the U.S.-Japan Digital Trade Agreement.

★   ★   ★

I WAS concerned about the South Korea leg of the journey. Trump did not have the personal rapport with President Moon that he had with Abe, and he was sympathetic to the argument that others had put forward for decades, that U.S. forces were no longer needed on the Korean Peninsula and that the United States was underwriting the security of a successful country with a strong economy that was now capable of defending itself.

The first event upon our arrival at Camp Humphreys, the largest U.S. Army garrison in Asia, home to United States Forces Korea and United Nations Command, was meant to demonstrate the strength of the alliance and to emphasize that U.S. military forces on the peninsula were critical to American as well as South Korean security. Soldiers, sailors, airmen, and Marines applauded as Trump and Moon entered the dining facility to join them for lunch. They shook hands with the leaders and posed for selfies. As the presidents sat down across from each other, the rest of us joined servicemen and -women at other tables. I had great discussions with motivated soldiers who had volunteered to serve on a frontier separating a tremendously successful free society from a destitute gulag state. As we were about to depart the dining facility for a meeting with commanders at the headquarters, I introduced Trump to a soldier from his old neighborhood in Queens.

Lunch with troops had been the perfect icebreaker. As Marine sergeant Cortney Wells told a reporter, "I think it's great, especially for the alliance," that the two presidents were together at Camp Humphreys. I agreed and hoped that the positive vibe would last.

The commander of U.S. Forces Korea, Gen. Vince Brooks, rode with Trump to headquarters where my old friend, Lt. Gen. Thomas Vandal, commander of the Eighth Army, greeted us. Moon and Trump sat behind the U-shaped table surrounded by American and South Korean general officers. As senior U.S. and Republic of Korea commanders showed slides depicting the North Korean threat and how the allied force would respond to various contingencies, I imagined how the prospect of a costly war on the peninsula might strengthen Trump's inclination to disengage rather than remain committed to deterring North Korean aggression. The briefings and the eighty-kilometer flight to Seoul resurrected Trump's view of the alliance as one-sided and South Korea's economic success as coming at the expense of the United States.

As our helicopter lifted off, he asked General Brooks how much the construction of Camp Humphreys had cost. Brooks told him that the cost was $10.8 billion, but he added that the Republic of Korea had covered $9.8 billion. Trump asked why it hadn't covered 100 percent.

I had briefed Trump on these figures and on the fact that Seoul paid the salaries of 8,600 Korean nationals who support the troops and their families at Camp Humphreys. I had heard it before, but I am sure Brooks was surprised when Trump stated that the agreement should be the equivalent of a cost-plus contract, with the South Koreans reimbursing all U.S. costs plus a profit margin.

As we flew over a massive Samsung semiconductor fabrication plant, Trump asked why we didn't have anything like that in the United States. It was a good question. In 1990, the U.S. share of chip manufacturing was 37 percent. By 2017, it had fallen to 13 percent.[4]

Even more troubling was that the United States and the world were wholly dependent on Taiwan's TSMC and South Korea's Samsung for the most advanced chips. The Samsung chip manufacturing plant, or fab, and other vast industrial infrastructure we overflew pushed trade issues to the top of the agenda. Almost nothing put Trump in a worse mood than reminders of the loss of U.S. manufacturing due to unfettered globalization.

On the way to the Blue House, I could tell that Trump was riled. I reminded him that Moon was expanding South Korea's defense capabilities and was open to renegotiating KORUS and ROK reimbursement for U.S. defense costs. "I know you will be direct about those issues in our meetings, but anything you say publicly that sounds like less than a full commitment to South Korea's defense will embolden North Korea and encourage Moon to abandon the maximum pressure strategy and accommodate China."

The ornate welcome ceremony at the Blue House improved Trump's mood. Discussions in the bilateral meetings were direct but cordial. I was glad that THAAD came up only as Moon lamented the more than ten billion dollars in revenue South Korean companies had lost after China penalized them in response to the deployment of the defensive systems. Trump promised to tell Xi that he had "picked the wrong Korea" to sanction. At the state dinner, held at the Blue House, Moon seemed keen to demonstrate that Abe was not the only world leader who knew how to get close to the American president, stating that "Trump's election victory one year ago is already making America great again."

During his remarks, Trump reverted to his reality-TV promoter persona: "We're going to have an exciting day tomorrow, for many reasons that people will find out." He was teasing a surprise visit to the demilitarized zone (DMZ), which he decided to make after having previously dismissed such a visit as "cliché." Once someone told him that President Obama had received favorable press coverage for his own visit there, however, Trump did not want to miss out.

Heavy fog between Seoul and the landing zone foiled the plan. A grumpy Trump sat in the back of the car waiting in vain for the fog to clear. I assured him that holding off was the right decision. Fog and multi-ship helicopter operations are a bad combination. Besides, his address to the ROK National Assembly would be much more important than a visit to the DMZ.

Pottinger and I had provided the content for Trump's speech with the severe polarization of South Korean politics in mind. In the speech, Trump congratulated South Koreans for their "miraculous" climb "from total devastation to among the wealthiest nations on earth" and emphasized the stark contrast between the two Koreas. He suppressed his reservations about the alliance and emphasized "peace through strength," with a message intended for Pyongyang that "anyone who doubts the strength or determination of the United States should look to our past, and you will doubt it no longer." It was a strong ending that garnered enthusiastic applause across party lines.

We boarded Air Force One. The images and messages of our unshakable alliances with Japan and South Korea communicated by the visits to Tokyo and Seoul would be important to set the conditions we desired for the next and most consequential leg of the journey.

*   *   *

MUCH OF the preparation for the trip to China, as before the summit with Xi at Mar-a-Lago, centered on what not to say on critical issues to avoid Chinese Communist Party traps. Xi, like other leaders, had been studying Trump to determine how to manipulate him into statements and actions to advance his own agenda. On the flight to Beijing, I again framed the discussion so Trump might direct his contrariness toward Xi rather than me.

"Mr. President, he wants you to use the words 'one China principle' instead of 'one China policy,' to make it seem like you endorse his position that there is only one China and that Taiwan is a part of China. He wants you to equivocate on Japan's Senkaku Islands to create ambiguity about whether the islands fall under the U.S.-Japan security treaty. He wants you to accept his offer to reduce tensions in the South China Sea if only you recognize a significant portion of his unlawful claim to ownership of it. He wants you to believe his false promises of cooperation on curtailing cyberattacks, fentanyl trafficking, and various forms of economic aggression so you will relax restrictions on Chinese investment in U.S. tech companies, lift export controls on sensitive technology, and rule out tariffs and other trade enforcement actions. He will continue to complain about military exercises in Korea to convince you to suspend them as the first step to alleviate pressure on North Korea and return to the failed approach of 'freeze-for-freeze' as the first concession of many just to secure a chance to talk with Pyongyang. But most of all, he wants you to endorse a 'new kind of great power relationship' to suggest that you endorse Chinese primacy in Asia."

I told Trump that the pomp and circumstance of what Chinese officials were calling the "state visit plus" was designed to create the impression for the Chinese people and international audiences that the Communist Party was all-powerful and that the balance of power in the world was shifting away from the United States and back to its natural hub in China.

The first event was a tour of the Forbidden City, the seat of Chinese emperors across five centuries.[5] As we passed through the West Glorious Gate, I looked for Pottinger, who had been walking behind us. I discovered later that guards had denied him access; as senior director for Asia, Matt knew too much. Our hosts clearly intended to use the visit to the Forbidden City to convey messages without the encumbrance of someone like Matt, who might subject those messages to skepticism and keen appraisal. The most important message associated with the visit to the Forbidden City was the inevitable return to an international system in which Chinese leaders granted privileges in exchange for recognition of China's superiority.

While the images broadcast that day to China and the world from the Forbidden City were meant to project confidence in the Chinese Communist Party, I sensed profound insecurity. Chairman Xi wanted to be seen as the unchallenged ruler of an increasingly powerful and apparently harmonious country. But like the emperors who had occupied the Forbidden City, Chairman Xi practiced a remote and autocratic style of rule vulnerable to corruption and internal threats.

As the tour ended, I was even more convinced that our dramatic shift in policy was needed and long overdue. I was struck by the fears as well as the grand ambitions that drive the Chinese Communist Party's efforts to extend China's influence along its frontiers and beyond and realize its dream of returning to a natural order with Chinese power at the center.

A welcome ceremony overlooking Tiananmen Square combined a military parade and a throng of Chinese and American elementary school children leaping up and down and enthusiastically waving the flags of the two nations.

We entered the Great Hall of the People for a restricted bilateral meeting, and Xi launched into a list of complaints ranging from U.S. air and naval movements through the South China Sea to U.S.-ROK military exercises to China's claims to ownership of the Japanese-administered Senkaku Islands.

During this spiel, it became obvious to me that Xi was backing away from his halting commitment to maximum pressure on North Korea. He used the same metaphor he had used in Hamburg— that "barefooted people do not fear those with fancy shoes"—and he signaled unwillingness to impose costs on the DPRK sufficient for maximum pressure to work, noting that breaking every tie with Pyongyang would only generate hatred. Xi urged us not to employ what he called long-arm jurisdiction to sanction Chinese banks, which Xi said would continue to move money for North Korea. Finally, in case we had missed his intention to back away from complete denuclearization of North Korea, he suggested that it would be acceptable if North Korea simply froze its nuclear and missile programs.

As Trump began to speak, I experienced a wave of apprehension that caused a sinking feeling in my stomach. The president agreed with Xi that military exercises with South Korea were "provocative" and went on to describe them as a "waste of money." Even worse, he seemed to agree with Xi's suggestion of a return of freeze-for-freeze. Trump did not refer to the talking points I had given him on the top issues of Taiwan, the South China Sea, and the Senkakus. His response to Xi's complaints about all three gave the impression of U.S. ambivalence over countering People's Liberation Army aggression across the region. Just when I thought it could not get worse, Trump offered to mediate on the Senkakus, implying that China had a legitimate claim to be adjudicated.

I passed Kelly a folded note. "He [Xi] ate our lunch . . . He [Trump] walked into the trap."

I hoped that some of Trump's comments would be lost in translation or were so opposed to U.S. policy that they would be dismissed as a negotiating trick to gain concessions on trade issues. At least his comments were not public. I would need time to talk with Trump after the next extended bilateral meeting and before the joint statements to the press.

The extended bilateral discussion consisted of Chinese and U.S. briefings to President Trump and Xi on the four high-level dialogues inaugurated at Mar-a-Lago. Tillerson covered the U.S.-China Diplomatic and Security Dialogue, highlighting the need for "risk reduction" in the South China Sea, space, and cyberspace. There was no Chinese response. Lighthizer presented on the U.S.-China Comprehensive Economic Dialogue, listing the key elements of Chinese economic aggression, which ranged from overcapacity, overproduction, and dumping of products to intellectual property theft to the lack of reciprocity in market access for U.S. goods and services.[6] Politburo Standing Committee member Wang Yang muttered that they took this very seriously—which, of course, they did not—while quoting Confucius on the "great pleasure to have guests come from afar." After the only woman present, Liu Yandong, simply listed the areas of supposed cooperation under the social and cultural dialogue, Tillerson summarized CCP suppression of nongovernmental organizations, interference with Chinese students in the United States, and the use of state media to advance biased or false pro-PRC and anti-American content. Because the U.S. attorney general was not present, I gave the final briefing on the U.S.-China Law Enforcement and Cybersecurity Dialogue. I looked directly at Xi:

> Mr. Chairman, if I were a pessimist, I would say that progress on law enforcement and cyber is a great disappointment. But I want to be positive. So, we might focus on the many opportunities to improve and strengthen cooperation. We could begin with two easy objectives: the repatriation of over thirty-nine thousand Chinese nationals who have final orders of removal from the United States and the improvement of mutual legal assistance by simply responding to basic requests for evidence, such as bank records on cases involving

transnational organized crime and narcotics trafficking. It is a priority for us that China stop the practice of sending so-called law enforcement teams to the United States to harass Americans. And we have the opportunity to deliver on a top priority for President Trump to end the Chinese manufacturing and distribution of the drug fentanyl and its precursor chemicals—a drug that killed over sixty thousand Americans last year. It is difficult for us to understand how your government, which has such a firm grasp on the activities of its people, is unable to stop drug manufacturing and trafficking. And finally, we have an opportunity to implement the cybercrime agreement made in 2015, especially ending the cyber-enabled theft of trade secrets and the activation of the hotline mechanism to improve coordination. Attorney General Sessions is looking forward to working on all these critical problems with your team. Consistent with President Trump's guidance, we will judge progress by our actions and results rather than words. Thank you.

Xi, who is usually stone-faced, betrayed a look of surprise at how direct I was. His only response was to thank me for what he described as my excellent briefing. But, as was the case with other attempts to form working groups with CCP officials, these comprehensive dialogues were doomed to fail.[7]

Over McDonald's hamburgers our hosts had provided, I got a moment to confer with Trump prior to the statements he and Xi would make to the press. Because I was certain that the room was wired, I did not refer to Trump's earlier statements, to avoid drawing attention to them. Instead, I played to our hidden Chinese audience, highlighting the issues Trump would raise, including the need for placing more pressure on North Korea, stopping the "lethal flow" of fentanyl, and ending the "massive distortion" associated with China's weaponization of its statist, mercantilist economic model against ours and other free-market economies.

"Okay, General," Trump said. I could tell he just wanted to relax.

During the reading of his statement, Trump looked at Xi and ad-libbed, "I don't blame you, I blame us." It was the perfect way to communicate to Xi that it would be unnatural for the United States to remain passive as the CCP engaged in economic aggression.

We moved on to our last meeting of the day, before a break at the hotel in advance of the state dinner. Trump was tired of meetings. "Why am I doing this meeting again?" he asked me on the way in.

"Premier Li Keqiang is the titular head of state, so we have to go along with that charade as a matter of protocol."

Trump grimaced as he took his seat across from Li.

When CCP officials are not reading vetted statements, they usually engage in obfuscation cloaked in feigned sincerity. But Li had a reputation for being a relatively liberal and less ideological pragmatist. He was direct, and the long soliloquy he delivered was revealing. He observed that China, having already developed its industrial and technological base, no longer needed the United States. He dismissed U.S. concerns over unfair trade and economic practices, indicating that the U.S. role in the future global economy would merely be to provide China with raw materials, agricultural products, and energy to fuel its production of the world's cutting-edge industrial and consumer products. President Trump listened for as long as he could and then interrupted the premier, thanked him, and stood up to end the meeting.

Li's arrogance revealed how, in 2017, the CCP viewed its centralized, statist economic system as bestowing advantages, especially the ability to coordinate efforts across government, business, academia, and the military. And, especially after the financial crisis of 2009, it considered decentralized free-market economic systems as unable to compete with China's centrally directed strategies, such as Made in China 2025, One Belt One Road, and Military-Civilian Fusion.

I heard arrogance, but, again, I sensed fear. It would take a few more years for the frailties in China's economic model to become obvious under the strain of Covid-19 and the country's zero-Covid policies. As the party continued to tighten its grip on power, it began to choke out its economy. Li and other party leaders seemed to recognize that they had only a narrow window of strategic opportunity to strengthen their rule and revise the international order in their favor. They had to realize the "China Dream" before China's economy soured, before the population grew old, before other countries realized that the party was pursuing national rejuvenation at their expense, and before unanticipated events such as the coronavirus pandemic exposed the party's vulnerabilities.

Li, who hailed from a rival faction and was once thought to be the party's future leader, would depart the Politburo in March 2023 and die of a heart attack under suspicious circumstances seven months later.

★   ★   ★

THE NEXT day, we departed Beijing on the way to the Asia-Pacific Economic Cooperation (APEC) conference in Danang, Vietnam. The remainder of the trip provided an opportunity for Trump to counter the CCP's effort to re-create a tributary system in Asia with an alternative vision of a free and open Indo-Pacific.

Our motorcade took us directly to the Ariyana Convention Centre. As we sat in a large conference room overlooking the white sand beach, I told Trump that his speech may turn out to be the most important of the trip. "Mr. President, the speech makes clear that the choice nations and companies face is not a choice between Washington and Beijing; it is a choice between sovereignty and servitude."

I thought he would be more excited about the opportunity to speak to a large audience of business and political leaders, but as he often did when he had insufficient sleep, he reverted to contrariness. "I don't think I like the phrase 'free and open Indo-Pacific.'"

I smiled to communicate that I knew what he was doing. "Mr. President, you know that it is the best phrase to counter the vision that China is trying to drive down everyone's throat. Believe me, the audience will love it, and you will come to love 'free and open Indo-Pacific' too."

The speech could not have gone better. The audience applauded the key lines, and Trump received a standing ovation at the end. Thanks to the hard work of the deputy assistant to the president for international economic affairs, Everett Eissenstat, Trump's main points would make it into the APEC communiqué, including the need to end "unfair trade practices," remove "market-distorting subsidies," and reform the World Trade Organization's "negotiating, monitoring and dispute settlement functions."

So far, the trip had been successful, but Trump's patience seemed to wear thinner with every mile traveled.

The corner suite at the Grand Hilton Resort overlooked a serene beach just south of where the first U.S. combat units of 3,500 Marines landed in South Vietnam on March 8, 1965. *Too bad such a nice accommodation is being wasted on me*, I thought, as I met with our travel team before briefing Trump on the next day's activities, which included the APEC leader meeting and lunch, travel to Hanoi, and a state banquet with North Vietnamese president Tran Dai Quang.

As soon as Eissenstat and I entered the president's room, I could tell that our pre-dinner prep session was unlikely to go well. Kelly wore a look of apprehension, and Trump looked like he had been woken from a nap. As I highlighted the next day's activities, he unleashed what seemed like pent-up animosity toward me. "Why do I have to do this? This is your fault, General." He hated preparing for engagements, and he saw me as the cause for his working so hard and being away from home for so long.

Although I did not need or expect him to do so, Kelly intervened: "Your national security advisor is just doing his job and trying to help you. There is no need to talk to H.R. like that. This meeting is over." Kelly was clearly frustrated with Trump's self-absorption, resistance to doing basic preparation, and tendency toward disrespecting and disparaging those who were trying to serve him.

One might think that getting dressed down by the president would be disconcerting. But I was unconcerned and not offended. I shrugged and smiled at Eissenstat as we departed: "That went well." I knew that at some point I would get used up by Trump. I had resolved to do the best I could to fulfill my duty to him until I was no longer effective.

It was already getting dark when we landed in Hanoi. As our motorcade wended its way through the city of ten million, people lined the streets, clapping and cheering to welcome Trump. Despite the devastation of the Vietnam War, nearly 80 percent of Vietnamese people hold a favorable opinion of the United States, and an equal percentage holds an unfavorable view of China.

Matt Pottinger checked reactions to the trip on social media. "You're not going to believe this," he said. "Trump just tweeted, 'Why would Kim Jong-un insult me by calling me "old," when I would NEVER call him "short and fat"? Oh well, I try so hard to be his friend—and maybe someday that will happen!'"

We both laughed.

The state dinner hosted by President Quang had set a positive tone for our meetings, but as I briefed a more polite Trump the next morning, he seized on what was meant to be a positive example of improving security cooperation with South Vietnam, the recent transfer of an ex-Hamilton-class high-endurance Coast Guard cutter to Vietnam, as more evidence of other nations taking advantage of U.S. largesse. I tried to explain that although it had cost $17 million to refurbish the cutter in advance of the transfer, that cost was far below what the Coast Guard would spend to dispose of the ship. Similar transfers, I told him, had saved the U.S. government over $150 million across the past two decades. But once Trump seized on a story that reinforced his preconceptions, facts were of little consequence.

As we walked up the steps of the bright-yellow Beaux-Arts-style Presidential Palace, which was constructed in the early 1900s to house the French governor-general of Indochina, I had a feeling that the bilateral meeting with President Quang, Prime Minister Nguyen Xuan Phuc, and other government officials might not go well.

Phuc opened with an enthusiastic welcome and praise for Trump's conducting the longest overseas trip to Asia by an American president.

Don't remind him, I thought.

He complimented Trump's speech at APEC and was direct about his own agenda: increased trade and arms sales. He highlighted a large liquefied natural gas project.

So far so good.

But then, a few minutes into the meeting, Quang thanked Trump for the cutter, which, as with a discussion of THAAD with the South Koreans, triggered a Trump tirade about how he was different from his predecessors and would no longer be giving away Coast Guard cutters or anything else for free.

Trump highlighted his desire for Vietnam to import more from the United States, then asked Quang, "Where do you buy your weapons?"

"Mainly from Russia," he responded.

"So, we are giving you Coast Guard cutters, but you are buying from Russia?"

Quang interjected, "But the ban on purchasing arms from the United States was lifted only last year."

I tried to get a word in; I sensed where this was going. "Mr. President, now that the ban on selling arms is lifted, we have a tremendous opportunity . . ."

Trump cut me off. "America has been a piggy bank that others pull from. We want a reciprocal deal." He turned to me and Tillerson and Kelly. "I'm mostly talking to my people. It's outrageous." He directed his anger mainly at Rex, me, and the rest of the staff as confused Vietnamese leaders looked on. They might have thought this strange behavior to be a ruse or a negotiating ploy. Trump turned to Tillerson with a look of disdain: "Rex—anything?"

Before Tillerson could respond, Trump asked Lighthizer to summarize trade issues. Lighthizer noted that the United States purchased 20 percent of Vietnamese exports but encountered non-tariff barriers for the import of U.S. goods.

Trump turned back to Quang. "If we can't do well with Vietnam, we should not do business with Vietnam." Finally, the discussion moved on.

Quang thanked Trump for his candid remarks, noted that U.S. imports were up 77 percent in the past year, and restated his desire to buy U.S. weapons.

The contrast between the architecture of the Presidential Palace and the Soviet-style Communist Party headquarters, the stark, foreboding building where Trump met with General Secretary Nguyen Phu Trong, served as a reminder that Vietnam was still a Marxist-Leninist communist country.

I could see the president was tired. Trump told Trong, "Work on expanding arms sales with Tillerson and McMaster. Next, I go to the Philippines. These twelve days have been complex. I have given so many speeches. So, I look forward to going home. But I like it here

too. I could stay longer." Years later, in 2024, as the two main parties' candidates faced off for an election rematch, I thought back to
the Asia trip and wondered how Biden and Trump, who would both
be octogenarians by the end of their terms, could perform well the
sometimes grueling job of president.

The clock was ticking on Trump's patience, but I concluded the
visit feeling optimistic. Vietnam was still a communist country in
which market-oriented economic reforms would proceed slowly and
the prospect for political reform would remain dim. But its resistance to Chinese dominance would lead to closer diplomatic, military, and economic ties to the United States.

The next stop, the ASEAN Summit in the Philippines, would provide Trump with an opportunity to strengthen the case for choosing
sovereignty over servitude.

*   *   *

FROM AIR Force One, the size and density of Manila, a city of
thirteen million people at the time, was striking. Ending the journey with the ASEAN Summit, a bustling conference for an organization that relies on consensus among nations that are often on
opposite sides of the most important issues before it, was bound to
try Trump's patience.

He was already beyond the point of wanting the trip to end. As
we departed the hotel to go to the Cultural Center of the Philippines for the "family photo" and the opening ceremony, no one
wanted to get in the "Beast," the president's armored car, with Trump
and me.

As I started to discuss his meetings with Prime Minister Turnbull of Australia and President Rodrigo Duterte of the Philippines,
Trump began to berate me, asking me why I had planned such a demanding and lengthy trip. Reminding him that I had recommended
breaking up the trip months ago would have done no good.

"Mr. President, I am doing the best job I can for you. If you are not
happy with me, I am ready to go whenever you say the word."

He turned away and looked out the window for the rest of the
short drive. As we pulled up to the cultural center, I warned him

that he would be expected to perform the ASEAN handshake with the other leaders, crossing his arms and simultaneously grasping the hands of the leader to his left and right.

The next day, Trump had an opportunity to revel in his contrarianism during his meeting with Duterte, whom most leaders in the free world viewed with unease due to the thousands of extrajudicial killings carried out under his "war on drugs." I reminded Trump that when Duterte took office, he traveled to Beijing and stated that it was "time to say goodbye to Washington." I recommended that Trump be tough with him on human rights abuses and warn Duterte that his apparent love for Xi and the CCP was bound to be unrequited. U.S. relations were still very strong with leaders across the Philippine government and security forces. Trump might remind Duterte, I said, of the assistance that U.S. special forces had provided in the protracted and deadly fight against Muslim separatist terrorists in the Philippine city of Marawi.

Instead, Trump praised Duterte.

Sarah Huckabee Sanders later said that "human rights came up briefly" in the bilateral meeting. What she did not say is that the topic came up in the form of Trump admiring how "strong" Duterte was in the fight against drugs and even suggesting that the United States should send apprehended drug traffickers to Duterte "because I know you'll take care of them."

Duterte had responded, "Yes, can do."

They both laughed, after which Duterte said he was "a big fan of Machiavelli. When choosing between being feared and loved, I prefer being feared."

Trump was not the first U.S. president to accommodate abusive regimes, but his praising Duterte got him nothing. Trump might have objected to a treaty ally who was happy to take U.S. military support while expressing admiration for China, who had deferred the Philippine territorial dispute with China in the West Philippine Sea, and who accepted infrastructure loans and investments that ceded massive influence to Beijing. But he did not.

Years later, Trump told an interviewer, "It's funny, the relationships I have, the tougher and meaner [leaders] are, the better I get along with them. You'll explain that to me someday, okay? But maybe it's not a bad thing. The easy ones I maybe don't like as much or don't get along with as much."[8]

I came to see Trump's embrace of Duterte, and his berating me in the hotel room and in "the Beast," as connected to his struggle for self-worth. If he was accepted by strongmen like Duterte, Putin, and Xi, he might convince others, and especially himself, that he was strong. And his attempt to elicit anxiety or anger in me through derogation may have been a response to his sense of losing control—control over his life on the extended trip and, as I responded that I was happy to leave whenever he wanted, control over me.

On the long flight home, after a call to update the cabinet on the results of the trip, I reflected on the past nine months. I believed that I was getting Trump what he needed, but I realized that I was not the person to give him what he wanted. He wanted a yes-man, someone who would tell him more of what I had heard in that first Oval Office meeting in February, that his instincts were always right, combined with various other forms of flattery and affirmation.

But to give him what he wanted would have done a disservice to him and the nation. I resolved to continue getting him the best advice until my time was up.

CHAPTER 16

WEAKNESS IS PROVOCATIVE

TRUMP EXPRESSES 'GREAT CONFIDENCE' IN SAUDI REGIME ACCUSED OF POLITICAL PURGE . . . The prince recently took a number of bold and unprecedented steps at home, consolidating power by arresting 11 princes . . . *LEBANON ACCUSES SAUDI ARABIA OF HOLDING ITS PM HOSTAGE* . . . Hariri travelled to Riyadh on Nov. 3 before abruptly resigning in a televised statement a day later . . . Trump speaks with Erdogan about crisis in Syria . . . **TRUMP TELLS TURKISH PRESIDENT U.S. WILL STOP ARMING KURDS IN SYRIA** . . . Mr. Cavusoglu said Mr. Trump gave instructions to U.S. generals and his national security adviser, **Lt. Gen. H.R. McMaster,** that "no weapons would be issued" to the Kurdish forces . . . *SYRIAN SURPRISE: HOW TRUMP'S PHONE CALL CHANGED THE WAR* . . . Erdogan Says He and Trump Were on Same 'Wavelength' in Phone Call . . . Pakistan frees Hafiz Saeed, alleged mastermind of Mumbai attacks . . . **NEW NORTH KOREAN MISSILE IS A 'MONSTER'** . . . New missile test shows **North Korea capable of hitting all of US mainland** . . . *MCMASTER: 'NOT MUCH TIME' LEFT TO DEAL WITH NORTH KOREA* . . . **TRUMP RECOGNIZES JERUSALEM AS CAPITAL OF ISRAEL IN REVERSAL OF LONGTIME U.S. POLICY** . . . Trump's Jerusalem decision promises upheaval . . . Hamas calls for Palestinian uprising over Trump's Jerusalem plan . . . TRUMP SETS OUT NATIONAL SECURITY STRATEGY OF 'PRINCIPLED REALISM' AND GLOBAL COMPETITION . . . "GEOPOLITICS ARE BACK AND THEY ARE BACK WITH A VENGEANCE," SAYS MCMASTER . . . President Trump unveiled his new national security strategy today, emphasizing a need for strategic competitiveness among rival powers, and building strength through prosperity domestically . . . **TRUMP GIVES GREEN LIGHT TO SELLING LETHAL ARMS TO UKRAINE** . . . *IRANIAN CITIES HIT BY ANTI-GOVERNMENT PROTESTS*

SOON AFTER we returned from the Asia trip, Trump asked me to join him for lunch in the small dining room adjacent to the Oval Office. We had a wide-ranging discussion about the many changes he had made to U.S. foreign policy, with an emphasis on what would be the main theme of his National Security Strategy: the need to compete to advance and protect America's interests. We were accelerating progress on countering China's economic aggression, maximizing pressure on North Korea and Iran, and implementing the South Asia strategy. Trump had also approved a Russia strategy to impose costs on the Kremlin for its destabilizing actions, strengthen U.S. and allied defenses, and deter further aggression.

"Mr. President," I said, "I think it is time to confirm your decision to provide Ukraine with defensive capabilities and, in particular, the Javelin antitank missiles. Your cabinet fully supports providing and selling those weapons to Ukraine. As you said many times, it was ridiculous for the Obama administration to give Ukrainians first-aid kits, but not give them what they needed to fight. I know Putin told you in his last phone call, 'If you want peace, do not give Ukraine weapons,' and I know that some people are telling you that Javelins could provoke Russia, but Putin's history shows that what provokes him is the perception of weakness."

I pulled out a large rectangular chart with a time line and photos. "Below this time line are events or decisions that portrayed American weakness or lack of will, and above it are subsequent acts of Russian aggression. Mounting opposition to the war in Iraq during the Bush administration in 2006 inspires cyberattacks on Estonia in 2007 and the invasion of Georgia in 2008. The 2014 invasion of Ukraine follows the Obama administration's unenforced redline in Syria."

"Okay, General. What do you want me to do?"

I handed him a presidential decision memo with three options. "Mr. President, initial the option you want. One: No Javelins. Two: Provide the full amount through foreign military assistance. Three: Provide half the Javelins through assistance and sell Ukraine the other half."

He initialed option three and signed the memo instructing the departments to execute the already congressionally authorized sale and provision of Javelins. But implementation of that simple decision would prove difficult. Members of the White House staff impeded it, and the Department of Defense placed restrictions on how the Ukrainian Army could employ the systems.

I was learning how difficult it is to implement even clear presidential decisions. I would have to spend more time following up on execution.

★   ★   ★

AS THANKSGIVING approached, two holiday phone calls confirmed my assessment at the UN General Assembly that a myopic focus on the military destruction of ISIS had ceded the initiative in Syria. The first call was with President Erdoğan of Turkey at 8 a.m. on November 24, the day after Thanksgiving. As Putin had done during a phone call the previous week, Erdoğan told Trump that there was no longer justification for U.S. support to the Syrian Democratic Forces (SDF) because ISIS had been defeated. They both lied—Putin because he wanted the United States out so Assad could regain control of northeastern Syria, and Erdoğan because he wanted to prevent the development of a Kurdish Army that might seek independence and lay claim to eastern Turkey.[1] Like Putin, Erdoğan also portrayed Assad as the inevitable winner in the Syrian Civil War to garner Trump's approval for a Turkey-Iran-Russia-brokered end of the war.

That, too, was a lie. Assad was weak. His military was devastated. He had control of only 42 percent of the populated area of the country and of only 8 million of the 21 million prewar population. Two hundred billion dollars in infrastructure had been destroyed, and neither Assad nor his Russian and Iranian sponsors had the money to reconstruct the country. The SDF sat atop 67 percent of Syria's oil reserves.

Trump knew that what he was hearing were falsehoods, but Erdoğan, like Putin, had figured out how to play to Trump's distaste for sustained military operations in the Middle East. Erdoğan described continued arms transfers to the SDF as a "waste of money." U.S. support for the SDF was "null and void" because "ISIS was defeated."

Trump fell for it. "You're right, it is 'ridiculous,'" he said. "I told

General McMaster no weapons to anyone, now that it is over. I told General McMaster that to his face!"

Erdoğan and Putin seemed also to have shared their assessment that I was the principal impediment to their agendas. Erdoğan insinuated that I had delayed his phone call, telling Trump that the two of them should speak more often. Trump responded that he would give Erdoğan a personal phone number so he could reach him anytime.

Erdoğan must have judged the phone call successful. He would, no doubt, share his assessment with Putin and probably with the Iranians, too. Trump had never told me to stop the delivery of weapons. His vacillation on the call was bound to encourage Turkish action against the SDF, which would, in turn, divert the SDF from the far-from-completed mission of defeating ISIS. I believed that Trump's eagerness to disengage might also encourage Russia and Iran to give the United States a push out the door with proxy attacks against our small force in Syria and Iraq. Trump's ambivalence toward Syria and the Middle East generally would encourage others, such as Israel, the United Arab Emirates, and Saudi Arabia, to hedge with Russia and accommodate Assad. Assad's remaining in power would mean no resolution of a war that had killed more than 400,000 people, wounded over 1.3 million, displaced over 5 million internally, and forced 6.3 million to flee the country. Iran was perpetuating the weakness of its Arab neighbors to pursue its hegemonic goals to establish a superhighway to the Mediterranean and place a proxy Army on Israel's border.

Putin and Erdoğan were playing Trump. If I allowed this situation to go unchallenged, I would be derelict in my duty as national security advisor. I insisted that we schedule an NSC meeting on Syria before the holiday break.

The second Thanksgiving call was with Prime Minister Saad Hariri of Lebanon later that morning. Hariri had withdrawn his resignation as prime minister, which he had announced under duress on video while visiting Saudi Arabia. Crown Prince Mohammed bin Salman had coerced the resignation because he thought Hariri was weak in confronting Hezbollah, the organization that had assassinated Hariri's father, Rafic Hariri, in 2005.

MBS had also ordered the detention of hundreds of Saudi royals, billionaires, and senior government officials at the Ritz-Carlton hotel in Riyadh. There were reports of abuse, and many detainees had to relinquish financial assets to gain release. Saudi authorities described the monthslong operation as a crackdown on corruption, but it was primarily a way for MBS to consolidate power.

The perpetual turmoil in Lebanon and MBS's draconian actions were consistent with Trump's earlier description of the region as "one big mish mosh of crap." But I hoped that Trump would also conclude that without sustained U.S. engagement, the situation in the Middle East could get worse. I delivered a message to Hariri, which I had coordinated several days earlier with the State Department and my Quint counterparts, urging him to do more to get Hezbollah back behind the buffer zone. I also asked him to tell us what we and our allies might do to help him rekindle the March 14 Alliance, the coalition of political parties and independents that he had led in 2005 after his father's assassination during the "Cedar Revolution" that compelled Syrian forces to leave Lebanon.

The United States could not solve Lebanon's problems, but the Obama administration's accommodation of Iran had strengthened Hezbollah and allowed the terrorist organization to turn Lebanon into a base for operations, with 150,000 rockets pointed at Israel. I wanted Trump to see that he had already begun to restore U.S. influence in the region after the Obama administration disengaged and that when he spoke about leaving the Middle East, he sounded like President Obama, undermined the gains he was making, and set back efforts to defeat jihadist terrorists, counter Iranian aggression, protect Israel, and make progress on a resolution of the Israel-Palestinian conflict.

Hariri thanked me for the work that I and many others had done to gain his release and convince MBS that he, Hariri, despite his shortcomings, was the best person available to counter Hezbollah's growing influence. There would always be crises and disappointments in the Middle East. Lebanon would be in political and economic free fall one year later, and in October 2018, a fifteen-man Saudi hit squad with close ties to MBS would murder and dismember Saudi journalist and U.S. resident Jamal Khashoggi in the Saudi consulate in Istanbul.

In March 2018, six months before Khashoggi's unconscionable murder, I hosted MBS at my home for dinner. The candid conversation convinced me that the crown prince was committed to a reform agenda that included promoting women's rights and combating extremist perversions of Islam. I was profoundly disappointed and disgusted, then, when I learned of Khashoggi's murder, but I still believed that disengagement from the Middle East would neither arrest the region's cascading crises nor moderate the behavior of MBS and the Saudi royal family. Indeed, years later, the Biden administration would alienate the Saudis and resurrect the Obama policy of accommodating Iran with disastrous results.

After the Thanksgiving weekend, I told Kelly that Trump's dissonance about the Middle East and the long delay in bringing him options in Syria were dangerous. I used an analogy that I knew would resonate with the chief of staff. Like Trump, Ronald Reagan had cared little about the Middle East before confronting a war in the Levant. He sent Marines to Beirut on an ambiguous multinational peacekeeping mission while his secretaries of state and defense pursued divergent approaches to the Lebanese Civil War. After suffering the largest single-day loss of life for the Marine Corps since the Battle of Iwo Jima in 1945, the United States conducted a humiliating retreat that led to the ascendency of Hezbollah in Lebanon and encouraged a new generation of terrorists, including Osama bin Laden. Without a clear mission for U.S. forces in Syria as part of a strategy to protect and advance vital American interests in the Middle East, we were set up for another tragedy.

Mattis, doubtful of Trump's willingness to sustain the effort in Syria, seemed eager to withdraw. Tillerson, cognizant of the role U.S. forces played not only in the defeat of ISIS but also in countering Iran, preferred a long-term effort in support of the SDF.

Finally, Kelly agreed to an NSC meeting on the last working day before the holiday break in December.

*   *   *

BECAUSE TRUMP would make decisions before that meeting that had implications across the region, our team endeavored to place

those decisions in broader context and to highlight potential consequences. Anticipating those consequences required listening to and
considering the perspectives of our friends in the region.

It was in that spirit that Mike Bell and I met with King Abdullah II
of Jordan and his ambassador, Dina Kawar, at the ambassador's residence in Washington around noon on the Monday after Thanksgiving. The king was concerned that Trump's engagement with
the Israel-Palestinian peace process was biased in favor of Israel and
against the Palestinians. With over two million Palestinians living
in the country, many of whom were classified as refugees, the Hash-
emite Kingdom would be in jeopardy if hope for a two-state solution
evaporated. As custodian of the Muslim holy sites in Jerusalem, the
king asked that the United States prevent any change to the status of
the disputed city.

I would summarize the king's concerns to Trump when I returned
to the White House, but Abdullah was bound to be disappointed. By
the time he and Queen Rania arrived at Quarters 13 that evening for
a dinner Katie and I hosted in their honor, Trump had made the decision to recognize Jerusalem as the capital of Israel and to move the
U.S. embassy there from Tel Aviv.

Kushner, advisor Jason Greenblatt, U.S. Ambassador to Israel David Friedman, and I had first discussed the embassy move on November 15. The Jerusalem Embassy Act, which Congress passed in
1995, directed the president to move the U.S. embassy from Tel Aviv
to Jerusalem, but each president since Bill Clinton had delayed the
move by signing a waiver every six months. Tillerson had convinced
Trump to sign the waiver in May, but when it was time to do so
again in November, Kushner thought it time to make good on the
president's campaign promise to comply with the act.

As we spoke, I drafted the following objectives:

Keep the President's campaign promise to move the Embassy.

Make progress toward a peace deal between Israel and the Palestinians.

Prevent large-scale violence.

Limit Iranian and Hamas influence in the Palestinian territories in Gaza and the West Bank.

Keep regional states on board with the peace process and normalization of relations with Israel.

Two days later, Tillerson joined us for a meeting in the Oval Office. I summarized the objectives and noted the potential for unrest in the region, a further deterioration in Israeli-Palestinian relations, and a reduction in the already dim prospects for an eventual two-state solution.

Tillerson again recommended that Trump sign the waiver because of those downside risks. Friedman argued that conventional approaches to broker peace had not worked, suggesting that actors in the region would respect Trump for doing what he had promised to do.

When Trump suggested that the embassy move might ease the peace process, it was clear he was not going to sign another waiver.

I assured everyone that the NSC process would get the president their advice and ensure that the departments and agencies were ready to implement his decision.

"Okay, General, run the process," Trump said. "But I want to make the decision soon."

An NSC meeting in the Situation Room on November 27 allowed Trump to hear from his principal advisors. Tillerson and Mattis recommended that the president renew the waiver to avoid sparking widespread violence, but once Trump had made the decision, all were prepared to implement it.

On December 5 and 6, Trump called Netanyahu, Abbas, King Abdullah, King Salman, and al-Sisi. I called my key counterparts, as did Tillerson, Mattis, and Pompeo. I had recommended that Trump explicitly hold out the possibility that a portion of East Jerusalem could become the capital of a future Palestinian state. Trump rejected the idea, but he would give reassurances that the United States remained committed to facilitating a lasting peace agreement and maintaining "the status quo at Jerusalem's holy sites, including the Temple Mount, also known as Haram al-Sharif."

Friedman told me later that he had been wary about bringing the decision to the president through the NSC process, but he was surprised by how our team had acted as honest brokers and coordinated a comprehensive plan for implementation. And despite the controversial nature of the decision, none of our deliberations leaked. I asked Friedman to share his views with Trump, explaining that those who had joined the administration to press their own agendas had tried to portray the NSC staff as the problem instead of the solution to overcoming bureaucratic inertia and resistance to policy changes. For several days after the announcement, Mike Bell held regular meetings to help the departments and agencies to integrate mitigating diplomatic, informational, and security measures.

*   *   *

IT WAS not getting any easier to coordinate with the secretaries of defense and state. The twice-weekly phone calls had worked well, but Mattis and Tillerson, who had requested them months earlier, often missed them. I concluded that I had no option but to resort to formal and informal written communications when their departments slow-rolled or acted contrary to the president's decisions and policies.

I wrote to Tillerson, noting that Trump had said clearly that it was "useless to talk to the Taliban when they think they are winning," but State Department officials, as they had done with approaches to Pyongyang, were pursuing talks with the Taliban in Doha, Islamabad, and Mecca.

I sent Mattis a memo noting that, despite the president's directive and many public statements on lifting restrictions on U.S. forces in Afghanistan so they could pursue the Taliban, the Obama administration rules of engagement had remained in place. Mattis finally lifted the restrictions and restored status-based targeting of the Taliban.

Our senior directors continued to coordinate directly with their counterparts at the deputy and assistant secretary levels, but even that became problematic toward the end of 2017, as Tillerson occasionally forbade acting assistant secretaries from attending meetings and Mattis issued what one of his assistant secretaries described as a "gag order" to preclude collaboration on contingency planning for North Korea and Iran.

It was difficult to get State and Defense even to comply with Trump's directives to stop certain activities. I discovered that contrary to the South Asia strategy, which called for the suspension of all aid to Pakistan with a few exceptions, when Mattis visited Islamabad in the coming weeks, the Pentagon was going to deliver a military aid package that included more than $150 million worth of armored vehicles.

I called for a meeting with Mattis, Tillerson, Dunford, and the deputy director of the Central Intelligence Agency, Gina Haspel. I started by noting that the president had been very clear on multiple occasions to suspend aid to the Pakistanis until they halted support for terrorist organizations that were killing Afghans, Americans, and coalition members in Afghanistan. We had all heard Trump say, "I do not want any money going to Pakistan."

Mattis noted the possibility that Pakistan might retaliate in certain ways, but others, including Ambassador David Hale, who had joined by video from Islamabad, did not share those concerns. Mattis reluctantly halted that shipment of assistance, but other aid would continue, prompting Trump to tweet on New Year's Day, "The United States has foolishly given Pakistan more than 33 billion dollars in aid over the last 15 years and they have given us nothing but lies & deceit thinking of our leaders as fools. They give safe haven to the terrorists we hunt in Afghanistan with little help. No more!"[2]

Pakistan was not changing its behavior, and almost as an insult, the government released Hafiz Saeed, the mastermind behind the 2008 Mumbai terrorist attacks, on the eve of Mattis's visit. Moreover, a recent event in Pakistan involving hostages had exposed the undeniable complicity of Pakistan's Inter-Services Intelligence with the terrorists.

News reports criticized the president's tweet as capricious and devoid of a coherent policy.[3] But halting assistance was a critical part of the South Asia strategy that Trump had approved at Camp David in August. A lunch that the president hosted with the vice president, Tillerson, Mattis, Kelly, and me on December 14 helped me understand why it was difficult to implement Trump's guidance on Pakistan or to foster cooperation on contingency plans for North Korea.

North Korea had recently tested an intercontinental ballistic missile judged capable of reaching the United States.

After lunch, Tillerson and Mattis pulled out a chart with a notional time line at the bottom. Diplomatic and then military actions were depicted from left to right. Diplomatic actions were in green and military actions in red. The premise was that diplomatic and military actions were separate rather than integrated and that we could put maximum pressure on North Korea with diplomatic and economic actions alone.

But military efforts such as the interdiction of ships evading UN sanctions and visible preparations to respond to DPRK aggression were essential to convince Kim Jong-un that his regime was safer without the weapons than with them. Unless Kim thought the United States, South Korea, and Japan might conclude that the risk of a nuclear-armed North Korea outweighed the cost of a military campaign to destroy its missiles and nuclear facilities, he had little incentive to give them up.

If we had to act militarily, Trump asked Mattis, "What more do we need to do to be ready?" Mattis's response portrayed the military as unprepared, lacking the training and range of capabilities necessary for war. Trump was surprised: "How could our military not be ready when we are spending seven hundred billion dollars on it?"

As we walked out of the dining room, I said to Kelly, "What the hell was that? It sounded like [Mattis] was describing the military of the 1970s."

Mattis, who viewed the president as someone prone to rash decisions, seemed to have been underselling U.S. military prowess to give Trump pause. That may also have been the reason the Pentagon, when asked to participate in contingency planning and a tabletop exercise on North Korea, had slow-rolled the effort.

Slow-rolling was not limited to contingency planning or the Defense Department. The president kept asking me, "Are we at maximum pressure on North Korea?" The answer was no, as the State Department opposed secondary sanctions on Chinese banks facilitating illicit North Korean financial transactions. The State

Department was also ambivalent about Nikki Haley's effort to secure additional UN Security Council sanctions.

Thanks to Haley's persistent diplomacy with the backing of
Trump—who had told Xi, "Oil should be cut off entirely. . . . We
have to get much tougher faster"—the UNSC resolution passed, au-
thorizing member states to "seize, inspect, freeze, and impound any
vessel in their territorial waters found to be illicitly providing oil to
North Korea through ship-to-ship transfers, or smuggling coal and
other prohibited commodities from the country."[4]

Despite that authorization, U.S. forces did not conduct any inter-
dictions. Slow-rolling is bad etiquette in poker and could be disastrous in national security.

★   ★   ★

TRUMP AND I agreed that the United States had vacated arenas of
competition vital to national security.

I told Trump in late November, "Your National Security Strategy
is more than an academic exercise. It is an opportunity to describe
the significant shifts in policy that you are making, persuade others
to support those changes, and overcome normal bureaucratic inertia and opposition from the people who reflexively oppose anything
you propose.

"And, Mr. President, you have to own this strategy for it to serve
its purpose."

Sitting across from the Resolute Desk, Schadlow briefed him on
the main themes and the priority actions the strategy directed.

Trump responded, "This is fantastic." He directed Stephen Miller,
who was in the meeting and had reviewed drafts of the document, "I
want more language like this in my speeches."

The National Security Strategy appealed to Trump in part because we had started with the president's views on foreign policy.
And he liked much of the language because he had spoken it in previous speeches and statements we had helped draft to give him an opportunity to preview the strategy's main themes and big ideas. The
strategy appealed to Trump the iconoclast because it explicitly broke
with previous policies that were based on fundamentally flawed

assumptions. And Trump embraced the main theme of the strategy that the United States needed to compete to promote American prosperity, preserve peace through strength, advance U.S. influence, and protect the American people, the homeland, and the American way of life.[5]

I thanked Schadlow and her team for delivering a sound and compelling document that would drive Trump's foreign policy priorities across the government and for doing so in record time. As the first National Security Strategy to meet Congress's expectation that it be published during the first year of a presidency, this NSS had been foundational to and ensured consistency across the many other public strategies that followed it, from the National Defense Strategy to the Nuclear Posture Review to the Ballistic Missile Defense Strategy to the counterterrorism and cyber strategies. The collaborative process that Schadlow ran allowed fellow senior directors on the NSC staff, officials from across the government, and outside experts to challenge previous policies and generate new ideas about how to compete effectively.

The other purpose I had in mind for the NSS was to help Trump reconcile his contradictory predilections, especially the need to advance American interests abroad and his desire to retrench. The National Security Strategy and Trump's speech announcing it stated clearly that, while the United States cannot solve the world's problems or pay for everything, it can and would continue to catalyze positive developments in key regions of the world. The strategy acknowledged that alliances made America stronger while urging allies to pull their own weight. It communicated to adversaries and rivals that competition would not foreclose on cooperation, but that cooperation would come with an expectation of reciprocity. Trump's short introduction stated that America would "promote a balance of power that favors the United States, our allies, and our partners" while never losing sight of "our values and their capacity to inspire, uplift, and renew."

With the benefit of hindsight, it is difficult to argue against the objectives and priority actions in the NSS, such as improving border security, accelerating defense innovation, modernizing the nuclear deterrent, and protecting the national security innovation base. Subsequent events, such as Russia's massive invasion of Ukraine in

February 2022, highlighted the strategy's call for pursuing U.S. "energy dominance" and bolstering critical supply chains.

*   *   *

DECEMBER 20 was Trump's last day in the White House before he headed to Mar-a-Lago for Christmas with his family. I went to see him in the Oval Office before we walked to the Situation Room.

"Mr. President, I know you are wary of an open-ended commitment in Syria, but I also know that you do not want to allow the return of ISIS or permit Iran to establish a land bridge across Iraq and Syria that strengthens Hezbollah and other Iranian proxies and threatens Israel."

Pompeo, Coats, and I had, over the previous three weeks, shown Trump that what he was hearing from Erdoğan and Putin was disinformation aimed at getting him to abandon the SDF and help Assad regain control of the oil-rich northeastern part of the country. And in those conversations, I told the president that ordering U.S. forces out of Syria prematurely would be the same as Obama leaving Iraq in 2011, which had set the stage for the rise of ISIS.

The meeting went well, and Trump approved the strategy. Tillerson explained Trump's decision in a speech at the Hoover Institution at Stanford University in January 2018, noting the 2011 mistake of premature disengagement from Iraq and pledging to "continue to remain engaged as a means to protect our own national security interest."[6] I had done my best to show Trump that the United States' leaving the Middle East would neither conciliate the region's violent passions nor insulate America from them.

Still, it would be a constant struggle to help Trump remember the logical argument that had helped him resolve his dissonance about the Middle East and set a clear long-term vision to advance U.S. interests there.

*   *   *

I WAS satisfied that we had ended the year with the National Security Strategy rollout and the clarification of U.S. policy in Syria. My

approach to transcend rather than get mired in the internecine battles for control of foreign policy was tough but was getting results.

And I was drawing strength from the best part of my job—
working with talented and dedicated people who wanted to make a
difference. I had blocked time to make the rounds to our directorates
to take stock of the year and listen to their ideas about priorities in
the coming year. I asked each directorate to clarify its major goals
and describe how it and the interagency team aimed to achieve those
goals. And, as always, I asked the directorates how I could help them
overcome obstacles and take advantage of opportunities to acceler-
ate progress. We held another all-hands meeting in which I recognized members of our team who had contributed to the success of
the Asia trip, the NSS, and the Syria strategy. I sensed that morale
was high. Within the National Security staff, we were building momentum.

And we created some holiday cheer. Our team put together a
fantastic party in the Eisenhower Executive Office Building. Tom
Bossert and I offered toasts to thank our staff and their families for
the important work they were doing. The Georgetown University
Chamber Singers, accompanied by the U.S. Army Band Woodwind
Quintet, sang Christmas carols. Katie and I got to wish everyone the
best for the holidays as we made our way through the progressive
cocktail and hors d'oeuvre gatherings that each directorate hosted.
To cap off the evening, I introduced DJ Max Powers and confessed
my ambition to be remembered as the funkiest national security
advisor. During the following week, Katie and I hosted *two* ugly-
sweater parties for our dedicated Secret Service detail so that both
shifts could attend one.

The White House got quiet after Trump left for Mar-a-Lago. I enjoyed giving evening tours to family and friends, to show them the
decorations in the Residence. Aunt Nan and Tish visited just before
Christmas. Our family went to see the musical play *An American in
Paris* at the Kennedy Center on December 23. On Christmas Eve, Fr.
Paul Hurley, Katie, and I wandered around a dark White House looking for light switches to illuminate the Christmas trees. Father Paul
said Mass at our home for our family and some of our Catholic neighbors, and I experienced the comfort of family, friendship, and faith.

Later that evening, we brought dinner out to our Secret Service detail, who had placed next to the armored SUV an illuminated blowup of Olaf, the friendly enchanted snowman from Disney's *Frozen*.

★   ★   ★

THE DAY after Christmas, I rushed out to the SUV to tell the Secret Service that I needed to make an urgent trip to Philadelphia. My father had suffered a stroke. Our team scrambled a second SUV and got us moving north fast on the interstate.

When I arrived at the county hospital, I quickly realized that I had to get my father out of there. The doctors and nurses were overwhelmed with emergency cases, including gunshot wounds. My dad was receiving little attention. A kind friend of Jared's arranged a flight for my dad to a teaching hospital, where he received dramatically better care, albeit too late to prevent severe damage to his speech and motor skills.

My gratitude for our Secret Service team would deepen as they got me to Philadelphia many times over the coming months as my father underwent extensive treatment and rehabilitation. It was sad to see this former hard-nosed athlete and tough soldier hobbled by the stroke, but he was cognizant that Katie, Tish, and my cousins were with him, and we enjoyed our time together. Fr. Vince Burns visited many times, as did troopers from the First Troop Philadelphia City Cavalry. When it was doubtful that my father would recover, Father Vince said Mass for us and administered the sacrament of the Anointing of the Sick.

As in combat, responsibility suppressed my sorrow over my father's condition. And there were signs of hope and positive momentum in the New Year. Widespread protests in Iran that had begun in Mashhad, the nation's second-largest city, indicated that maximum pressure was the right policy toward that country. I recommended that, in contrast to the Obama administration's silence during massive protests in 2009, Trump tweet his support for the protestors: "The world is watching!" and "Oppressive regimes cannot endure forever."[7] As some in the U.S. media criticized Trump for his tweets, Iranian protesters chanted, "Our enemy is right here, they are lying that it is America."

To put more international pressure on the regime, Ambassador Haley and I planned a visit of the UN Security Council ambassadors to the capital, during which Haley took them to the Washington Navy Yard to see a collection of rockets and missiles that Iran had provided the Houthis for attacks against the UAE, Saudi Arabia, and shipping in the Bab al-Mandeb Strait. Years later, after the Biden administration resurrected the policy of accommodation with Iran and removed the terrorist designation from the Houthis, the latter would acquire more advanced missiles from Iran and use them to disrupt shipping in the Bab al-Mandeb after Hamas's October 7, 2023, murderous attack on Israel.

★   ★   ★

WHEN I met with my senior directors in early January 2018, they described frustrations with the State and Defense Departments. Although officials in both departments wanted to collaborate, the secretaries were impeding efforts to work together. I asked them to help make this the year of implementation, but they complained that it was getting more difficult to keep the departments and agencies aligned. I told them that "to overcome the obstacles that we are encountering, we will continue to lead by charm. Focus on policy objectives as a way to resolve differences. Communicate through multiple channels at multiple levels. Be good listeners and make every initiative their idea. And be radically transparent in everything we do."

But my colleagues were far from transparent with me. Kelly had begun to meet with Tillerson and Mattis. One day, when I walked in on him having breakfast with Tillerson and Tillerson's chief of staff, I made light of the situation, "Chief, I'll tell you the same thing I told Rex and Secretary Mattis months ago, whenever you are ready to expand your club, I am embarrassingly free."

Tillerson and Mattis have gotten to him, I thought.

Kelly was also making it more difficult to schedule the meetings that were necessary to keep the president informed and engaged with his foreign policy agenda. The chief of staff had instructed the assistant in the Oval Office to call him whenever I was in with the president alone. His intention was to impose order, but he was making it harder for me to do my job.

In retrospect, the constant strain of coping with Trump's tirades seemed to have blinded Kelly to some of the hard-won accomplishments of the past year. In a principals committee meeting, he said that Trump had to "eat the Obama strategy for the first year." I was speechless: it was exactly the opposite of what we had done.

Kelly and I could have been better partners. He seemed to have been persuaded by the Tillerson and Mattis mantra "There is only one secretary of state." But there was also only one president, and it was Trump's foreign policy. As Tillerson and Mattis intensified efforts to get rid of me, Kelly pressed the Army to nominate me for four-star commands. When he raised the possibility with me, I reminded him that I had decided when I took the job not to compete for promotion and to retire when I was done.

Late in January 2018, Kelly raised the prospect of my leaving. I said that I was happy to go whenever the president wanted to make a change. "I'll go talk to him about it now," I said as I got up to leave.

Kelly said, "No, don't do that."

It seemed that he wanted more time to talk with Trump about who might succeed me. I would do the same in the coming weeks.

CHAPTER 17

ALLIES, AUTHORITARIANS, AND AFGHANISTAN

TRUMP TO DAVOS: 'AMERICA IS OPEN FOR BUSINESS' . . . Trump praises African leader after disparaging comments . . . *TRUMP ARRIVED IN DAVOS AS A PARTY WRECKER. HE LEAVES PRAISED AS A PRAGMATIST* . . . Vice President Mike Pence: US and allies will take whatever 'action is necessary' in defense against North Korea . . . Fred Warmbier hopes his presence at Olympics is reminder of brutality of the Kim regime . . . **US STEPS UP EFFORT TO AVERT CONFRONTATION WITH TURKEY OVER SYRIAN KURDISH MILITIA** . . . Scores of Russian mercenaries reportedly killed by US airstrikes in Syria . . . *PUBLIC REPORTS 'CLEARLY SHOW' ASSAD'S USE OF CHEMICAL WEAPONS: MCMASTER* . . . H.R. McMaster says US in no rush to leave Syria, urging 'economic consequences' for Iran and Russia . . . **AT MUNICH SECURITY CONFERENCE, FRAYED RELATIONS ON DISPLAY AS GLOBAL CRISES GROW** . . . Putin's 'Invincible' Missile Is Aimed at U.S. Vulnerabilities . . . *MCMASTER CAUGHT IN THE MIDDLE AS MATTIS AND TILLERSON MANEUVER TO CONSTRAIN TRUMP ON NATIONAL SECURITY ISSUES* . . . US Maintains 'Maximum Pressure' on North Korea Ahead of Possible Summit . . . **TRUMP FIRES TILLERSON, TAPS POMPEO AS NEXT SECRETARY OF STATE** . . . Putin tightens grip on power with overwhelming Russian election win . . . **PRESIDENT TRUMP CONGRATULATES PUTIN ON RE-ELECTION**

"I THINK that this trip qualifies you as a globalist, Mr. President," I said as Gary and I sat down across from Trump on Air Force One.

We were on our way to Davos, Switzerland, for the annual meeting of the World Economic Forum, which according to its website, "engages the foremost political, business, cultural and other leaders of society to shape global, regional and industry agendas." Davos also provides fodder for conspiracy theorists who allege that the forum is a secret society that controls the world's governments and economies and material for satirists who note that attendees fly there on private jets to lament global warming.

Trump wanted mainly to promote his trade and economic agendas and to tout the success of his economic policies. One month earlier, on December 22, 2017, he had signed the Tax Cuts and Jobs Act (TCJA) into law, reducing the corporate tax rate from 35 percent to 21 percent. But I saw Davos as an important opportunity to clarify the nature of the competition with the Chinese Communist Party and counter the softheaded cosmopolitanism that gave China and other authoritarian rivals space to undermine the international order. The main events would be Trump's speech to the forum and a dinner with CEOs of European companies that invest and manufacture in the United States.

Trump is not a morning person. I could tell that he was grumpy as Gary and I joined him, Jared, and Ivanka at the dining room table in his hotel suite on January 26.

"Mr. President, you will recall that you have three bilateral meetings this morning: Prime Ministers May and Netanyahu and President Paul Kagame of Rwanda, who will soon take over as the chairperson of the African Union."

Trump got red-faced and breathed heavily through his nose, the usual buildup to the eruption of his temper. "Why the hell am I meeting with Kagame? Whose idea was that?" he said, looking at me. I had briefed him on the meeting before, but he had clearly forgotten.

I smiled and pointed across my chest: "It was Gary's idea, Mr. President."

"Mr. President," Gary said, "Kagame wants to help improve your relationship with African leaders. It will be a positive meeting. He's not expecting an apology."

The Kagame meeting got off to a rough start when Kagame told Trump that some African leaders were still upset about his reported description of their countries as "shitholes," and Trump responded, "Tell me who they are, and I will cut off their aid."

An affable conversation followed, and Kagame, who valued his relationship with the United States, would go on to promote goodwill between Trump and African leaders.

Trump's speech before the World Economic Forum was, in part, a counter to Xi's much-touted 2017 Davos performance, in which he expressed support for globalization. After a musical interlude, World Economic Forum founder Klaus Schwab gave Trump a warm introduction. Trump took credit for U.S. economic growth, wage growth, and low unemployment and then got the crowd's attention:

"The United States will no longer turn a blind eye to unfair economic practices, including massive intellectual property theft, industrial subsidies, and pervasive state-led economic planning. These and other predatory behaviors are distorting the global markets and harming businesses and workers, not just in the U.S., but around the globe."

I thought that "Trump the globalist" had done a great job putting his National Security Strategy and the pillar of "advance American influence" into practice. Yet the media coverage of his speech relative to Xi's speech in 2017 was absurd. CNN, which had described Xi's speech as a "robust defense of globalization," highlighted in 2018 the reaction of self-described "ethical jeweler" Pippa Small, who said that Trump had almost made her cry because it was "all about money." She was, of course, attending the World Economic Forum, not an art festival.

There was much more to be done to compete with China on the battleground of perception—especially among the Davos crowd. Many World Economic Forum attendees and the press would continue to fawn over Xi as they paid lip service to "ESG" (environmental, social, and governance) concerns while investing in a country whose governance practices included genocide, forced labor, and technologically enabled Orwellian means of stifling human freedom.

My successor would say that Trump's National Security Strategy was written, filed away, and never returned to again. But work was under way across the government to implement the strategy and to effect major shifts in U.S. foreign policy, the most important of which was the abandonment of "cooperation and engagement" with China and the recognition that the United States had to compete. In many one-on-one meetings with CEOs of some of the largest U.S. companies, I listened to complaints about various forms of Chinese economic aggression, after which my interlocutor would invariably say to me, "Please do not say I told you this." CEOs would support a competitive approach to the CCP, but they had allowed their companies to become overly reliant on staying in the party's good graces. Although Trump would vacillate between his desire for a trade deal with China and the actions necessary to counter the weaponization of its mercantilist model (such as investment screening, tariffs, and export controls), the general direction of U.S. policy toward the CCP had shifted fundamentally and would endure into the Biden administration.

★   ★   ★

ON JANUARY 30, I welcomed the Warmbier family to my office. "It is an honor to meet you," I told them. "I know that there is nothing I can say to lessen your sorrow, but please accept my deepest condolences on the loss of Otto." Later, Otto Warmbier's parents, Fred and Cindy, and his brother, Austin, and sister, Greta, would attend that evening's State of the Union address as guests of the First Lady.

Otto had been a student at the University of Virginia when, on his way to study abroad in Asia, he joined a tour of North Korea. The North Korean regime's thugs arrested him under false charges and sentenced him to fifteen years of hard labor. They tortured him nearly to death and released him just before he died from his injuries.

In his address, Trump would condemn the "criminal regime" and pledge "to honor Otto's memory with American resolve." I promised the same to that extraordinary family. But I was concerned that the maximum pressure Trump wanted placed on North Korea was dissipating.

Ambassador Haley had secured new UN sanctions, including a reduction in refined oil imports by 90 percent. But while South Korean president Moon was speaking the language of maximum pressure, he was doing everything he could to initiate an inter-Korean dialogue and suggesting sanctions relief to allow a North Korean contingent to participate in the upcoming Winter Olympics in PyeongChang, South Korea. Moreover, China was resisting additional sanctions.

I believed that maximum pressure could work. This was no time to let up.

Kim Jong-un appeared to be under duress in his New Year's Day speech, in which he announced his willingness to begin a North-South dialogue and send a joint delegation to the upcoming Olympics. Then, on January 9, Moon met with Kim at the DMZ. My South Korean counterpart, Chung Eiu-yong was ecstatic when he called me that evening, telling me that Kim was "sending a message of hope."

I told him, "I am not so sure. What if Kim is just desperate for sanctions relief and is trying to drive a wedge between us? The one thing that could blow up the relationship between our presidents is South Korea appearing as a neutered bystander in a conflict between the United States and North Korea."

I did not tell Chung that Trump had been asking me, "Why don't we get out of South Korea and let Russia and China deal with North Korea?" Or that as Trump complained about the trade deficit with South Korea, he had asked me, "Why are we defending people who hate us?"

I suggested to Chung that we get together with our Japanese counterpart, Yachi Shotaro in San Francisco as soon as possible to ensure that Seoul, Tokyo, and Washington stayed aligned.

On Saturday, January 13, as we had in the first trilateral, I met separately with Yachi and Chung prior to dinner. Then, over steaks and cabernet at the Leatherneck Steakhouse on the top floor of the Marines' Memorial Club and Hotel, I stressed to Yachi and Chung the importance of our three nations sticking together. "Kim may be smarter than he looks," I suggested. "If he creates the impression that U.S. defense of the peninsula is unappreciated or unnecessary, he will amplify voices of those in the United States who are anxious to retrench and bring U.S. troops home. Getting U.S. forces off the peninsula could allow a possibly nuclear-armed North Korea to coerce both of your countries. We have to stick together, not allow the pressure to dissipate, and adhere to the principles we established in our last meeting."

We agreed that there would be no concessions to get to the negotiating table, such as a freeze-for-freeze, and no lifting of sanctions before there was irreversible momentum toward denuclearization. We were already trying to plug leaks in the pressure campaign as joint exercises scheduled at the time of the Olympics were "deconflicted." I was worried that Chung and especially his boss were willing to do just about anything to have a sustained dialogue with Kim Jong-un.

Chung's description of the "peace Olympics," in which North and South would march under a unified banner in the opening ceremonies, contrasted starkly with the unspeakable brutality inflicted on Otto Warmbier. I promised the Warmbiers that I would do all I could to increase the pressure on the Kim family dictatorship. Vice President Pence, who would lead the delegation to the Olympics with his wife, Karen, and Ivanka, invited Fred Warmbier to accompany him to PyeongChang.

Pence shared our assessment that Kim was mounting the charm offensive to relieve the pressure on his regime. I warned Pence that Moon would try his best to play matchmaker between the U.S. delegation and the North Korean delegation led by Kim Jong-un's sister Kim Yo-jong and the nonagenarian nominal head of state, Kim Yong-nam. In a lengthy discussion in the Oval Office, Trump thought it would be good for Pence to meet Kim Yo-jong in passing, to deliver a tough message such as "This could end badly or end well for you. The choice is yours." But Tillerson, who reflexively opposed anyone but him conducting interactions classified as diplomacy, disagreed. Frustrated with Tillerson's position, Trump looked at Pence: "Okay, if they ask for a meeting, you decide."

Pottinger, Hooker, and I followed up with Pence and his chief of staff, Nick Ayers, before Pence departed for the Olympics. We agreed that the vice president should avoid efforts by Seoul to arrange a photo op that might be represented as an indicator that the United States was backing off maximum pressure. If a chance meeting occurred, the key messages to communicate would be that "the president and our military are ready, President Trump has decided that he will not accept North Korea as a nuclear weapons state, pressure will mount, and time is running out. You have a better future available."

And to eliminate Moon as a middleman who, we suspected, was telling Kim and Trump what he thought each of them wanted to hear, Pence would make it clear that "no one speaks for the United States except the United States."

Moon tried and failed to set up Pence and Kim's sister for a conversation or at least a photo opportunity. Although neither party spoke to the other, hopes were rekindled that the Olympic spirit might be the beginning of the long-awaited thaw in relations between North and South and would finally transform the government in Pyongyang into something less brutish and dangerous.

Moon's deep desire for dialogue and North Korea's warped charm offensive in PyeongChang, complete with a unit of two hundred young women cheerleaders, were not the only reasons I was worried that pressure on the North was dissipating. In Washington, Tillerson, despite Trump's "wasting his time" tweet, continued to pursue talks with Pyongyang. In a meeting with Trump, the secretary of state talked about "peeling off layers" of sanctions in return for progress in negotiations, exactly what we had all vowed to avoid.

Language in the State of the Union address and the attendance of victims of North Korea's brutality were meant to keep the pressure on Pyongyang, but even Trump, who had been strong in his message to Xi and Putin on North Korea, told Moon the week before the speech that he "would be willing to meet Kim Jong-un."

Trump dictated to me the language he wanted Moon to use: "At some time, it would be good to meet because we would get along, and it would be a good result for the world."

Maximum pressure required a strong, consistent message from the president and everyone who spoke for him. But consistency, I had learned, was not Trump's strong suit. And his inconsistency was not limited to North Korea.

★　　★　　★

TRUMP'S VACILLATION on Syria and the Middle East broadly had, as I had feared, created a vacuum that others, including Russia and Turkey, were filling. In late January, Erdoğan ordered an offensive in the northwestern part of Syria to protect Turkey against what he described as a Kurdish "terror Army." The stated objective of the offensive, which was centered on the town of Afrin, was to create a nineteen-mile-deep "safety zone" within Syria devoid of Kurdish fighters and to prevent pockets of territory under Kurdish control from coalescing into a single area. I had been planning for some time to visit Turkey to work with Erdoğan's closest advisors to identify ways to resolve some of our problems, and accentuate areas in which our interests aligned, but Tillerson had opposed my traveling. I decided that we now needed direct communication between me and Erdoğan's highly centralized Office of the President to prevent a further deterioration in the relationship. I accepted the invitation of my counterpart, Ibrahim Kalin, to meet with him and Hakan Fidan, director of the National Intelligence Organization, on February 11 in Istanbul. I suggested that, while we conducted a two-plus-two meeting, our teams work separately and then brief us on their ideas. Kalin agreed.

For that trip, I took with me Nadia Schadlow, who had replaced Dina Powell as deputy national security advisor for strategy after Dina departed the administration in January; Fiona Hill, our senior director for Europe and Russia; and representatives from the key departments, including Col. Rich Outzen from the State Department.

Over dinner at the Palazzo Corpi, a magnificent 1882 mansion with elegantly frescoed walls, Consul General Jennifer Davis described a relationship on the rocks. The Turkish government was harassing embassy and consulate local staff. The state-controlled media spewed a steady stream of anti-American propaganda, including unfounded accusations that the United States was behind the 2016 coup attempt against Erdoğan. Prospects for the future of the relationship were grim, Davis said, due to the conservative Islamist ideology and anti-Western populism animating Erdoğan and his party.

The U.S. relationship with Turkey would require a sustained effort. I knew that I would not be around long enough to see it through, but if I could deliver a well-reasoned assessment of the relationship, a mutual understanding of our interests, and agreed priorities for solving problems, others could follow through and at least prevent the relationship from foundering completely.

The next morning, our party made the short drive to the Yildiz Palace complex and grounds, first used as an imperial estate during the reign of Sultan Ahmed I, in the early seventeenth century. Kalin and Fidan met us on the steps of the Mabeyn Köşkü, one of several imperial Ottoman pavilions and villas, a fitting venue evocative of Erdoğan's and his party's sentimental nostalgia for the Ottoman Empire.

I thanked Kalin and Fidan for hosting us in such a historic and elegant place. I told them that maybe memories of the Russo-Turkish wars and the Ottoman-Persian wars to which the buildings there bore witness might make easier our task of arresting the drift in our relationship. I wanted first to hear their assessment, because I "believe that the growing distance between us could be the most profound shift in the geopolitical landscape since the end of the Cold War. And I believe that shift is terrible for both of our nations."

As expected, Kalin, who did most of the talking, complained heavily about U.S. support to the Syrian Democratic Forces and the U.S. failure to extradite Erdoğan's arch-nemesis, Muhammed Fethullah Gülen.

When he finished, I pulled out a chart that was a by-product of the strategies for Syria and Turkey that Trump had approved during the week before Christmas. It listed the strategic objectives of major actors in the Syrian Civil War, including Iran, Israel, Jordan, Russia, Syria, Turkey, and the United States. The objectives were arranged in boxes and color-coded for each country. It was a striking depiction of the general alignment between U.S. and Turkish objectives and divergence between Turkey and the Syria-Russia-Iran axis. The one outlier was the Turkish objective of curtailing U.S.-SDF ties.

Our discussion confirmed two obstacles on each side that were preventing an improvement in our relationship. For Turkey, it was Gülen and U.S. support to the SDF. For the United States, it was the unjust imprisonment of American chaplain Andrew Brunson and the purchase of the Russian S-400 air defense system. I told them that I would regret to see it, but we would soon have to take measures to impose costs on Turkey for both. The end of Turkey's participation in the F-35 program was a certainty if the S-400 sale proceeded. I don't think they believed me.

As I had warned Kalin and Fidan, Brunson would be released only after Trump placed punitive tariffs on Turkey in August 2018 that resulted in an 18 percent devaluation in the lira. Trump also terminated Turkish participation in the F-35 program.[1]

Tillerson had follow-on meetings in Ankara, but both of us would be gone two months later. Two years later, when a Russian and Iranian offensive in Idlib Province killed approximately sixty Turkish soldiers and drove nearly one million more refugees toward the Turkish border, I wondered if Fidan and Kalin remembered our discussion. My hope was that, in the long term, the importation of Russian arms and Turkey's deepening dependence on Russian energy would embolden Moscow to use its leverage against Ankara and thereby revive unhappy memories of Turkey's experience with the Russian Empire. And, I thought, Iran's hegemonic aspirations in the region would eventually collide with Turkey's interests in Syria and the Middle East. But Erdoğan's and his AKP party's sympathies for Islamist parties, their close relationship with Qatar, and their antipathy to Israel would, in the near term, keep Erdoğan close to Tehran and Moscow.

On the flight home, I debriefed the cabinet, including Tillerson, who would visit the Turkish foreign minister and Erdoğan the following week, and Mattis, who would meet his Turkish counterpart at a NATO ministerial meeting. I suggested that we refine our Turkey strategy with an emphasis on the modest objective of avoiding a complete breakup while developing contingency plans for the worst-case scenario, including the relocation of U.S. military assets currently in Turkey. Years later, when Erdoğan would say after the horrible attacks on Israel of October 7, 2023, that Hamas was not a terrorist organization but a "liberation group," I thought it might be time for the NSC to dust off that plan.

*   *   *

TURKEY WAS not alone in taking advantage of the ambiguous U.S. policy in Syria. Moscow apparently concluded that if Trump had one foot out the door, it was time to give him a little push. On February 7, 2018, Russian mercenaries and other pro-Assad forces reinforced with tanks and artillery attacked U.S. forces, and the Kurdish and Arab militiamen they were advising, in northeastern Syria.

The mercenaries were from the Wagner Group, a state-funded private military company owned by Yevgeny Prigozhin, the Russian oligarch known as "Putin's cook," a man indicted by U.S. special investigator Robert Mueller and sanctioned by the Trump administration for his role in sowing disinformation during the 2016 U.S. presidential election. (Prigozhin would meet his demise in an unexplained plane explosion in 2023 after marching on Moscow with a force composed largely of ex-convicts.)

The attack on the U.S.-SDF base was ill-conceived and poorly executed. U.S. forces and their partners killed more than two hundred Russian mercenaries while suffering no casualties. The mercenaries' immediate objective was to gain control of an old Conoco oil plant needed to defray the costs of the war and reconstruction. But I thought a secondary objective may have been to cause U.S. casualties and, as with the "Black Hawk Down" incident in Somalia in 1993, catalyze the withdrawal of U.S. forces.

No battle like that between Russians and Americans had ever occurred, even at the height of the Cold War. But Putin was eager to sweep the crushing defeat under the rug. He used Prigozhin's Wagner Group to give him deniability, and he did not want to cope with negative news that might interfere with his engineering a lopsided victory in the forthcoming presidential election.

One week later, I was shaking the hand of Putin's right-hand man, Nikolai Patrushev, at the U.S. consulate in Geneva. Patrushev had wanted to meet for a long time, but I had again delayed, in deference to Tillerson. By early 2018, it was clear that Tillerson's solo effort to find areas of cooperation with Russia had achieved disappointing results and that it was time to establish more direct channels of communication between the White House and the Kremlin, other than the occasional phone calls and meetings between Trump and Putin.

No one on our team believed that the Geneva meeting would solve our problems with Russia. Events of the following month confirmed that assessment—including the Skripal poisoning and a chest-thumping speech in which Putin announced new nuclear weapons and showed an animated video depicting these weapons descending on what appeared to be Mar-a-Lago.

After introductions, I offered coffee to the Patrushev delegation, but none of them touched the light refreshments we had on hand. Fiona Hill; director for Russia Joe Wang; our State Department consul general, Ted Allegra; and I sat down across from Patrushev, two of his senior staff, and a notetaker. Patrushev had the air of self-confidence of a former KGB officer and the sullenness of a patriot full of resentment after witnessing the downfall of the system to which he had sworn allegiance.[2]

I wanted Patrushev to understand that the United States was determined to oppose future Russian aggression in Ukraine or the Black Sea region. I did not mention the failed Russian attack in Syria. Instead, I made the general point that the next act of Russian aggression in Syria or Ukraine could trigger a major military confrontation, even if Moscow intended to act below the threshold of what might elicit a military response from NATO.

I wondered if Patrushev had ever smiled. I thought his face might crack and fall off if he did. But he did sort of smirk when I thanked him for providing the U.S. Congress with what seemed to be the only issue members agreed on—sanctioning Russia for its subversive activities. I noted that the first major foreign policy legislation to emerge from the U.S. Congress after President Trump took office was the Countering America's Adversaries Through Sanctions Act, which passed in the Senate in a 98–2 vote after the House passed it 419–3. Patrushev's half smile seemed meant to communicate that despite the Kremlin's denials, Russia was, of course, deeply engaged in cyber-enabled information warfare, including the sustained attacks on me that peaked in August 2017.

I ended the meeting by expressing hope that "Russia will stop acting reflexively against the United States, at least in areas in which those actions cut against Moscow's interests."

The meeting confirmed for me that Trump, like his two predecessors, was bound to be disappointed in his effort to build a better relationship with Putin. Putin and Patrushev had low opinions of American resolve, and although Trump had approved extensive sanctions on Russia and decided to provide and sell defensive weapons to Ukraine, his mixed messages would not disabuse Putin of that opinion. I was sure there would be more challenges to come.

★　　★　　★

ON SATURDAY, February 17, I arrived at the Munich Security Conference in time for a large dinner at which Prime Minister Netanyahu was to deliver the keynote address. Netanyahu moved from the seat across the table to sit next to me. He was concerned about Hezbollah's improved capabilities, including precision rockets, and the likelihood that it and other Iranian proxies, including Hamas and Palestine Islamic Jihad in Gaza and the West Bank, could attack in the coming year after the election in Lebanon.

He thanked me for the close coordination with his team, and I took advantage of the opportunity to voice my concerns about his hedging approach to Russia. "Prime Minister, you know that Putin is using a 'bait and switch'—baiting you with the promise to curtail Iran's presence and influence in Syria while actually enabling Iran's proxies on your borders."

Netanyahu smiled and said he had better return to his seat.

Getting others to see and act on the threat from Russia was the main theme of my trip. In separate meetings with German minister of foreign affairs Sigmar Gabriel and defense minister Ursula von der Leyen, I tried to convince them that the Russia-to-Germany natural gas pipeline Nord Stream 2 was a bad deal and that it was past time to reverse Germany's effective disarmament since the end of the Cold War. It would take Russia's massive reinvasion of Ukraine in February 2022 to kill Nord Stream 2 and impel German chancellor Olaf Scholz to declare a *Zeitenwende*, or watershed moment, and begin to rearm. Obviously, Scholz and much of Europe were too late to prevent the first major war in Europe since World War II.

In the speech I delivered at the conference—which immediately followed a speech by Russian foreign minister Sergey Lavrov—I emphasized the need to counter the proliferation and use of the most destructive and heinous weapons on earth, defeat jihadist terrorists, and reform international institutions that had been subverted and turned against their purpose. But what made news was the response I gave to a question from the member of the Russian Duma, the lower house of the Federal Assembly. As I mentioned in chapter 1, he suggested cooperation between Moscow and Washington in the area of cyber-security. After joking that I doubted there would be any Russian cyber experts available because they were all engaged in subverting our democracies, I described evidence cited in the Mueller investigation's indictments of Russians for election interference in 2016 as "incontrovertible."

My statement incensed Trump and almost certainly accelerated my departure from the administration. Press reports refracted my answer through the lens of the false accusations of "collusion." Trump remained unable to recognize that he could both accept that Russia had conducted a cyber-enabled information warfare attack during the 2016 election and reject assertions that the attacks were intended to bias or had succeeded in biasing the results in his favor. Partisan politics had helped the Russians and their alt-right fellow travelers and undermined the most important requirement for success in the White House or any organization: trust.

When I saw Trump on February 20, a year after he had hired me, I said, "I know you're angry with me, but I was only calling out the Russians, not agreeing with those accusing you of so-called collusion or claiming that Russia affected the election result." He was civil, but I could tell he was still angry. He avoided eye contact with me for the rest of our meeting.

When Gary Cohn told me he planned to announce his departure from the White House on March 6, I told him, "I think I'll be close behind you. I'm thinking right after the NATO summit in August."

Gary replied, "I don't think it'll be that long."

The first deliberately leaked stories about my impending departure had appeared on March 4.

*   *   *

ON THE afternoon of March 8, I hosted South Korea national security advisor Chung Eui-yong in my office for a one-on-one debrief on his meeting with Kim Jong-un in Pyongyang three days earlier. Separately, Deputy Director of the CIA Gina Haspel met with South Korea's director of national intelligence, Suh Hoon, who had also attended the meeting with Kim. We then summarized the results for select members of the cabinet, including Mattis and Deputy Secretary of State John Sullivan—Tillerson was traveling in Africa—in a conference room in the Eisenhower Executive Office Building. Our plan was to meet with Trump the following morning before asking Chung and Suh to join him in the Oval Office.

All was going according to plan until I received a note that the president had heard about our meeting in the EEOB and wanted to see Chung and Suh right away. I asked Pottinger to take over for me, tapped Haspel on the shoulder, and walked with her to the Oval Office. I politely apologized to the administrative assistant who tried to stop us as we entered the Oval. I felt it important to pre-brief Trump.

"We believe that Kim is feeling the effects of the pressure campaign and wants a way out," I told him. "That is the main reason he wants to meet with you. We also think that President Moon and his team want desperately to get talks started and are probably telling you and Kim what they think each of you wants to hear. You have two choices: say you will talk now or tell Kim that you will wait until you see progress toward denuclearization. In either case, we should make no concessions just for talks, and we should keep the pressure up." I turned to Haspel: "Gina, what would you like to add?"

Haspel didn't get a chance to respond; Kelly opened the door and ushered in the others who had been in the meeting at the EEOB. I walked over to the door and asked, "What the hell are you doing? We were pre-briefing the president."

Kelly responded, "Everyone else should be here, too."

It was more evidence that he was trying to squeeze me out—but more important: Trump was not going to get anything out of a discussion with eight people in his office.

Although I knew Trump would find the prospect of a summit with Kim irresistible, I wanted to suggest that he send a strong message back to Moon that we would not let up on the pressure. I caught Pottinger's eye, and we both smiled in resignation as Chung and Suh entered the room.

Chung sat down next to Trump and relayed Kim Jong-un's invitation to meet with Trump. When Trump immediately answered yes, Chung just about fell out of his chair. Then Trump asked Chung and Suh to make the announcement to the press from the White House.

Kelly and I would exchange words as I departed the Oval Office, and I let him know what I thought about how he handled this situation. But there was no time for hard feelings.

I sat with Chung at the conference table in my office and drafted a statement on a legal pad in long hand. Chung and Pottinger reviewed it. Our team quickly typed it up. I called President Moon's office on my secure line, handed the phone to Chung, and left him and Suh alone there to update Moon and get his approval on the statement.

Sarah Huckabee Sanders arranged for Chung to address the press at the "sticks" outside the entrance to the West Wing. Once everything was set, I asked Chung and Suh to excuse me—Katie and I were hosting a long-planned farewell dinner for Gary and Lisa Cohn. "Eiu-yong, break a leg," I told Chung. "I'll see you tomorrow for breakfast."

The next morning, Chung and I agreed that we should meet again with our Japanese counterpart, Yachi Shotaro, to ensure that we stayed aligned. Then I assembled our team to establish principles for a summit between Kim and Trump.

A summit with Kim presented opportunities. Trump was unconventional, and conventional approaches had not worked. A top-down process with North Korea seemed better than previous bottom-up, protracted negotiations with North Korean officials who had no real decision-making authority and who were fully vested in the status quo.

Kim Jong-un had a tremendous capacity for brutality, but no one knew how he would respond to President Trump's argument that denuclearization was in the North Korean leader's interest. To maximize the opportunity and protect against the downside, I drafted a short list of risks and mitigating measures. I asked Matt and Allison to work with State and Defense on actions necessary to achieve a favorable outcome. I also asked them to list the concrete steps necessary to reach verifiable denuclearization before the end of Trump's first term.

When we met in San Francisco on the weekend of March 17–18, Chung, Yachi, and I agreed again not to repeat the failed pattern of the past, to continue to enforce sanctions on Pyongyang, and to make no concessions, such as suspending military exercises, as a part of a freeze-for-freeze.

Yachi asked to meet me alone at the end of the conference. Trump had fired Tillerson five days earlier, and Yachi had read press reports of my own imminent departure. As we sat in front of the fireplace in the library of the Marines' Memorial Club and Hotel, he told me that he and Prime Minister Abe did not want me to leave. He noted that I had helped Trump put sound policies in place and had worked well with Japan and other allies.

I answered obliquely, "Whenever I depart, I will be deeply grateful to have had the opportunity to work with you and Abe-san."

Our conversation was confirmation that I had reached the point at which I was used up. How could I speak for the president and have influence with my foreign counterparts if they knew I was leaving and was at odds with the president?

★　　★　　★

WHEN I returned to Washington, I reminded Trump, "I am ready to leave whenever it is best for you. My plan is to retire from the Army. I'll do all I can to help whomever you select as my replacement."

"Who do you think would do a good job?"

"Rick Waddell, whom you know, is competent, effective, and knows what you want to achieve. Steve Biegun would also do a great job for you," I said, referring to the then vice president of international governmental affairs for the Ford Motor Company

"What do you think of John?" Trump asked, clearly referring to John Bolton.

"Mr. President, if you trust him and value his judgment, that's what's most important." What I thought was that Trump and Bolton would be oil and water.

"Thanks, General. You're doing a great job."

He was polite, but we had both come to the conclusion that it was time for me to move on. I was worn out with Trump. Collating his diverse positions into diplomatic and national security frameworks to implement his decisions was necessary, but seemed bureaucratic to him. Trump did not fully understand my role relative to his cabinet officials and he had begun to blame me for the slow-rolling and freelancing of his secretaries of State and Defense. Members of his "MAGA" base misinterpreted my efforts to translate Trump's priorities into a workable foreign policy and national security strategy as impeding rather than advancing his agenda. And as Trump was subjected to a $40 million investigation with regular leaks and media hysteria over "Russian collusion," I was pressing him to acknowledge the Kremlin's sustained campaign of political subversion against the United States, which he thought might bolster those who were attacking the legitimacy of his presidency.

*   *   *

JUST A few days after Russian agents deployed the nerve agent in Salisbury, poisoning Sergei Skripal and his daughter, a story appeared in the *New York Post* with the headline "Putin Heaps Praise on Trump, Pans U.S. Politics." When I walked into the Oval Office that evening, on another matter, the president had a copy of the article and was writing a note to the Russian leader across the page with a fat black Sharpie. He asked me to get the clipping to Putin. I took it with me. When I got home that night, I confided to Katie, "After over a year in this job, I cannot understand Putin's hold on Trump."

News was breaking about the poisoning in England, and I was certain that Putin would use Trump's annotated clipping to embarrass him and provide cover for the attack. The next morning, I stuck to procedures and gave the clipping to the White House Office of the Staff Secretary, which manages any paper coming into and out of the Oval Office. I asked them to take their time clearing it and to come back to me before sending it to Putin via his embassy in Washington. Later, as evidence mounted that the Kremlin and, very likely, Putin himself had ordered the nerve agent attack on Skripal, I told them not to send it.

I told Trump, "Mr. President, do you remember the article and note you told me to send to Putin? I didn't send it. Putin would almost certainly have used the note to embarrass you, alleviate pressure over the Skripal incident, and reinforce the narrative that you are somehow in the Kremlin's pocket."

Trump was angry. "You should have done what I told you to do, General."

"Mr. President, you can be angry at me, but you have to know that I was acting in your interest."

Trump's anger passed, but each of these confrontations eroded our relationship further. Another was just around the corner.

Soon after this incident, Trump had wanted to call Putin to congratulate him on his election victory. I explained that Putin's victory had been rigged, thanks to the Kremlin's control over the media, its quelling of the opposition, the disqualification of popular opposition candidates such as Alexei Navalny, and restrictions on election monitors.

A call was arranged anyway, and the day before it, I told Trump I knew he was going to congratulate Putin, but that he should know that "the Kremlin will use the call in three ways: to say that America endorsed his rigged election victory, to deflect growing pressure over the Salisbury nerve agent attack, and to perpetuate the narrative that you are somehow compromised." I then asked Trump the following: "As Russia tries to delegitimize our legitimate elections, why would you help him legitimize his illegitimate election?"

I suggested that he focus on condemning the Salisbury attack and Assad's continued use of chemical munitions and warning that there would be consequences for these and other acts of aggression. But at this stage in our relationship, my advice on Putin and Russia had become pro forma. I knew that Trump would congratulate Putin and go soft on Salisbury and Syria.

Trump had taken the early morning call from the Residence. Because I had briefed him the day before, I listened in from my office. As expected, he congratulated Putin up front.

Soon after the call, it became apparent that a member of the White House or NSC staff had leaked the preparation materials for the call. In all-capital letters at the top of the first briefing card in the stack we prepared routinely for head-of-state calls were the words "DO NOT CONGRATULATE." Even though Trump probably never saw the packet, the leak was a perfect opportunity to portray me and the NSC staff as untrustworthy.

Those pushing for Bolton to replace me also reportedly got involved. Sean Hannity called President Trump to claim that he knew it was one of the staff in my front office who had leaked the prep materials, but that person never had access to them. The White House chief of staff's office seemed to reinforce the message that the NSC staff was untrustworthy, with many stories highlighting how incensed Kelly was about the leak.

All this broke during Trump's meeting with Saudi crown prince Mohammed bin Salman in the Oval Office. Several news outlets pointed out that Trump's congratulatory words to Putin had come at a strange moment, given the recent Skripal poisonings. Tweets from prominent Republican lawmakers disapproving of Trump's congratulatory message prompted a response that emphasized Trump's hopes for his relationship with Putin:

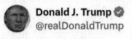 **Donald J. Trump** ✔
@realDonaldTrump
···

I called President Putin of Russia to congratulate him on his election victory (in past, Obama called him also). The Fake News Media is crazed because they wanted me to excoriate him. They are wrong! Getting along with Russia (and others) is a good thing, not a bad thing.......

11:56 AM · Mar 21, 2018

 **Donald J. Trump** ✔
@realDonaldTrump
···

.....They can help solve problems with North Korea, Syria, Ukraine, ISIS, Iran and even the coming Arms Race. Bush tried to get along, but didn't have the "smarts." Obama and Clinton tried, but didn't have the energy or chemistry (remember RESET). PEACE THROUGH STRENGTH!

12:05 PM · Mar 21, 2018

After the call to Putin, Trump had asked me, as he had before, to invite Putin to the White House. Wearily, I told him, "Mr. President, I will invite him if you really want me to—but I think we should deal with the Skripal poisoning and the situation in Syria first."

He responded, "I like getting out of Syria." Putin, like Erdoğan, was doing all he could to reinforce that predilection.

I responded, "Mr. President, you approved a long-term, low-cost strategy for Syria in December."

Trump's ambivalence was dangerous. Turkey's incursion and the Wagner Group were cases in point. And Assad had begun to use chemical weapons again. Moreover, with Tillerson gone, we had lost an advocate for a sustained effort in Syria. Mattis had even suggested that Assad's use of chlorine gas was not as serious as the use of sarin, prompting me to correct him and to note that the intergovernmental Organisation on the Prohibition of Chemical Weapons did not make that distinction.

Mattis was recommending against another U.S. military response, based on concerns over escalation. He told Trump, "Nothing is limited if we do this" and "You will not be able to stop this." But the lack of a response, along with Trump's desire to get out of Syria, had emboldened Turkey and Russia. As Turkish forces closed in on the Syrian city of Manbij and threatened the viability of the SDF, I scheduled a call with Erdoğan and arranged a principals small-group meeting for Tuesday, March 20.

I welcomed everyone to the meeting. We had circulated a paper the night before that laid out two basic options: declare victory and withdraw, or sustain control of territory in Syria until ISIS is defeated and a political resolution to the civil war is in place that denies Iran control of Syria. "Ladies and Gentlemen, I think we need a session with the president to remind him why we are in Syria and remind him that Syria is connected to our vital interests in the Middle East, including Israel's security."

Mattis responded, "Our situation [in Syria] may be untenable." He told us that he had already prepared a withdrawal plan.

I noted that the president had approved, and Tillerson had announced, a Syria strategy that rejected withdrawal because it would repeat the mistake of disengaging prematurely from Iraq. We needed to send a strong signal to Erdoğan not to attack Manbij. I suggested that Mattis consider reinforcing our troops in Syria, which he had the authority to do.

It seemed that Mattis and others had concluded that Trump had already made up his mind to get out. Kelly refused to schedule a meeting with Trump. If the president was not hearing the voices of his NSC, he would listen exclusively to his New York "friends" and to members of the neo-isolationist right, such as Sen. Rand Paul. I gave Trump a one-page paper to remind him why we were in Syria. I don't know if he read it. As I had feared, Trump, without the benefit of reviewing his Syria strategy, had told his supporters at a political rally in Ohio on March 29 that "We'll be coming out of Syria like very soon. Let the other people take care of it now."[3]

And another contentious phone call, this time with Erdoğan, was only two days away.

Mattis came into my office after the principals small-group meeting on Syria. "Is there a problem between us, H.R.?"

"Hell, yes, there's a problem between us, Mr. Secretary." Ylli rushed out of the office and closed the door behind him. "The problem is, Mr. Secretary, that you have been slow-rolling and obstructing our ability to get options to the president and prepare for contingencies." I recounted the failure to act on the bridging strategy or change the rules of engagement in Afghanistan, the continuation of aid to Pakistan, and the use of "peaceful pressure" and his "gag order" that frustrated the table-top exercise on North Korea.

"What has been my greatest disappointment in this job is that we could have accomplished so much more if you had allowed me to work with you and Tillerson."

I ended with "You know what, Mr. Secretary? I hope you get John Bolton, because you deserve John Bolton."

Mattis, red-faced, said, "At ease, Lieutenant General. You can't talk to me that way." His use of "at ease," a military term employed to order a subordinate to stop talking, revealed part of the problem in our relationship: Mattis regarded me as a subordinate, and he expected deference rather than collaboration.

CHAPTER 18

THE LAST 385 YARDS

President Trump is on the verge of firing his national security advisor, H.R. McMaster . . . NATIONAL SECURITY ADVISER H.R. MCMASTER IS EXPECTED TO LEAVE TRUMP ADMINISTRATION . . . Saudi Crown Prince Mohammed bin Salman arrived in Washington Tuesday at the start of a visit aimed at wooing US backing on issues ranging from business to confronting Iran . . . **MCMASTER, LEAVING WHITE HOUSE POST, WILL RETIRE FROM ARMY THIS SUMMER** . . . *TRUMP REPLACES H.R. MCMASTER AS NATIONAL SECURITY ADVISER WITH JOHN BOLTON* . . . Trump expelling 60 Russian diplomats in wake of UK nerve agent attack . . . **WHITE HOUSE PRAISES MCMASTER ON HIS LAST DAY** . . . For McMaster, Pomp Under Bittersweet Circumstances . . . *WHITE HOUSE STAFFERS BID FAREWELL TO MCMASTER WITH A 'CLAP OUT'* . . . White House employees gave a lengthy round of applause Friday afternoon for ousted national security adviser H.R. McMaster on his final day on the job . . . "Throughout my career it has been my greatest privilege to serve alongside extraordinary servicemembers and dedicated civilians."

ON MARCH 22, 2018, as I sat in our living room with Afghanistan's national security advisor, Haneef Atmar, I knew Trump's call was coming. We had just finished our lunch with Saudi Arabia's minister of state, Dr. Musaed al-Aiban, and the UAE's national security advisor, Sheikh Tahnoon bin Zayed Al Nahyan, during which we had discussed how to bolster Afghanistan and pressure Pakistan to curtail its support for the Taliban, the Haqqani network, and other terrorist organizations.

"The new strategy is working," Atmar told me. "The Taliban are taking heavy losses, and many of them no longer believe that they can simply wait for the United States and international forces to leave." Then he asked me directly, "How much longer will you stay?"

His timing was uncanny. Before I could answer, Quinn Lorenz, my deputy chief of staff, politely interrupted our discussion to tell me I had an urgent call on my secure phone.

It was the president, and Atmar would soon have his answer.

*　　*　　*

AS I walked into the auditorium at the EEOB on the morning of March 23, everyone stood and gave me a long ovation. I made eye contact with as many people as I could as I said thank you over and over. When they stopped cheering and sat down again, I told them:

"The purpose of this final all-hands meeting is to thank you for the privilege of working alongside you and for your extraordinary service to the president and the nation. I am proud of you and I hope you are proud of what we accomplished together, from the shift to competition with China to a comprehensive strategy to counter and deter Russian aggression, to the maximum pressure strategies on Iran and North Korea, to fundamental shifts in policies toward Cuba and Venezuela, to the first sound and sustainable strategy for South Asia and the war in Afghanistan, to an approach to the Syrian Civil War and the Middle East grounded in the realities of the region and our vital interests."

"You have helped strengthen our national defense and returned America to competitive arenas that we had vacated based on flawed assumptions about the nature of the post–Cold War world. I have one final request. I ask that you stay on and do your best to help Ambassador Bolton and President Trump. I am not going to say goodbye today because I am not leaving immediately. But I promise not to hang around too long, either. I look forward to staying in contact with all of you and seeing you down the road."

As I walked back to the West Wing, I felt a combination of relief, gratitude, and regret. Relief that Katie and I had clarity about my departure. Gratitude for the opportunity to serve in what I think is one of the best jobs in the world and to do so alongside so many talented and dedicated people. And regret over leaving unfinished much of the important work that was under way and over the opportunities missed or realized only partially.

I wanted to use the two weeks I had left to resolve unfinished business, including mitigating the Turkish incursion and responding to indications of more chemical attacks in Syria, resolving the Gulf mini-crisis, unveiling tariffs on China for intellectual property theft, and trying to convince Trump that steel and aluminum tariffs on China were fine on national security grounds, but that tariffs on some of our closest allies were counterproductive. But the most important immediate task was to obtain Trump's decision on how to respond to Russia's brazen use of a banned nerve agent in the poisoning of Sergei Skripal.

*   *   *

IT WAS standing room only in the Oval Office for our early afternoon meeting with Trump, who was about to depart for Mar-a-Lago. Trump and Pence sat in front of the fireplace, and key members of the national security team filed in. Rick Waddell stood behind the couch where Deputy Attorney General Rod Rosenstein, FBI director Christopher Wray, and Acting Secretary of State John Sullivan were seated. I stood behind Mnuchin, Haspel, Coats, and Mattis.

"Good afternoon Mr. President and Mr. Vice President. The purpose of this meeting is to present courses of action for your decision on our response to Russia's poisoning of Skripal and his daughter. The timing of your decision is important because we will use the weekend to coordinate our response with the United Kingdom and other allies and partners. I will ask Ricky to summarize the courses of action."

I handed Trump and Pence a card with bullet list descriptions of each option; the courses of action were differentiated mainly by the numbers of Russian officials expelled and by whether we would close a consulate connected to Russian intelligence collection and subversion. Trump listened and then, despite having been presented with the intelligence multiple times, asked if we were sure it was Russia and Putin who had ordered the hit on Skripal. I had come to understand that Trump was skeptical of intelligence, in part, because he associated the entire intelligence community with his anger over the Mueller investigation and the Obama administration's misuse of Foreign Intelligence Surveillance Act warrants to surveil a Trump campaign aide.

Haspel answered that the evidence and intelligence were overwhelming. She went on to state that the attack had endangered hundreds and maybe thousands of people.

I added, "Mr. President, I know you are wondering why Vladimir Putin would order something like this. It is because he is making a statement to anyone who might want to cooperate with us and because he thinks he can get away with it."

I knew what Trump was thinking: *Why do we care about this?*

"Mr. President, we did not develop these options just to support our British allies. We prioritized American interests. If attacks like this are normalized, no one is safe. And the intelligence agents we would expel and the consulate we would close are involved in espionage against the United States, including political subversion and information warfare."

Trump seemed to listen to me more intently than usual. Maybe it was because I was on the way out. Finally, he referred to the list of options we'd given him and chose the third one, which would close the Russian consulate in Seattle and expel sixty undeclared intelligence officials. I left the White House reflecting on the privilege of serving as national security advisor. On the day after I was fired, I had helped Trump make an important decision.

The next day, Saturday, March 24, I had the honor of talking with cadets of the West Point rugby team before their match against the Naval Academy midshipmen. I saw in that team what I had tried to foster in Washington, with mixed results—bonds of trust and mutual respect. The Army ruggers hung on to a narrow lead with an impressive try line stand at the end of the match.

I would come to see their victory as a metaphor for what I would experience over the next forty-eight hours.

In the car on the way to and from Annapolis, I made a number of phone calls to European allies to urge them to match the strong actions Trump had approved. The response from Germany, France, and Italy on the Skripal assassination attempt was disappointing. Other European countries stepped up, especially those who had experienced subjugation under the Soviet Union, such as the Baltic States, Poland, and the Czech Republic. But the scale of expulsions of Russian personnel in embassies and consulates abroad would never match those in the United States, simply because there were far fewer undeclared Russian intelligence agents in those countries.

On Sunday, Rick Waddell called me from Air Force One on the way back from Mar-a-Lago. I could hear concern in his voice. He had briefed Trump on the numbers of European expulsions and, consistent with his expectation for reciprocity, Trump was angry.

"Rick," I said, "did you explain that there are far fewer Russians in those countries to expel?"

"I did," Rick replied, "but the president was not in a listening mood, if you know what I mean."

"Oh yes, I do."

I called Kelly. "Chief, this is a disaster. It will be blood in the water for Putin if we renege on this," I said, referring to how the perception of weakness emboldens the Russian dictator. "I'm on my way out. It's up to you to resolve this."

Kelly called the president and persuaded him to stick with the decision he had made in the Oval Office on Friday.

Trump was right to be angry: some of our European allies were not stepping up to confront Putin. Years later, in August 2020, German chancellor Merkel would describe as "shocking" the poisoning of Putin political opponent Alexei Navalny with the same nerve agent used in the attempted murder of the Skripals over two years earlier. But her weak response to the Skripal poisoning may have been all the encouragement Putin needed.

*   *   *

"HELLO, AMBASSADOR. It's good to see you."

Bolton and I sat at the small conference table in front of the bookcase in my office.

"You know that the Smithsonian will provide any art you select," I said and explained that I had selected *Lee Surrendering to Grant at Appomattox*, by Alonzo Chappel, to help us remember that we had been more divided in the past (the Civil War was our most destructive war), that our republic required constant nurturing and improvement (the war ended the criminal institution of slavery), and that military victories required the consolidation of those victories into sustainable political outcomes (the failure of Reconstruction and the rise of Jim Crow in the South were cases in point). And the other painting, Charles Willson Peale's *Washington at Princeton*, was meant to remind visitors to the office that there were opportunities in even the most desperate situations and that, in war, bold action was often less risky than inaction.

"John, we have a process that is working, but it is a constant fight to overcome friction." I then dove into the top priorities. "There is too much for us to cover. You know the issues, so I want to focus on just four topics—North Korea, China, Russia, and Syria."

"On North Korea, maximum pressure is starting to kick in, but pressure could dissipate based on the upcoming summit, and we risk returning to the pattern of previous failed efforts."

On China, I passed Bolton a copy of the Indo-Pacific strategy and highlighted the work on countering Chinese economic aggression. "We are at the start of a bipartisan shift from cooperation and engagement to competition." I told him that, on Russia, "Putin knows that Trump would like to disengage from sustained military operations abroad, especially in Afghanistan, Syria, and Iraq. You saw the response to the Skripal poisoning, but Trump made that decision reluctantly. Trump still believes he can 'make a deal' with Putin, and Putin believes he can convince Trump to withdraw from Europe, South Asia, and the Middle East, so he can fill the vacuum."

Finally, I predicted that due to recent incidents and to Trump's ambivalence to the mission, another crisis was coming in Syria. "The president has been talking about 'getting the hell out' of Syria, and I think you should revisit Syria with him as soon as possible. You will find that when presented with good analysis and multiple options, Trump will make tough decisions. The problem is that he finds it very difficult to stick with them. On issues like trade agreements and tariffs, there are those who'll try to manipulate him by telling him that he'll look weak unless he takes a certain action. What you can do is help elevate discussions and focus on objectives. You'll have a honeymoon period with him, but every time you help him go beyond his predilections and prejudices to make one of those tough decisions, he'll feel a degree of resentment toward you. That resentment will build over time and erode your relationship with him and your effectiveness."

Bolton thanked me for my candid assessments, but I could tell he was getting impatient. He had a great deal more experience than I did in playing Washington's power game. He didn't need my advice. But I was sure he had never seen anything like the Trump White House. I couldn't help but think he was like the dog that caught the car.

Over lunch in the Ward Room of the Navy Mess, I told Bolton I wished him the best and that he had full access to the NSC staff. He complimented the work we had done to effect long-overdue shifts in U.S. foreign policy. "The National Security Strategy is excellent," he said. "And I intend to keep it unchanged."

"Oh, and John, you have great international counterparts. Two of them, Mark Sedwill and Philippe Etienne, are coming to dinner at my house tomorrow. You're welcome to join them."

"Thank you, General. Unfortunately, I have a prior commitment."

"Good luck, Ambassador. I am at your disposal anytime before and after I depart."

We shook hands.

I never spoke with him again.

*   *   *

KATIE AND I would miss Fort McNair and Quarters 13. I was glad our last official dinner was with the national security advisors of two of America's closest allies, the United Kingdom and France. I had planned our dinner before I knew the date of my departure, so the conversation with Mark and Philippe turned toward a retrospective on our work together. My friends were concerned about the durability of the policy shifts we had helped implement. I tried to reassure them, but they were right to be concerned.

The president, disregarding my metaphor of "shooting all our allies to get to China," would use national security as the justification for steel and aluminum tariffs not only on China, but also on some of our closest allies. Although he held true to the principle of no major concessions to North Korea before Pyongyang took major steps toward denuclearization, he would cancel U.S.-South Korean military exercises. And after having hosted the Warmbiers and decrying the "savage" regime in North Korea, Trump would say that he and Kim Jong-un "fell in love" during their June 2018 Summit in Singapore.[1] Trump even absolved Kim of personal responsibility in Otto Warmbier's death, saying he "took [Kim] at his word." Pressure on the North dissipated, and under the Biden administration, China and Russia reverted to enabling rather than isolating Pyongyang.

Trump was right to provide defensive capabilities to Ukraine, but he would withhold that assistance to seek an advantage over Joe Biden in the 2020 presidential election.

He acted directly against Iran and its proxy network with the killing of Qasem Soleimani and Abu Mahdi al-Muhandis in Baghdad on January 3, 2020, but subsequent decisions not to respond to multiple Iranian attacks emboldened Tehran and raised doubts among U.S. allies in the Gulf concerning America's reliability.

Trump established the first sound long-term, low-cost strategy for Afghanistan and South Asia, but then abandoned that strategy and replicated the Obama policy of negotiating a withdrawal time line with a terrorist organization—setting the stage for the Biden administration's humiliating retreat from Kabul in August 2021.

On Russia, Trump imposed tremendous costs on the Kremlin, recognized the folly of Germany's and others' dependency on Russia for oil and gas, and urged NATO nations to rearm to deter Russia.

But he would continue to delude himself about Putin, who continued to play him like a fiddle. I found myself yelling at the television in July 2018 as Trump described Putin's denial of interference in the 2016 election as "strong and powerful."[2]

After dinner, Sedwill, Etienne, and I walked north along the Tidal Basin, toward the Washington Monument and the White House.

"I'm going to miss working with you guys," I told them, "but I think we got a lot done together in the past year."

They agreed that we had begun to adapt to the most significant geostrategic shifts since the end of the Cold War. But they wanted to talk about what was happening in the United States. Although they had their own problems in the United Kingdom and France, Sedwill and Etienne shared their grave concerns about polarization in American society and the crisis of confidence in the United States' democratic principles, institutions, and processes.

When we turned the corner and began to walk down Second Avenue, the street that separated the fronts of the homes there from a large parade field, I pointed out Grant Hall, a three-story building directly across from Quarters 13. On the third floor is a courtroom that was constructed hastily for a military trial that took place in May and June 1865. Eight defendants were accused of conspiring with John Wilkes Booth, the assassin who fatally shot Lincoln in Ford's Theatre on April 14. David Herold, who was with Booth when Union soldiers shot the assassin, was sentenced to be hanged, along with three others, including Mary Surratt—the first woman executed by the U.S. government. I pointed out the area just outside the courthouse where a makeshift scaffold was erected to accommodate their simultaneous executions. Afterward, the four were buried in pine boxes on the site of the hanging.

For Mark and Philippe and the other guests I subjected to these walks, I hoped to point out that our maladies were not unprecedented. We had been through worse times. My optimistic message was based on my belief that our republic has a tremendous capacity for improvement. The United States always was, and remains, a work in progress.

I joked with Sedwill about how his country had made 1814 a difficult year for the United States, with British troops setting nearly every U.S. government building ablaze, including the White House and the Capitol. "So, if we could recover from that and the Civil War, I think we can overcome today's problems."

What I did not foresee were the events that followed the 2020 presidential election, including Trump's persistent false claims of widespread election fraud and his encouragement of a mob to conduct the most significant attack on the U.S. capital since August 1814.

Despite the profound tragedy and disappointment of January 6, I do not think my confident message to Sedwill and Etienne was misplaced. American institutions held. And the courts heard and rejected Trump's false claims of widespread fraud. But those institutions should not have had to withstand an attack inspired by a chief executive sworn to "support and defend the Constitution."

★   ★   ★

BY FRIDAY, April 6, I had said farewell and thank you to members of our team, colleagues across the administration, and my international counterparts. Katie's sister and sister-in-law happened to be visiting from California with four of their high school–age children, so they, along with my daughter Colleen and son-in-law Lee, joined me in my office on my last day.

My nephew Patrick told Katie that "If President Trump says something about my hair, I'm going to say, 'I like your hair, too.'"

Katie said, "You had better not."

Pence came into the office and spoke to all of us before asking us to walk down to the Oval Office. Trump was gracious. Spotting Patrick's surfer haircut, he told him, "I like your hair." Patrick just replied, "Thank you, Mr. President."

Trump asked Katie, "Do you think John will do well?"

Confused, she replied, "Do you mean John Kelly?"

"No," he said. "John Bolton."

"You hired him, Mr. President. I hope he does."

Then Trump pointed his finger at my four nieces and nephews: "Your uncle is a great guy, very tough, and he did a fantastic job for me. Make sure he only writes nice things about me."

I shook Trump's hand and told him again that I was grateful for the opportunity to serve him and the nation.

He asked me, "What are you going to do?"

I told him I'd like to teach and write.

"If you need a letter of recommendation, let me know."

"Goodbye, Mr. President."

★   ★   ★

WHEN WE returned to the office, Katie and I stayed behind to thank members of our team. Ylli said, "You have one more call. He wanted it to be the last one you received in the office."

I picked up.

"General McMaster, it's Senator McCain. I want you to know that I am proud of you, admire you, and consider it a privilege to have served with you."

"Senator, the privilege has been mine. I cannot thank you enough for your example, mentorship, and friendship over the years. It is me who admires you."

McCain had been diagnosed with an aggressive cancerous brain tumor and would pass away fewer than five months later, but he had nonetheless taken the time to phone me. As he had done when he was tortured by the North Vietnamese as a prisoner of war, he was still thinking of everyone but himself.

When I started to leave, Ylli recommended we stop in to say goodbye to the team in the Situation Room. We did so, and as Katie and I left the Situation Room, I saw the vice president outside the West Wing entrance. As we stepped out into the parking lot, Pence offered his hand, and I realized that NSC and White House staff had lined our path from the door to the Suburban, parked about two hundred yards away.

As people clapped and yelled out, I held Katie's hand and waved goodbye, mouthing the words "thank you." It was humbling. Time slowed down, and the walk seemed to last almost the entire thirteen months of my tenure. Highlights and low moments came to mind as I tried to look every person in the eye. Katie saw that a member of the White House staff was crying, and she began to cry, too. We were both touched by the expression of support. As we approached the car, Katie and I went to opposite sides. Secret Service agent Matthew helped Katie, who was now sobbing, into the backseat. I hugged the leader of our detail, Brent, and said thank you. He had decorated our Suburban with an American flag and a three-star general officer flag. Katie was apologizing for crying. I turned to her and said, "I never expected anything like that. Thank you for doing that with me."

I felt a tugging sensation as we pulled away from people who had been with us through the crucible of the Trump White House. I realized that I was also experiencing emotions associated with the end of my last tour of duty in the U.S. Army.

As I had learned in three real wars, combat brings out the best in some people and the worst in others. In the war with ourselves in Washington, those who had fought alongside me had done their best to help America compete, renew its confidence, and build a better future.

As we rode past the Jefferson Memorial, Katie and I took in the cherry blossom trees. They were in full bloom because the winter had been so cold.

POSTSCRIPT

Trust is the coin of the realm. When trust was in the room . . .
good things happened. When trust was not in the room, good
things did not happen.
—SECRETARY OF STATE GEORGE P. SHULTZ

DESPITE THE chaos in the White House, Trump administered
long-overdue correctives to unwise policies. The system our NSC
team established proved effective. For many months, our NSC
decision-making process helped Trump reshape foreign policies
in the face of efforts to undermine and marginalize it. The policy
options it produced rested on a solid foundation of comprehensive
analysis, sound assumptions, clear objectives, and realistic con-
cepts for integrating all elements of national power and the efforts
of likeminded partners. Results included a fundamental shift in
national security strategy and new policies toward China, Russia,
North Korea, Iran, Venezuela, and Cuba. Trump repaired frayed
relationships with Israel and its key Muslim-majority neighbors
and pursued normalization of relations between them that many
dismissed as a futile endeavor. He unveiled long-term strategies to
defeat the Taliban, ISIS, al-Qaeda, and other terrorist organizations
from Afghanistan to Syria, strategies based on objectives rather
than arbitrary time lines. His administration strengthened defense,
lifted senseless restrictions on America's warriors, recapitalized the
nuclear deterrent, and initiated long-term strategies to compete in
space and cyberspace.

Trump overruled the bureaucracy and defied foreign policy

experts to move the U.S. embassy to Jerusalem; stop providing aid to Pakistan, whose Army was funneling support to enemies; cut off hundreds of millions of dollars to the corrupt United Nations Relief and Works Agency for Palestine Refugees in the Near East (UNRWA) that was abetting Hamas in Gaza; and withdrew from the United Nations Human Rights Council (UNHRC), which counts among its members some of the greatest human rights abusers.

The wisdom of those policies and decisions became obvious to many only after the Biden administration disastrously reversed them. A short list of those reversals includes the relaxation of security on the Mexican border; greenlighting Russia's Nord Stream 2 pipeline while canceling a U.S.-Canada pipeline; restricting U.S. energy production and export while relaxing sanctions on Venezuela and Iran and asking those hostile dictatorships to export more oil and gas; supplicating to the Islamic Republic of Iran and lifting the financial and economic pressure on the regime even as it intensified its proxy wars across the Middle East; and lifting the terrorist designation from the Houthis in Yemen even as they and other members of Iran's network of terrorists were increasing the stockpiles of weapons they would unleash after the October 7, 2023, Hamas assault on Israel. The Biden administration restored funding to the UNRWA and rejoined the UNHRC and other international organizations without demanding reforms. But after presiding over their most humiliating foreign policy failure, the fall of Afghanistan and the deadly, humiliating retreat from Kabul, the Biden administration claimed that it had been bound to adhere to the Trump administration's negotiated time line for withdrawal.

In fairness, some of President Biden's foreign policy storms gathered in an atmosphere of inconsistency that Trump had created before he left office. Trump abandoned his South Asia strategy, and his betrayal of our Afghan allies was forged in a withdrawal agreement signed by his envoy, Ambassador Zalmay Khalilzad, in February 2020. In contrast, when the Obama administration sought to get out of Iraq, it felt no comparable compulsion to negotiate with al-Qaeda before departing.

Trump also reversed course on Pakistan, inviting its virulently anti-American prime minister, Imran Khan, to sit next to him in the

Oval Office. Just like his two predecessors, Obama and Bush, Trump foolishly asked a Pakistani leader to help resolve the security problems in Afghanistan, problems for which the Pakistani Army was largely responsible.

After making the righteous decision to kill Qasem Soleimani and his Iraqi terrorist puppet, Abu Mahdi al-Muhandis, in Baghdad on January 3, 2020, Trump chose not to respond to subsequent Iranian and Iranian-proxy-force attacks on U.S. and allied nation forces, aircraft, and facilities, including shipping and oil infrastructure.

Following his approval of the most significant shift in U.S. foreign policy in decades from engagement with China to competition with it, Trump vacillated. He swung between the use of trade enforcement mechanisms and pursuit of a "BIG deal." As presidential scholar Fred Greenstein observed, "Presidents who stand firm are able to set the terms of policy discourse" because "they serve as anchors for the rest of the political community."[1] Rather than anchoring U.S. policy, Trump often unmoored it.

In his first year, Trump articulated a clear direction for much of his foreign policy agenda in the National Security Strategy and other complementary strategies. Regrettably, after that first year, he abandoned significant elements of his foreign policy. Due in part to Trump's inconsistency and then Biden's fecklessness, the world became a more dangerous place. Troubles arose across South Asia, Ukraine, the Black Sea, Gaza and the broader Middle East, the South China Sea, the Taiwan Strait, and the Korean Peninsula. Future American presidents will have much work to do to recover from the cascading crises set in motion in the early 2020s. Their ability to do so will depend in large measure on the factors I observed nearly thirty years ago in a book about Lyndon Johnson's Vietnam War decisions: the president's "character, his motivations, and his relationships with his principal advisors."[2]

Presidential character—or patterns of thought, feeling, and behavior that characterize the way a person deals with the challenges and opportunities of the presidency—is rarely subjected to scrutiny in a methodical way.[3] There are plenty of psychological and political science constructs to use, but the simplest and clearest comes from the Stoic philosophers Epictetus, Marcus Aurelius, and Seneca.

Epictetus defined the discipline of perception as the quality of "clear judgment in the present moment." Trump could see the contours of complex situations and was in the habit of challenging assumptions and conventional wisdom. But his conflicted vision of the world and America's role in it clouded his judgment. As the countless examples in this book attest, Trump's anxieties and insecurities rendered him vulnerable to advisors keen to advance their own priorities and to foreign counterparts who knew how to conjure his emotions and direct them toward retrenchment or other agendas. The neo-isolationist alt-right often used the same talking points as Vladimir Putin, Xi Jinping, and Recep Tayyip Erdoğan to try to persuade Trump: allies are freeloaders, and sustained military commitments abroad are futile and wasteful.

Marcus Aurelius observed that discipline of action requires toleration of those who are "meddling, ungrateful, violent, treacherous, envious, and unsociable," in recognition that they can harm you only if you allow them to. But Trump was obsessed with critics to the point of distraction. He often demonstrated the ability to make tough decisions, but after criticism from his political base, he was prone to abandoning those decisions. His self-absorption and preoccupation with political pugilism often distracted him from the tasks at hand. His intolerance of criticism rendered him distrustful and vulnerable to manipulation by Iago-like figures who merely had to insinuate that a member of his inner circle was disloyal.

Seneca emphasized the need to have control over one's own mind to govern oneself, accept things as they are, and manage one's thoughts and emotions, in recognition that there is much in life that is outside our control. Trump was understandably angry over false charges of collusion with Russia and the considerable bias against him in the mainstream media. But he proved unable to channel his emotions toward constructive purposes. It was easy for people to stoke his anger and direct it against others to increase their influence or remove obstacles to their agendas. Trump's sense of aggrievement reinforced his penchant for seeking affirmation from his most loyal supporters rather than broadening his base of support. And his anger at some for obstructing implementation of his decisions inspired an unhealthy distrust of the people and institutions that are essential to carrying forward a president's agenda. Trump's indiscipline made him the antagonist in his own story.

Trump lacked basic knowledge of how the government runs, and his impatience with learning about the roles of his senior officials and about alternative models for decision-making limited his ability to lead. When there was conflict, he avoided it or, at times, stoked it.

But his senior team, including me, should have done better to resolve those conflicts ourselves. I was able only to attenuate rather than overcome tensions with Secretary of State Rex Tillerson and Secretary of Defense James Mattis, who prioritized their control of policy over collaboration.

Tillerson and Mattis were not just confident in themselves; they also lacked confidence in a president they regarded as impulsive, erratic, and dangerous to the republic. Regrettably, we all diminished one another's efforts and our ability to make the most of our opportunity to help Trump make decisions, stick with those decisions, and act in the interest of the American people.

Ultimately, Trump's deficiencies in the disciplines of perception, action, and will produced a tragic ending to his presidency on January 6, 2021. His ego and love of self distorted his perception of the 2020 presidential election. His sense of betrayal drove him to abandon his oath to "support and defend the Constitution," a president's highest obligation.

Fortunately, the safeguards that America's founders built into the Constitution foiled Trump's attempt to usurp it. Yet there was still human suffering on that day at the Capitol. Five people died. More were wounded. The mob desecrated our most cherished democratic symbol, the people's House of Representatives. The attack on the U.S. Capitol stained our image, and it will take a long-term effort to restore what Donald Trump, his enablers, and those they encouraged took from us that day.

*   *   *

A FEW months after I departed the White House and retired from the Army, President Trump called me.

"I miss you, General. You did a great job for me and the country."

"Thank you, Mr. President. I considered serving as your national security advisor a privilege, and if I had the opportunity to go back to February of last year at Mar-a-Lago, I would do it again."

We both knew, however, that based on the nature of our experience together since he hired me, we could never work together again.

★   ★   ★

I HOPE that young people who have persevered through these pages will conclude that, even under challenging circumstances, there are tremendous rewards associated with service under any administration. As political partisans remain at war with one another, America needs people who are determined to stay above the fray and fulfill their duty to the Constitution and to their fellow citizens. The job one does in service to the nation is larger than any one individual.

My tour of duty in the Trump White House, like my previous thirty-three years as a soldier, gave me the opportunity to serve with talented and dedicated people committed to defending and strengthening our republic. Our nation is in need of honorable people, whether in a uniform or civilian clothes, who rise above faction in their desire to work for the common good.

ACKNOWLEDGMENTS

Friends and esteemed colleagues on the National Security Council staff, my Secret Service detail, and many others across the Trump administration inspired me to write our story. They wanted me to explain how, despite the often-described chaos in the White House, we came to work every day motivated by our oath to support and defend the Constitution and our desire to help President Trump advance the interests of the American people. Many participated in the oral history project that informed this book. Several read and helped improve portions of the manuscript. I shall leave them unnamed, so there is no ambiguity concerning my sole responsibility for the book's contents.

As with my previous book *Battlegrounds*, I could not imagine writing this one anywhere but at the Hoover Institution at Stanford University. I am indebted to many Hoover Institution fellows who listened to my ideas and helped shape this project from the outset. The professionals on the Hoover Institution staff provided resources and support. I am especially grateful to Jaime Walter, who cheerfully fixed my innumerable IT issues, and to the late Karen Weiss Mulder, who provided the Hoover fellowship with the resources we needed and inspired us with her empathetic and relentlessly positive attitude.

I could not have completed this project without the assistance of my senior research program manager, Chelsea Berkey, who led our team of student research assistants, organized materials to aid in the writing, helped me conceptualize the book, and organized readers' criticisms and suggestions to ease the seemingly endless redrafting. She was ably assisted by my longest-serving research assistant, Emma Bates, who remained on the team after graduating from Stanford and "defecting" to the University of California, Berkeley to pursue her doctorate in history. I wanted this book to appeal to younger generations. The advice that Chelsea, Emma, and our research assistants provided helped me draw out the themes of greatest interest to them. My assistant, Laurie Garcia, remained the glue that held our team together. She protected the time I needed to complete the project and vastly improved the manuscript with her superb copyediting.

My students and research assistants organized evidence, reviewed literature, and prepared chronologies. In the ongoing seminar associated with writing this book, they heard me think out loud and helped me clarify and sharpen the analysis. They conducted and transcribed nearly one hundred interviews across five years with those who served in the Trump administration and with keen observers of the administration in Congress and the press. Historians and researchers will be able to access those oral histories at the Hoover Institution Library and Archives. I want to express my deepest thanks to the following current members and alumni of the research team: Sylvie Ashford, Marco Baeza, Emily Bauer, Sophia Boyer, Carter Clelland, Fiona Clunan, Jonathan Deemer, Hannah Delaney, Kyle Duchynski, Lisa Einstein, Allyse Feitzinger, Sydney Frankenberg, William Healzer, Jacqueline Henley, William Howlett, David Jaffe, Josiah Joner, Matt Kaplan, Ethan Lee, Olivia Morello, Paul Nelson, Eva Orozco, Dylan Rivera, Hiroto Saito, Kathleen Schwind, Arelena Shala, Mac Simpson, Elizabeth Spaeth, Ethan Sperla, Samantha Thompson, Theo Velaise, and Kate Yeager. Two brilliant high school interns, Grace McGoran and Jane Martin, helped with research and book summaries.

In addition to former Trump administration officials whom I have left unnamed, I inflicted the manuscript on friends and colleagues who I knew would give me unsparing criticisms and insightful suggestions. Jeffery Chen, Rodes Fishburne, Jordan Grimshaw, Stephen Kotkin, Zachary Shore, Lewis Sorley, Marin Strmecki, and Wright Thompson helped me improve the book tremendously.

I had the good fortune of beginning this project with editor Jonathan Jao and finishing it with Sean Desmond. Desmond helped me chisel away, sometimes reluctantly, what was unnecessary and adjust proportions to improve the story's continuity and rhythm. It was a pleasure to work again with Sean and the entire HarperCollins team as we got the book across the finish line. I hope that my first editor, the late Buz Wyeth, would have been proud of us. I want to thank my agents, Rafe Sagalyn and Binky Urban, for sticking with me through two books across the past six years.

The historians and civil servants of the National Security Council's Directorate for Records Access and Information Security Management were extraordinarily helpful. Senior Director Ellen Knight, Anne Withers, and Mike Smith helped me access my papers, cleared my notes, declassified documents, and approved the manuscript for publication. Our NSC director for national security strategy and history, Dr. Seth Center, provided advice throughout the project. He and John Powers conducted a series of oral history interviews in the weeks following my departure from the White House that prevented me from having to rely on stale memories.

I could not have completed this or any project without the support of my family. My wife, Katie, as she did during my tour of duty in the Trump administration and across thirty-four years of service in our Army, inspired me and did her best to keep me in good humor, especially as deadlines approached. Our daughters, Katharine, Colleen, and Caragh, and my sister, Letitia, were sources of strength as Katie and I experienced the maelstrom of Washington and as I resurrected some of the less pleasant memories in the telling of this story. They and my sons-in-law—Lee Robinson, Alex Pittman, and Charles England—read portions of the manuscript and provided helpful suggestions. Completing a book requires solitude, but I often found myself in the happy position of being interrupted by our six grandchildren. Those interruptions may have delayed the delivery of the manuscript, but the children's joyful presence provided needed relief from the task. I hope that they one day read this book and realize that, even under difficult circumstances, the rewards of service more than compensate for any difficulties encountered.

If you've read this far, you may have concluded that I require a lot of help. That is true. Across my career, I had the good fortune to work with talented people who compensated for my many deficiencies. Of course, any errors that remain are mine alone.

NOTES

A Note on Sources

During my tour of duty in the Trump White House, I carried note-
books that I filled with my summaries of conversations, assessments
of critical challenges, ideas to advance U.S. interests, tasks to complete, and priorities and guidance for our staff. These were sufficient
to jog my memory as I performed my duties and as I endeavored
to resurrect the memories contained in this book. I also consulted
a range of draft and final documents that crossed my desk across
those thirteen months. During the last two years of the Trump presidency, I had the opportunity to access these materials in the Office of
Records Access and Information Security Management at the White
House, take notes, and have those notes cleared for use. These note-
books and other materials can be accessed at the Donald J. Trump
Presidential Library through the National Archives and Records Administration.

My daily calendar, also in that records collection, contains the
dizzying list of appointments, meetings, and phone calls that filled
my 457 days as national security advisor. Although it contains few
details, it helped me remember the context of many of the events
recounted here and clarify the order in which those events occurred.
My tremendous research assistants at Stanford University provided
additional chronologies of world events and press reporting on
Trump and his administration that often provided color and helped
me understand better the contrast between the reality on the inside
of the White House and perceptions on the outside.

As a historian, I felt a duty to capture my experience while it was still fresh in my memory. Days after I left the White House, I conducted a series of classified oral history interviews with Director for National Security Strategy and History Dr. Seth Center and National Archives Archivist John Powers. Those interviews are now largely declassified and can be found in the same records collection.

I wanted this book to place my experience in the context of those alongside whom I served. I wanted to include the perspectives of other members of the Trump administration and of those who observed the administration closely. Although my editor convinced me that such a book would be unmanageable, I relied heavily on a collection of more than ninety oral history interviews that my student research assistants conducted over the course of five years. Archivists at the Hoover Institution are curating that collection so researchers and historians can access it.

My editor also forced me to cut extensive historical background and details of policy formulation and implementation. Much of that background and many of those details are contained in *Battlegrounds: The Fight to Defend the Free World*, which I hope readers will regard as a companion to this book.

The vast body of memoirs and secondary source accounts of the Trump administration were useful for my understanding how memories and accounts of Trump's first year in office were refracted through the lenses of partisanship and either advocacy for or condemnation of the president.

During the preparation of this book, as during my time as national security advisor, I relied heavily on NSC teammates and colleagues in the administration who read drafts and provided helpful corrections and suggestions.

I quote myself and others only when my memories of conversations were clear or I had verbatim notes to access. Foreign leaders are almost always paraphrased here, due to the practice of regarding what they say as privileged foreign government information. Because President Trump used aberrant language to convey fantastic ideas in the process of thinking aloud, I included only conversations that proved relevant to his frame of mind, decisions, and policy outcomes.

Sources

Chapter 1: "You're Fired"

1. Philip Elliott, "Donald Trump Just Hired John Bolton. Here's Why That Makes Some Nervous," *Time*, March 23, 2018, https://time.com/5212129 /john-bolton-hr-mcmaster-donald-trump/. See tweet at https://twitter.com /realDonaldTrump/status/976948306927607810.

2. Nicolle Wallace, "White House Preparing for McMaster Exit as Early as Next Month," NBC News, March 1, 2018, https://www.nbcnews.com/politics/donald -trump/white-house-preparing-mcmaster-exit-early-next-month-n852371.

3. BBC, "Vladimir Putin Praises 'Outstanding and Talented' Trump," BBC News, December 17, 2015, https://www.bbc.com/news/election-us-2016-35124280.

4. John Santucci, "Trump Says 'Great Honor' to Get Compliments from 'Highly Respected' Putin," ABC News, December 17, 2015, https://abcnews.go.com /Politics/trump-great-honor-compliments-highly-respected-putin/story ?id=35829618. The full quote is in Jennifer Mercieca's book *Demagogue for President: The Rhetorical Genius of Donald Trump* (College Station: Texas A&M University Press, 2020).

5. Mike Calia, "Trump Criticizes National Security Advisor H. R. McMaster's Comments About Russian Meddling in the 2016 Election," CNBC, February 18, 2018, https://www.cnbc.com/2018/02/18/trump-criticizes-mcmaster-comments -about-russian-meddling-in-election.html.

6. John Kiriakou and Brian Becker, "'Russiagate' Morphs into a War on Dissent," Sputnik, February 21, 2018, https://sputnikglobe.com/20180221 /russiagate-morphs-into-war-on-dissent-1061850185.html.

7. Jane Mayer, "Is Ginni Thomas a Threat to the Supreme Court?" *The New Yorker*, January 21, 2022, https://www.newyorker.com/magazine/2022/01/31 /is-ginni-thomas-a-threat-to-the-supreme-court.

Chapter 2: "You're Hired"

1. United States District Court for the District of Columbia, "Government's Motion to Dismiss the Criminal Information Against the Defendant Michael T. Flynn," *United States of America v. Michael T. Flynn*, Defendant, Case 1:17-cr -00232-EGS Document 198, Filed 05/07/20, 2, https://cdn.cnn.com/cnn/2020 /images/05/07/flynn.pdf.

2. Patrick Radden Keefe, "McMaster and Commander," *The New Yorker*, April 23, 2018, https://www.newyorker.com/magazine/2018/04/30/mcmaster-and -commander.

3. Eliot Cohen and Max Boot, "The Full Transcript," interview by Susan Glasser, *The Global Politico* (podcast), *Politico Magazine*, December 18, 2017, https://www .politico.com/magazine/story/2017/12/18/the-full-transcript-eliot-cohen-and -max-boot-216112/.

4. Peter Rodman, *Presidential Command: Power, Leadership, and the Making of Foreign Policy from Richard Nixon to George W. Bush* (New York: Vintage Books, 2010), 284.

5. In possession of the author. Also available at the library of the US Army Armor School, Fort Knox, KY.

6. "President Trump Announces H. R. McMaster as National Security Advisor," YouTube video, February 20, 2017, https://youtu.be/KxfRDfv9tM8.

Chapter 3: "Love All, Trust a Few"

1. For more on the organization of the National Security Council and the Homeland Security Council, see "National Security Presidential Memorandum—2," *Federal Register* 82, No. 21 (January 28, 2017), https://www.govinfo.gov/content/pkg/FR-2017-02-02/pdf/2017-02381.pdf.
2. Ryan Browne, "Pence and Kaine: VP Opponents, US Marine Dads," CNN Politics, July 23, 2016, https://www.cnn.com/2016/07/23/politics/mike-pence-tim-kaine-marine-dads/.
3. Frank Hoffman, "Black Swans and Pink Flamingos: Five Principles for Force Design," War on the Rocks, August 19, 2015, https://warontherocks.com/2015/08/black-swans-and-pink-flamingos-five-principles-for-force-design/.
4. Keith Kellogg, *War by Other Means: A General in the Trump White House* (Washington, D.C.: Regnery Publishing, 2021), 107.
5. Jeffrey Goldberg, "The Lessons of Henry Kissinger," *The Atlantic*, December 2016, https://www.theatlantic.com/magazine/archive/2016/12/the-lessons-of-henry-kissinger/505868/.
6. Daniella Diaz, "A History of Trump's Thoughts on Afghanistan," CNN, August 21, 2017, https://www.cnn.com/2017/08/21/politics/history-president-trump-remarks-afghanistan-tweets/index.html.
7. Kenneth Harris, "Wartime Lies," *New York Times*, April 27, 1997, https://archive.nytimes.com/www.nytimes.com/books/97/04/27/reviews/970427.27harrist.html?scp=80&sq=cross%2520word&st=cse.

Chapter 4: DJT and LBJ

1. Greg Jaffe, "Three Words—Radical Islamic Terrorism—Expose a Trump Administration Divide," *Washington Post*, March 1, 2017, https://www.washingtonpost.com/world/national-security/three-words—radical-islamic-terrorism—expose-a-trump-administration-divide/2017/03/01/11137f78-fe98-11e6-8f41-ea6ed597e4ca_story.html.
2. Donald J. Trump, *The Art of the Deal* (New York: Random House, 1987), 39.
3. H. R. McMaster, *Dereliction of Duty: Lyndon Johnson, Robert McNamara, the Joint Chiefs of Staff, and the Lies That Led to Vietnam* (New York: HarperCollins, 1997), 71.
4. "Alexander Haig," *The Economist*, February 25, 2010, https://www.economist.com/obituary/2010/02/25/alexander-haig.

Chapter 5: Intrigue, Elbows, and Separate Agendas

1. R. D. Hooker Jr., *The Good Captain: A Personal Memoir of America at War* (Havertown, PA: Casemate Publishers, 2022), 1.

Chapter 6: A Well-Oiled Machine—Really

1. Fox News, "'Fox & Friends' Exclusive: Trump Blasts NYT Op-Ed Writer, Says 'It May Be a Deep State Person,'" Fox News, September 7, 2018, https://www.foxnews.com/politics/fox-friends-exclusive-trump-blasts-nyt-op-ed-writer-says-it-may-be-a-deep-state-person.

2. John H. Durham, "Report on Matters Related to Intelligence Activities and Investigations Arising Out of the 2016 Presidential Campaigns," United States Department of Justice, Submitted to Attorney General Merrick B. Garland, May 12, 2023, https://www.justice.gov/storage/durhamreport.pdf.

3. According to the *Guardian*, he posted these three tweets in a thirteen-minute period on the morning of March 4, 2017. See Chris Johnston, "'This Is McCarthyism!': Trump Accuses Obama of 'Wire-Tapping' His Office Before Election," *Guardian*, March 4, 2017, https://www.theguardian.com/us-news/2017/mar/04/donald-trump-accuses-obama-of-wire-tapping-his-office-before-election.

Chapter 7: Deep Contradictions

1. Carl von Clausewitz, ed. and trans. Michael Howard and Peter Paret, *On War* (Princeton, N.J.: Princeton University Press, 1976), 88.

2. For more on this visit, see H. R. McMaster, *Battlegrounds: The Fight to Defend the Free World* (New York: HarperCollins, 2020), 155–95.

3. See McMaster, *Battlegrounds*, 195–97.

4. Husain Haqqani and Lisa Curtis, "A New U.S. Approach to Pakistan: Enforcing Aids Conditions Without Cutting Ties," Hudson Institute, February 6, 2017, https://www.hudson.org/national-security-defense/a-new-u-s-approach-to-pakistan-enforcing-aid-conditions-without-cutting-ties.

5. For more on the visit to Pakistan, see McMaster, *Battlegrounds*, 195–213.

Chapter 8: Tightrope

1. Mark Landler, Ellen Barry, and Jason Horowitz, "Trump's 100 Days on World Stage: Rallying Some and Repelling Others," *New York Times*, April 28, 2017, https://www.nytimes.com/2017/04/28/world/trumps-100-days-on-world-stage-rallying-some-and-repelling-others.html?searchResultPosition=3; Rosie Gray, "The Entertainment Presidency," *The Atlantic*, April 30, 2017, https://www.theatlantic.com/politics/archive/2017/04/the-entertainment-presidency/524877/; Tina Nguyen and Abigail Tracy, "Trump's 100 Days of Failure," *Vanity Fair*, April 28, 2017, https://www.vanityfair.com/news/photos/2017/04/donald-trump-100-days-failure.

2. Zbigniew Brzezinski, *Power and Principle: Memoirs of the National Security Adviser, 1977–1981* (New York: Farrar, Straus and Giroux, 1983), 55–57.

3. H. R. McMaster, "Lt. Gen. H.R. McMaster on Foreign Policy; Sen. Schumer on President Trump's First 100 Days," interview by Chris Wallace, Fox News, April 30, 2017, https://www.foxnews.com/transcript/lt-gen-h-r-mcmaster-on-foreign-policy-sen-schumer-on-president-trumps-first-100-days.

4. Donald Trump, "FULL TRANSCRIPT: President Donald Trump's Interview with 'Face the Nation,'" interview by John Dickerson, *Face the Nation*, CBS, April 30, 2017, https://www.cbsnews.com/news/trump-interview-full-transcript-face-the-nation/.

5. Greg Miller and Greg Jaffe, "Trump Revealed Highly Classified Information to Russian Foreign Minister and Ambassador," *Washington Post*, May 15, 2017, https://www.washingtonpost.com/world/national-security/trump-revealed-highly-classified-information-to-russian-foreign-minister-and-ambassador/2017/05/15/530c172a-3960-11e7-9e48-c4f199710b69_story.html.

6. "National Security Adviser on President Trump's Meeting with Russian Officials," C-SPAN video, 00:01:38, May 15, 2017, https://www.c-span.org/video /?428556-1/national-security-adviser-president-trumps-meeting-russian -officials.

7. Miller and Jaffe, "Trump Revealed."

8. Fred Kaplan, "The Tarnishing of H. R. McMaster," *Slate*, May 16, 2017, https:// slate.com/news-and-politics/2017/05/h-r-mcmasters-reputation-is-being -destroyed-by-trumps-deceit.html.

9. Clausewitz, ed. Howard and Paret, *On War*, 119–21.

Chapter 9: Travels with Trump

1. "PM Netanyahu and His Wife Sara Welcome U.S. President Donald Trump and His Wife Melania at BGI Airport," Prime Minister's Office, gov.il, last modified May 22, 2017, https://www.gov.il/en/departments/news/eventairport220517.

2. Donald Trump, "Remarks with President Mahmoud Abbas of the Palestinian Authority in Bethlehem, Palestinian Territories," May 23, 2017, https://www .govinfo.gov/content/pkg/DCPD-201700352/pdf/DCPD-201700352.pdf.

3. Sarah Wildman, "Donald Trump at Yad Vashem Leaves a Bizarrely Chipper Note for Posterity," Vox, May 23, 2017, https://www.vox.com/world/2017 /5/23/15680314/trump-holocaust-memorial-guest-book-notes-so-amazing.

4. Winston Churchill, "Speech Delivered at the University of Zurich," September 19, 1946, Council of Europe, transcript, https://rm.coe.int/16806981f3.

5. Carl von Clausewitz, ed. and trans. J. J. Graham and F. N. Maude, *On War* (London: K. Paul, Trench, Trubner and Company, 1940), 142.

6. Clausewitz, ed. Graham and Maude, *On War*, 144. Translated also as "resistant medium."

Chapter 11: Winning Friends and Influencing Foes

1. Statement by Secretary Tillerson, July 4, 2017, https://eg.usembassy.gov/n -07042017/.

2. Jonathan Capehart, "Trump's White-nationalist Dog Whistles in Warsaw," *Washington Post*, July 6, 2017, https://www.washingtonpost.com/blogs/post -partisan/wp/2017/07/06/trumps-white-nationalist-dog-whistles-in-warsaw/.

3. Laurie Kellman, "Carter National Security Adviser Zbigniew Brzezinski Dies," PBS, May 27, 2017, https://www.pbs.org/newshour/nation/carter -national-security-adviser-zbigniew-brzezinski-dies.

Chapter 12: Knives Out

1. DFRLab, "#FireMcMaster, Explained," Medium, August 7, 2017, https:// medium.com/dfrlab/firemcmaster-explained-9e9018e507c2.

2. Lee Stranahan and Garland Nixon, "Establishment Media Frenzy over Trump Supporters' Call to #FireMcMaster," *Sputnik*, August 8, 2017, https:// sputnikglobe.com/20170808/establishment-media-frenzy-over-trump -1056271718.html. Laura Ingraham tweeted on August 3, 2017: "Obama holdovers at NSC or State Dept who are leaking sh[oul]d do real time for these leaks. Why has McMasters [*sic*] fired actual Trump supporters?" After the leak of my letter to Susan Rice allowing her to keep her security clearance,

Sean Hannity tweeted on August 3, 2017: "What is this? Does H.R. McMaster need to go? Susan Rice? Omg"; see Natasha Bertrand, "The Knives Are Coming Out for H. R. McMaster," *Business Insider*, August 4, 2017, https://www .businessinsider.com/hr-mcmaster-steve-bannon-russia-trolls-2017-8. For an example of an article defending me, see Dov Zakheim, "The 'Alt-right' Plot Against McMaster, Spurred by Its Jewish Fellow Travelers," *Haaretz*, August 10, 2017, https://www.haaretz.com/opinion/2017-08-10/ty-article/.premium/the -plot-against-mcmaster/0000017f-e56f-d97e-a37f-f76f61f40000.

3. "Statement by Senator John McCain on General H. R. McMaster," Press Releases, McCain.senate.gov, last modified August 14, 2017, https://webarchive .loc.gov/all/20170815131900/https://www.mccain.senate.gov/public/index .cfm/press-releases?ID=2EAD1145-92A8-49AD-B36D-E648F9F97B62.

4. Chas Danner, "Trump and Kushner Push Back on Right-Wing Campaign to Fire McMaster, for Now," *Intelligencer*, August 5, 2017, https://nymag.com /intelligencer/2017/08/trump-and-kushner-are-protecting-mcmaster-for-now .html.

5. *Times of Israel* Staff and Agencies, "Israeli Officials Say Under-Fire McMaster a Great Friend of Israel," *Times of Israel*, August 5, 2017, https://www.timesofisrael .com/israeli-officials-say-under-fire-mcmaster-a-great-friend-of-israel/.

6. Clint Watts, "Russian Bots Tweeting Calls to Fire McMaster, Former FBI Agent Says," interview by Lulu Garcia-Navarro, *Weekend Edition Sunday*, NPR, https:// www.npr.org/2017/08/20/544817844/russian-bots-tweeting-calls-to-fire -mcmaster-former-fbi-agent-says.

7. "Select Committee to Investigate the January 6th Attack on the United States Capitol," *Final Report*, H.R. Rep. No. 117-663, at 520 (2022), https://www.govinfo .gov/content/pkg/GPO-J6-REPORT/pdf/GPO-J6-REPORT.pdf.

8. Valerie Wirtschafter, "Audible Reckoning: How Top Political Podcasters Spread Unsubstantiated and False Claims," Brookings Institution, February 2023, https://www.brookings.edu/articles/audible-reckoning-how-top-political -podcasters-spread-unsubstantiated-and-false-claims/.

9. Jenna Johnson and John Wagner, "Trump Won't 'Rule Out a Military Option' in Venezuela," *Washington Post*, August 11, 2017, https://www.washingtonpost .com/news/post-politics/wp/2017/08/11/trump-wont-rule-out-a-military -option-in-venezuela/.

10. NBC News, "Hagel's Predecessors Decried White House 'Micromanaging,'" NBC News, November 24, 2014, https://www.nbcnews.com/politics/first -read/hagels-predecessors-decried-white-house-micromanaging-n255231.

11. This quotation is from an off-the-record interview that is part of a forthcoming oral history collection on Trump's foreign policy at the Hoover Institution Library and Archives.

Chapter 13: Movement in a Resistant Element

1. Donald J. Trump, "Remarks by President Trump on the Strategy in Afghanistan and South Asia," *The White House*, August 21, 2017, https://trumpwhitehouse .archives.gov/briefings-statements/remarks-president-trump-strategy -afghanistan-south-asia/.

Chapter 14: Contradiction and Contention

1. Ameenah Gurib-Fakim and Landry Signé, "Investment in Science and Technology Is Key to an African Economic Boom," Brookings, January 26, 2022, https://www.brookings.edu/articles/investment-in-science-and-technology-is-key-to-an-african-economic-boom/.

2. Eli Watkins, "Tillerson on North Korea: Diplomacy Will Continue 'Until the First Bomb Drops,'" CNN, October 16, 2017, https://www.cnn.com/2017/10/15/politics/rex-tillerson-north-korea-cnntv/index.html.

Chapter 15: Asian Odyssey (20K Miles with Trump)

1. "How Renewed U.S. Sanctions Have Hit Iran Hard," BBC News, May 2, 2019, https://www.bbc.com/news/world-middle-east-48119109. See also Kenneth Katzman, Summary, "Iran Sanctions," Congressional Research Service, April 22, 2019, 1, https://crsreports.congress.gov/product/pdf/RS/RS20871/291.

2. "Research Starters: U.S. Military by the Numbers," The National WWII Museum—New Orleans, https://www.nationalww2museum.org/students-teachers/student-resources/research-starters/research-starters-us-military-numbers; "The War in the Pacific: By the Numbers," Collection of the National WWII Museum, p. 23, https://www.ww2classroom.org/system/files/essays/wip003_0.pdf.

3. Lawrence Korb, "Trump's Defense Budget," Center for American Progress, February 28, 2018, https://www.americanprogress.org/article/trumps-defense-budget/#:~:text=Shortly%20after%20taking%20office%2C%20President,the%20proposed%20FY%202017%20budget.

4. Antonio Varas, Raj Varadarajan, Jimmy Goodrich, and Falan Yinug, "Government Incentives and US Competitiveness in Semiconductor Manufacturing," BCG and Semiconductor Industry Association, September 2020, p. 10, https://www.semiconductors.org/wp-content/uploads/2020/09/Government-Incentives-and-US-Competitiveness-in-Semiconductor-Manufacturing-Sep-2020.pdf.

5. For more on this visit, see McMaster, *Battlegrounds*, 89–104.

6. Much of the information we presented came from CEOs of some of the largest U.S. companies, many of whom would explain how their companies had been victims of Chinese economic aggression. They would always preface those explanations with a request that they remain anonymous lest their company suffer CCP retribution.

7. In 2020, Lighthizer would secure the U.S.-China Phase One Economic and Trade Agreement only after imposing tariffs on Chinese exports and threatening more.

8. Orion Rummler, "Trump Says He Gets Along Better with World Leaders 'the Tougher and Meaner They Are,'" Axios, September 14, 2020, https://www.axios.com/2020/09/14/trump-woodward-foreign-leaders.

Chapter 16: Weakness Is Provocative

1. But Hajin, the last town liberated in ISIS's physical "caliphate," would not fall until the summer of 2018, and U.S. counterterrorism operations against the remnants of ISIS continue in Syria to this day.

2. "Tweets of January 1, 2019," The American Presidency Project, January 1, 2018, https://www.presidency.ucsb.edu/documents/tweets-january-1-2018.

3. Jonathan Landay, Arshad Mohammed, and John Walcott, "'A Mad Scramble': How Trump Tweet on Pakistan Blindsided U.S. Officials," Reuters, January 11, 2018, https://www.reuters.com/article/us-usa-pakistan-aid-idUSKBN1F030Q/.

4. United Nations Meetings Coverage, "Security Council Tightens Sanctions on Democratic People's Republic of Korea, Unanimously Adopting Resolution 2397 (2017)," 8151st Meeting (PM), SC/131141, December 22, 2017, https://press.un.org/en/2017/sc13141.doc.htm.

5. The White House, *National Security Strategy of the United States*, December 2017, https://trumpwhitehouse.archives.gov/wp-content/uploads/2017/12/NSS-Final-12-18-2017-0905.pdf.

6. Rex Tillerson, "Remarks on the Way Forward for the United States Regarding Syria," Hoover Institution, January 17, 2018, https://tr.usembassy.gov/remarks-way-forward-united-states-regarding-syria/.

7. See @realDonaldTrump at https://twitter.com/realDonaldTrump/status/947181212468203520.

Chapter 17: Allies, Authoritarians, and Afghanistan

1. "U.S. Stops Sale of F-35 Fighter Jets to Turkey over Use of Russian Defense System," CBS, July 17, 2019, https://www.cbsnews.com/news/f-35-us-stops-sale-of-fighter-jets-to-turkey-citing-use-of-russian-s-400-air-defense-system/.

2. For more on this meeting, see McMaster, *Battlegrounds*, 25–35.

3. Ryan Browne and Barbara Starr, "Trump Says US Will Withdraw from Syria 'Very Soon,'" CNN, March 29, 2018, https://www.cnn.com/2018/03/29/politics/trump-withdraw-syria-pentagon/index.html.

Chapter 18: The Last 385 Yards

1. The Associated Press, "Trump on Kim Jong-un: 'We Fell in Love,'" *New York Times* (video), September 30, 2018, https://www.nytimes.com/video/us/100000006136380/trump-kim-jong-un-we-fell-in-love.html.

2. Jeff Mason and Denis Pinchuk, "Trump Backs Putin on Election Meddling at Summit, Stirs Fierce Criticism," Reuters, July 16, 2018, https://www.reuters.com/article/idUSKBN1K6011/.

Postscript

1. Fred I. Greenstein, "'The Qualities of Effective Presidents': An Overview from FDR to Bill Clinton," *Presidential Studies Quarterly* 30, no. 1 (2000): 178–85, http://www.jstor.org/stable/27552077.

2. McMaster, *Dereliction of Duty*, 324.

3. See James David Barber, *The Presidential Character: Predicting Performance in the White House* (Englewood Cliffs, NJ: Prentice-Hall, 1972), 8; see also Alexander George, "Assessing Presidential Character," *World Politics* 26, no. 2 (Jan. 1974): 234–82, https://doi.org/10.2307/2009901.

INDEX

ABOUT THE AUTHOR

H. R. McMaster is the Fouad and Michelle Ajami Senior Fellow at the Hoover Institution at Stanford University and Distinguished University Fellow at Arizona State University. A graduate of the United States Military Academy at West Point, McMaster served as a U.S. Army officer for thirty-four years and retired as a lieutenant general in 2018. He remained on active duty while serving as the twenty-fifth assistant to the president for national security affairs. McMaster holds a PhD in history from the University of North Carolina at Chapel Hill. He is the author of two bestsellers, *Dereliction of Duty* and *Battlegrounds*.